A Birth day present to my
son Charles
July 19 1882

J. G. Gunderson


25

THE

# RESURRECTION OF OUR LORD

THE CROALL LECTURE FOR 1879-80

# THE RESURRECTION

OF

# OUR LORD

By WILLIAM MILLIGAN, D.D.

PROFESSOR OF DIVINITY AND BIBLICAL CRITICISM IN
THE UNIVERSITY OF ABERDEEN

London

MACMILLAN AND CO.

1881

# PREFACE.

I REGRET much that the publication of the following Lectures has been so long delayed. Literary engagements which it was impossible to lay aside rendered an earlier preparation of the Notes impossible; and without them it seemed to me that the Lectures ought not to be given to the public. Considering the importance of the subject, I could have wished to devote even much longer time to this part of the work than I have been able to secure for it. With some verbal alterations, and the insertion of a few passages omitted in their delivery, the Lectures are now published exactly as they were preached. I issue them under a deep sense of their deficiencies; and my utmost hope is that they may help to direct the attention of others to the great subject of which they treat, so that it may be more thoroughly studied and more successfully unfolded. The field of thought embraced by the Resurrection of our Lord, in the light in which it is here presented, demands greater attention at the hands of our Scottish Theologians than it has hitherto received ; and it is by the united labours of many, rather than by the efforts of a few, that, at least in Theology, the truth is won. May the Risen Lord bless to the edifying of His Church the effort now made to set forth the glory of His Resurrection and of His Resurrection-state.

THE UNIVERSITY, ABERDEEN.
*May* 1881.

# CONTENTS.

## LECTURE I.

### *The Fact of the Resurrection of our Lord.*

## LECTURE II.

### The Evidence for the Resurrection of our Lord.

# CONTENTS.

## LECTURE III.

*Theories opposed to the Fact of the Resurrection of our Lord.*

## LECTURE IV.

*Bearing of the Resurrection of our Lord upon His
Person and Work.*

# LECTURE V.

*Bearing of the Resurrection of our Lord upon Christian Life and Hope.*

# LECTURE VI.

*Bearing of the Resurrection of our Lord upon the Church and the World.*

# LECTURE I.

" Why seek ye the living among the dead ?  He is not here,
but is risen."—LUKE xxiv. 5, 6.

THESE words were addressed by angels, on the morning
of the Resurrection, to the first visitors at the tomb
of Jesus ; and they may be fitly adopted to express
at once the principle and the aim of the present
course of Lectures.  I have to speak of the Resurrection of our Lord,— perhaps to some who do not
believe the fact, certainly to many who are not
thoroughly persuaded of it, and not less certainly to
many more who, while they admit it, are very
insufficiently alive to its vast and far-reaching issues.
Even the Church of Christ—and the remark applies
more especially to our Scottish Churches—seems not
yet to have realised the full importance of the truth
with which we have to deal.  Her faith may be as
lively and her love as sincere as that of the women in
the text ; but when she comes with grateful offerings
to the tomb of her Lord, she too often seeks the living
among the dead, and the words spoken to these

B

women have to be addressed to her, " He is not here, but is risen."

Two preliminary remarks have to be made, that the position which I am to occupy in connexion with the subject before us may be better understood :—

1. It is not my intention to make any appeal to those whose views of God and His relation to the world exclude the possibility of miracles. We shall, indeed, see hereafter that the Resurrection of our Lord is not a single or isolated fact,—a miracle like that of the multiplying of the bread or the walking on the sea — the absence of which would not have materially affected the general character of His Mission ; but that it is, in the highest sense, a natural and necessary part of that scheme of the Divine government by which man and nature are carried onward to the destiny awaiting them. Yet, in whatever light we look at it, its miraculous character is undeniable. It supposes a direct and immediate interposition of Divine power. It cannot be resolved into any of those processes around us to which our own experience bears witness. It is not a step in the ordinary evolution of the human race. Though contemplated from the first in the plan of the Creator and Governor of the world, it was, when it took place, a new beginning, a new creation,—in the strict sense of the word—a miracle.

To argue, therefore, with those in whose eyes the miraculous and the historical exclude each other, would be vain.  No amount of proof can be sufficient to convince them.  In their view, a miracle is forbidden, alike by the experience of the past and by the necessary laws of history.  The evidence may be varied, and clear, and strong ; but somewhere or other there must be delusion or mistake.  The weight of an alleged fact, as it claims to be miraculous, or is believed to be so, may be estimated, and the influence exercised by the belief must be allowed for ; but the fact itself can only be set aside.  With those who entertain such views, it is of no use to reason upon grounds of evidence.  The principles from which we severally start are contradictory of each other.  Till the controversy regarding them is settled, no further progress can be made.  To engage in any discussion of that kind would here, however, be out of place. I address those, and those alone, who believe in a personal and free Ruler of the Universe, and in whose eyes a miracle is not inconsistent with just conceptions of Divine wisdom and goodness.

2. It is not my intention to discuss the authenticity or genuineness of any of those books of Scripture which contain a great part at least of the evidence of the fact before us.  Individual passages may occasionally require to be defended, but the books themselves must be accepted in the form in which we have them.  This remark applies not only to those Epistles of St. Paul which even the most negative criticism accepts, but to the Acts of the

Apostles, to the three earlier Gospels, and to the Gospel of St. John. It may indeed be said that I thus ignore the present state of criticism upon what must necessarily form the very foundation of the argument. But the course to be pursued is both justifiable and necessary.

The criticism of the books of Scripture is a subject, the details of which are far too minute for discussion in a public audience ; and, even were it otherwise, the discussion would occupy the whole time at our disposal. It is well, too, to remember that the assertion, so often and so confidently made, that modern inquiry has demonstrated the untrustworthiness of those books to which we appeal, may be met with as repeated and as confident a denial. It has done nothing of the kind. Although it has modified in various respects our conceptions of the different books of the New Testament,—of their origin, their structure, and their aim,—it has failed to establish in the case of any one of them the full extent of its negative conclusions. Even those who differ from us will admit that, were it not for the miracles related in them, they would be entitled to take their place as historical documents by the side of other documents of similar antiquity.

Their relation of miracles cannot be allowed to disturb this conclusion. Were it otherwise, we should be at once compelled to bring argument respecting any part of their contents to an end. If, at the bidding of some particular system of philosophy, and without evidence on other grounds that a New Testament book is unworthy of trust, we reject its statements whenever it relates a miracle, we shall have no point at which to pause, and no principle upon which to accept its narratives, even when they have nothing to do with miracles. We shall find that it is not merely the force of a particular expression, or the correctness of a particular statement, which has been rendered uncertain, but the drift and tenour of each book, as a whole. So essentially is the miraculous interwoven with the structure of each, that, when we remove it, the aspect of the history is completely changed. Except on our own notions of probability, no one portion will have better authority than another. All historical statement will be at an end ; and, so far as the New Testament is itself concerned, we may close inquiry into its facts, because there is nothing to inquire into.

Once more, it is an important consideration upon this point, that we are not wholly dependent for evidence upon the direct statements of the New Testament, that the miracle of the Resurrection was wrought. Other important lines of evidence come in, not indeed sufficient of themselves, but involving facts which can hardly be accounted for on any other supposition than that the Gospel narratives of the Resurrection are true. Thus the general trustworthiness of our records, provisionally assumed, may ultimately be confirmed by the extent to which they harmonize with the best explanation of a series of important and entirely independent phenomena. We may not, indeed, fully comprehend them until we read them in this light. If the argument now to be urged for the Resurrection of our Lord can be made to shape itself into a whole, consistent not only with the special statements of certain books sought to be discredited, but with the general revelation of Scripture as to the purposes of God, and with undeniable facts of history, it is not too much to say that that alone will go far to dispel the doubts about our records, awakened by the bold language of some later inquirers.

We need not therefore attempt to settle these questions of criticism before we proceed further, and we may, for the time at least, accept as generally credible the books that have come down to us with the most powerful evidence in their favour.

With these two preliminary remarks let us turn directly to the subject before us,—the Resurrection of our Lord. The precise nature of the fact first demands our attention. Only when we have formed as distinct a conception of it as possible, shall we be able to judge aright of the evidence necessary to establish it, as well as of the relation in which it stands to the other points to which our attention must be directed. These points will be—The Person and Work of our Lord Himself; Christian Life and Hope; and the Mission and Functions of the Church.

On the nature of the fact there are especially two mistakes to be avoided.

1. There is the view of those who, while they adopt the language of the New Testament, hold that the Resurrection of our Lord is to be understood in a spiritual, not in a literal sense. According to them, it took place only in the hearts of His disciples. No *body* capable of being recognised by the senses came forth from that tomb in the garden where it had been laid by loving friends. But these friends who had lost the bodily presence of their Master were still possessed by His spirit. He lived and worked in their hearts after His death, and this was His real Resurrection : the spiritual alone is real.[1] It is not necessary to ask whether a clear and definite idea can be attached to this view. One thing is obvious—it is not that given us in Scripture. Words denoting material objects are often indeed used there in a spiritual sense ; and, had we no more than the word " resurrection " and its cognates to consider, they might perhaps be treated in that way. But the act itself comes before us in so many connexions, both of word and thought, that, if it can be so disposed of, all fixed interpretation of Scripture becomes impossible. In particular, the Resurrection of Christ is constantly associated with His Death, as one of two

---

[1] This, so far as I can understand the language, is the view of Dr. Abbott in his work, entitled, " Through Nature to Christ." See especially Chap. xxii.

truths which constitute a unity of the closest kind, so
that if the former is to be thought of as only spiritual,
the latter must equally be so ; and again, it is the
pledge and earnest of our own resurrection, so that
upon the same supposition the resurrection of Christians is "past already," and St. Paul was mistaken
when, in his Second Epistle to Timothy, he declared
that certain teachers of this doctrine had "erred concerning the truth."[1]

2. There is the view of those who imagine that, at
His Resurrection, our Lord either entirely laid aside
the material body in which He had previously lived
—thus becoming a purely spiritual Being ;[2] or who
so far modify this hypothesis as to allow that, while
essentially or mainly spiritual, He yet assumed
material substance and form at special moments and
for special purposes.[3]  But again, this view is inconsistent with the whole tenour of Scripture upon the
point.  It is constantly implied there that the life of
our Lord after He rose was that of the *man* Christ
Jesus.  Whatever difficulties may attend the reception of the fact, one thing is clear, that the Apostles
and early disciples of Christ did not think of His
resurrection - state as simply spiritual, but that the
very substance and essence and peculiarity of their
faith was this, that the same Son of man with whom

[1] 2 Tim. ii. 18.

[2] Such is the view of Keim in his "History of Jesus of Nazareth."

[3] This was the opinion of Rothe, as expressed by him in his
"Theological Ethics."

they had companied during the years of His ministry
had been brought back by the glory of His Father
from the grave. Nor was it otherwise with the
enemies of Christ. They understood the doctrine of
the Resurrection in this sense ; and it was because
they did so that their opposition was excited to the
keenest pitch against its preachers. There was nothing in the mere proclamation of a life continued
after death thus to provoke their rage. It was the
assertion that Jesus Christ had risen in the body
which drew forth at one moment their ridicule, at
another their persecuting spirit. Around that fact,
in its plain and literal acceptation, the infant Church
closed her ranks, struggled for existence, and ultimately prevailed. The very word " resurrection "
indeed has no meaning if we do not understand it in
this sense. It is the raising again of what has fallen,
the setting up again of what has been broken down.
If Jesus only lived in the spirit after death, it would
be an abuse of language to call such an entirely new
life a resurrection.

These remarks apply in part to the modification of
this theory formerly spoken of ; besides which, it too
is destitute of all Scripture proof. We never read
there of such transitions from one state to another as
are supposed. What the Risen Lord is at one moment
He always is. If the properties of His being at
times present phenomena incompatible with human
experience, it is not because they belong now to a

heavenly, and now again to an earthly, existence.
What connects Him with heaven shines through the
scenes that tell us most of His connexion with earth;
what connects Him with earth appears in the scenes
that are most closely associated with heaven. After,
not less than before, His Resurrection, our Lord is one.

We must dismiss, therefore, both these views of
our Lord's resurrection-state, as well as every other
sharing their fundamental principle, that His risen
body, whatever its peculiar substance or form, was not
a body in any true sense of the term. Upon this
general point the whole New Testament teaches with
a voice so definite and clear that it is unnecessary to
appeal to particular passages; and we shall hereafter
see that with a bodily, not a merely spiritual, resurrection are connected the most elevating considerations which it addresses to man in his relation both to
the present and the future. The existence of this
teaching is admitted. The opponents of the Resurrection for the most part simply contend either that
there are ways of explaining it other than that of
acknowledging the reality of the fact, or that the
whole story is a fable.

Thus far it is not difficult to come. It is much
more difficult to proceed farther, and to form anything like a distinct conception of what the resurrection-body of our Lord really was. Were it possible,
indeed, to adopt the idea generally entertained, that
" the very body which hung upon the cross and was

laid in the grave, rose again from the dead,"[1] it would
be easy to conceive of it. But, in the light of the
collected statements of Scripture upon the point,
such a view cannot be successfully maintained. It
is true that the body of the Risen Saviour was, in
various important respects, similar to what it had
been. Many passages, often quoted to establish a certain greatness of change which had come over it, are
insufficient for the purpose ; [2] others distinctly illustrate the similarity of its new to its old condition.

It still retained the print of the wound inflicted
by the spear of the Roman soldier, and the marks of
the nails by which it had been fastened to the cross.
Upon one occasion the Risen Jesus even appealed to
Thomas, upon another to all the disciples gathered
together at the time, to convince themselves by these
proofs, that it was no other than Himself who had
appeared among them. He calmed their fears by the
words, " A spirit hath not flesh and bones as ye see
me have;"[3] and when they believed not for joy and
wondered, He asked if they had any meat, and ate a
piece of a broiled fish before them.[4] In addition to
this, many little particulars, not so much expressly
mentioned as rather suggested by the narratives of
the Gospels, lead us to the same conclusion. Thus,
for example, we are entitled to infer that the features
of our Lord's countenance conveyed to the beholder
much the same impression as they had formerly

[1] Note 1.　　　[2] Note 2.　　　[3] Note 3.　　　[4] Note 4.

done; that the tones of His voice had not materially changed; and that His general form did not contradict the recollections of it which His disciples cherished.[1] All these things speak not only of a bodily and material structure, but of one closely corresponding to that which our Lord possessed before His crucifixion.

Much of the manner of His intercourse with the disciples, after the great event, confirms what has been said. He was not a new Redeemer. He was their old Master and Friend. He reminded them of the words that He had spoken while yet present with them;[2] He sent messages to them in which their former intercourse was implied;[3] and He accepted their tokens of joyful homage, when they hailed Him as One who, although thought lost, had been restored.[4] There can be no doubt that He Himself wished to be recognised by them as essentially the same as ever, and that they acknowledged Him to be so.

While all this, however, was the case, it is impossible not to see that, whatever the amount of likeness, a marked change had taken place in our Lord's resurrection - body ; and the same narratives which tell us of the likeness tell us also of the change. Thus, not only on the day of His Resurrection, but on the first day of the following week,—the

[1] John xxi.     [2] Luke xxiv. 44.     [3] Matthew xxviii. 10; John xx. 17
[4] Matthew xxviii. 9; John xx. 20.

very occasion, that is, when He invited Thomas to
put his fingers into the prints of the nails, and his
hand into His side,—we are told that He came and
stood in the midst of the disciples although the doors
were shut; and from the marked manner in which
the Evangelist repeats the statement, it is clear that
he regarded this mode of entrance as supernatural.[1]
At Emmaus He as suddenly vanished out of the
sight of the two with whom He had sat down to eat.[2]
He seems to have passed from place to place with
a rapidity beyond that of ordinary locomotion. We
never read of His retiring as of old for rest or food
to the homes of any of His disciples. We are told
nothing of His hunger, or thirst, or weariness. Even
when He allayed the fears of His disciples by
showing them His hands and His side, He indicated
that He was not exactly what He had been, by
speaking *not* of His "flesh and blood," but of His
"flesh and bones;"[3] while the fact of the Ascension,
and every notion that we can form of the heavenly
abode, are incompatible with the idea that the resurrection-body of Jesus was subject to the same conditions of ponderable matter as before. Nor is this
all, for the manner of our Lord's intercourse with His
disciples after His Resurrection bears hardly fewer
marks of change than the nature of His person. He
no longer accompanied them, as He had been wont to
do, upon their journeys, but sent them forth alone,

---

[1] Note 5.        [2] Luke xxiv. 31.        [3] Note 6.

and met them at the close.[1]   When Mary Magdalene,
in the first joy of her discovery that He was again
before her, would have clung to Him, He said,
"Touch Me not, for I am not yet ascended to My
Father;"[2] and, when He came in contact with the
others, there was a mysteriousness in His bearing,
and a reserve in His manifestations of Himself, very
different from what had been exhibited by Him
during His previous life.

Facts like these undoubtedly lead us to infer that
after His Resurrection our Lord was not the same as
He had been before He died, and that the body with
which He came forth from Joseph's tomb was different
from that which had been laid in it, and was already
glorified.

But there are other considerations tending in the
same direction; and, as the point with which we are
now dealing is one of the most momentous in our
whole inquiry; as it has the closest bearing upon the
evidence; and as it alone makes unspeakably precious
what would otherwise have little influence upon
either our life or hope, it is necessary to examine
them:—

1. First, then, it ought to be observed that the
Glorification of Jesus began at His Resurrection, not
at His Ascension.  All allow that the Saviour, now
exalted in the heavens, has a body different from
that which He possessed on earth.  When did He

---

[1] Matt. xxviii. 10-17.                    [2] Note 7.

assume it? There is not a word in the New Testament to favour the idea entertained by many that
He assumed it only at the moment when, on the
Mount of Olives, He took His last farewell of His
disciples, and returned to the immediate presence of
the Father.[1] Nay, more, it is impossible not to feel
that this idea elevates the Ascension to a place of
importance never assigned to it in Scripture. The
sacred writers draw no such distinction between the
Resurrection and Ascension as to lead to the inference
that the latter stands on the same level as the former,
or that it is to be viewed as one of the great redemptive acts of Jesus. They deal only with two such acts
in the later period of His history—His Death, and His
Resurrection.[2] The Ascension is subordinate to these.
Three of the four Evangelists do not even mention it;[3]
while the words of one of the three, and the other acts
recorded by him of his Risen Master, lead directly to
the conclusion that he associated everything essential
to the Glorification of Jesus with that moment when
He left the "linen cloths lying" in the grave, and
"the napkin that was about His head rolled up in
a place by itself."[4] It is the same with St. Peter and
St. Paul in their discourses and their letters. The
Resurrection is their central theme. Even when the

---

[1] Note 8.

[2] Luke xxiv. 26; Rom. x. 9, xiv. 9; 1 Cor. xv. 3-4; 1 Thess. iv. 14;
1 Peter i. 19-21; Rev. i. 18 ; John ii. 22, etc.

[3] The words of Mark xvi. 19 do not belong to the true text of that
Gospel.                              [4] Note 9.

former speaks of the ministry of Christ as extending
from the baptism of John to the day that He was
taken up, the event upon which he fixes as standing
in need of "witnesses," is the Resurrection;[1] and
when the latter, in 1 Timothy iii. 16, gathers together
six parts of "the mystery of godliness," he does not
say "received up *into* glory," but "received up *in*
glory,"—the glory was already there.

There is no better foundation for the still more
prevalent idea that the change produced upon the
body of our Lord was *gradual*,—that it began at His
Resurrection, went on in a progressive course during
the forty days that elapsed between the Resurrection
and the Ascension, and was only completed at the
latter.[2] No evidence can be adduced in support of
such a view. Some of the most marvellous appearances of the Risen Saviour, those removing Him
furthest from the condition of ordinary humanity,
belong to the very day of His Resurrection ; and the
language of St. John, when he describes each of the
appearances recorded by him as a "manifestation"[3]
of Jesus, implies more than that our Lord simply
made Himself known to His disciples upon these
occasions. At Cana of Galilee, when He turned the
water into wine, we are told that He "manifested"
His glory,[4] that is, that He caused rays of His hidden
glory to shine forth. In like manner He now

[1] Acts i. 22.        [2] Note 10.        [3] John xxi. 14.
[4] John ii. 11.

" manifested " Himself, that is, He revealed Himself
out of a hidden glory into which He had passed;
and this glory could only be the glory of His
eternal state, not waiting to be begun, but begun
already.[1]

2. The view now taken is further confirmed by
the fact that the triumph of our Lord began at His
Resurrection, and neither at His Ascension nor at
any point intermediate between that event and His
Resurrection.　His work of redemption, in so far as it
involved suffering, was then complete.　Nay, not
only all positive suffering, but all humiliation, the
thought of which it is not possible to separate from
that of suffering, then terminated for ever.　Sorrow
could no longer touch His soul, such sorrow at least
as He had known when He was " the Man of sorrows
and acquainted with grief."　He Himself had said to
His disciples at the last supper, that " henceforth,"
from that moment onward, He should drink only the
" new wine " of His Father's kingdom.　When His
soul was thus delivered, His body must have enjoyed
a parallel and equal deliverance.　There could be no
dualism in His resurrection-state even for forty days,
—the spirit free, the body bound, the one drinking
a full cup of gladness, the other still tasting the cup
of woe.　When the reward began, the glory in all
its parts must have begun also; and, if the latter was
not perfect, neither was the former.　Scripture says

[1] Note 11.

C

nothing in this matter of degrees of glory rising
successively above each other.

3. A third point must still be noticed, the bearing
of which upon the question now before us we cannot
overlook. Our Lord's Resurrection is the type and
model of our own. Through union with Him we live.
In conformity to Him lie both our present and our
future glory. Whatever is told us of our own destiny
must have had its analogy in Him. Were it not so,
the whole argument of the Apostle Paul in 1 Cor. xv.,
and other similar passages of his Epistles, would be
undermined. It would be impossible to accept the
doctrine of the Second Adam, or to see how the Risen
and Glorified Lord can be the "first fruits of them
that sleep."

But we are left in no doubt as to the teaching of
Scripture with regard to the general nature of that
body with which believers rise. Thus, in Matt. xxii.
30, our Lord Himself says that "in the resurrection
they neither marry nor are given in marriage, but are
as the angels of God in heaven." In 1 Cor. xv. 50,
we read, "Now this I say, brethren, that flesh and
blood cannot inherit the kingdom of God; neither
doth corruption inherit incorruption." In 1 Cor. vi.
13, we read again, with the same idea at the bottom
of the words, "Meats for the belly, and the belly for
meats: but God shall destroy both it and them."
Passages such as these, even if they stood alone,
would be sufficient to show that the body with which

the believer rises from the grave cannot be the same
as it is now; and that the heavenly world demands
an organization and functions different from those
possessed by us in our present state. "Flesh and
blood cannot inherit the kingdom of God." [1]  Before
they are fitted for a world in which there is neither
change nor death, they must be changed; they must,
in whatever way we endeavour to conceive of it,
become different from what they are.   But the passages just quoted do not stand alone.  There is another,
in which St. Paul expressly describes the change upon
those who shall inherit the kingdom denied to "flesh
and blood."  "There is sown," he says, "a natural
body; there is raised a spiritual body.  There is a
natural body, and there is a spiritual body." [2]  By
the first of these expressions we are not to understand
something conformable to nature, but the psychical,
the soulish, something adapted to the psychical, the
soulish, life in man,—that life which is possessed by
us in common with the lower animals, and as it
is when viewed apart from the higher spiritual
principle which fits us for communion and fellowship
with God.  By the second we are not to understand
the thin, the ethereal, the ghostly, but the pneu-
matical, the spiritual, something adapted to the
spiritual life in man,—that life possessed by us when
God dwells in us, and we in Him.  The words say
nothing in either case of the material particles of our

[1] 1 Cor. xv. 50.          [2] Note 12.

bodies. They do not describe them as being on this side the grave gross, sluggish, and ponderable, as on the other side refined, quick, imponderable. For aught we know, the particles of the body in this dim spot of earth may be of the same nature as they shall be in the bright home of heaven. There is no need to imagine that they must differ in their essence; they may be only subject to a different law. Modern science throws light upon this supposition; and, by what it has revealed to us of the structure of the universe, may be even said to lend it a degree of probability which it might not otherwise possess. Spectral analysis favours the idea that, to the remotest systems of the infinite depths of space, the constituent elements of all created bodies resemble one another; while it has also shown that they are more or less the same as those of earth. Does any one suppose that, considering the different relations in which these bodies stand to the centre of their own systems, or to the systems rolling around them, the laws of relationship between them and all that moves upon their surface will also be the same? This cannot be. The particles constituting a living creature upon one planet may, when transferred to another, be themselves the same, but the laws under which they repel or combine with one another, as well as their functions and powers, may be different. The amount of gravity, for example, at the surface of the various bodies of the solar system, is very different.

Thus also with our bodies. The laws of relation among their particles may change in the transition from the natural to the spiritual body; but it does not follow that the particles themselves must so change their nature as not to deserve the name of bodily particles at all. In its fundamental atoms the "spiritual" body may be as truly a body as the "natural" one.

As, too, our experience affords analogy to the nature of the change referred to, so also it helps us to comprehend the principle by the operation of which that change appears to be effected.

Even in our present state we have well-authenticated instances of the wonderful influence that can be exercised by the spirit over the body;[1] and we have only to suppose, what we must suppose, that in the state of the redeemed the spirit shall be endowed with a glorious strength, far surpassing the highest measure attainable by it in this world, in order to feel that the body may then also be so changed as to be no longer involved in the same conditions as before. In this way the "spiritual" body for which we wait may still be a body, although its needs, its functions, and its powers may be wholly diverse from what they at present are.

But what befalls us must have befallen our Lord. As our great Forerunner in the way to heaven, as our Pattern and Exemplar within the veil, He did not

[1] Note 13.

take upon Him our nature only for the three and
thirty years of His life on earth. He took it into
union with His own Divine nature for ever. He
formed with it an indissoluble tie. He bound it to
Himself in such a way that it was necessary for Him
to share its fortunes whatever they might be, whether
of weakness or strength, of joy or sorrow, of fixity or
change. To think that at any future time, or in any
future circumstances, our body may be one thing,
while our Lord's body was, in the same circumstances,
a different thing, would be to deprive the Incarnation of its meaning, and to invalidate the force of
the encouragement which it supplies.

It follows from all this that the body with which
Jesus rose was not the same as that with which He
died. At some moment or another of those mysterious hours during which He lay in the tomb in the
garden, a great change took place : the "natural"
became a "spiritual" body ; what was sown in "corruption," in this corruptible and mortal flesh, was
raised in "incorruption :" what was sown in "weakness" was raised in "power."

The remarks now made would in all probability
be more easily received were it not for the totally
unfounded impression, that if the resurrection-body
of our Lord was thus an already glorified body, the
change must have been such as would at once strike
the eye with tokens of the unearthly or the heavenly.
It is supposed that the words "glory" and "glorify"

refer to an outer, not an inner glory, to a glory like
that which surrounded Jesus when He was transfigured ; and the idea takes firm possession of the
mind that, when He rose in glory, His raiment and
His countenance must have shone with a brightness
at least equal to that which was exhibited on the
Holy Mount. There is no ground whatever for thinking so. Properly interpreted, " glory" and " glorify"
speak neither of angelic brightness in the countenance, nor of rays of golden light encircling the brow.
They speak of the glory of sonship, of the glory of
the revelation of the Father's love in the suffering
and sacrifice and death of His well-beloved Son, and
of that glory at length owned and adored by an assembled Universe.[1] No statements of the condition of
our Lord after His Resurrection speak of an outward
glory. The opposite rather is implied when Mary
Magdalene believed Him to be the gardener ; and
when His disciples, after He did make Himself known
to them, experienced none of those emotions with
which the three favoured Apostles were overwhelmed
at the spectacle of the Transfiguration. Upon our
Lord's body, as it came from the tomb, there may
have been neither outward nor visible change. The
change which it had undergone may have consisted
altogether in this, that it was now so plastic under the
power of the Spirit that both spirit and body coalesced
into a perfect unity: the old struggle between the

[1] Note 14.

limitation of the one and the illimitableness of the other was entirely and for ever closed.[1]

To all that has now been said different objections may be offered.

1. The view taken of our Lord's resurrection-body may be said to be self-contradictory and impossible. The objection would have weight were it necessary to believe either that the personality of our Lord, in the apparently inconsistent acts related of Him, was really different,—in one, Divine, in another, human,— or that these acts, instead of being a natural expression of what He was, were due to a special exercise of miraculous power. Both these suppositions are unnecessary. If we accept the doctrine of the Incarnation, if we believe that the Eternal Word became flesh and tabernacled among us, we must believe that our Lord, from that point onwards, always existed, not in one state or condition only, but simultaneously in two. The two indeed were combined into one united state; yet in such a manner that, at any instant, either of them might easily be more prominent than the other, might easily manifest itself as His leading characteristic, because in closer correspondence than the other with the particular stage of His history at the time. Thus, during His life on earth, when our Lord moved mainly amidst earthly things, what predominated in Him were the points of His connexion with earth: after His Resurrection, when

[1] Note 15.

He moved mainly amidst heavenly things, the points
of His connexion with heaven came prominently forward.　In neither case was the less prominent nature
laid aside.　In the former He was still Divine, though
constantly exerting, in order to maintain the limitations of His human state, the same act of self-sacrifice
as that made by Him when He assumed humanity.
In the latter He was still human, though the limitations of His humanity were, for the most part,
swallowed up in the illimitableness of His heavenly
condition.　The more retired aspect, therefore, if we
may so speak, of His compound nature might at any
moment assert itself, without doing violence to the
other.　It might come forward in answer to the
demands of surrounding circumstances: it might
withdraw to a subordinate position when the demand
passed away.　In all this too, it will be observed, there
is no miracle specially performed for the occasion.
The personality as a whole remains the same: it does
not change the completeness of its compound state; all
that we can say is that, for adequate reasons, one part
of it is for the time more prominent than the other.

Illustrations of what has been said are afforded
during our Lord's life before the cross, by His walking
on the Sea of Galilee, by His Transfiguration, by His
slipping out of the hands of the mob at Nazareth, by
His sudden withdrawals from the crowds at Jerusalem
when they threatened His life too soon.[1]　Why may

[1] Note 16.

not illustrations of the same general principle, although from the opposite point of view, be afforded by His life after His Resurrection? And, if He had not then completely laid aside His human nature, why may He not have shown by such proofs as men can best understand that His humanity was real? Unless, therefore, we either hold any union of the Divine and human to be impossible, or merge the two completely into one, making the Divine the human or the human the Divine, it seems not unreasonable to say, that the one element might occasionally assert pre-eminence, even in the condition in which the other generally ruled. Nor is it possible to say that in all this there is anything contradictory to the nature of matter. We know indeed too little of the essence of matter, too little of the laws which govern the movements of its infinitesimally minute molecules, too little of its relation to spirit, and of what may be the effect of its complete subserviency to spirit, to entitle us to say that the existence of such a body as that now spoken of is impossible. Is it even more wonderful than the fact of which we are told by our physicists, that in the instant or half instant needed to flash the electric spark from Europe to America, the molecules not only of three thousand miles of wire, but of the sheathing in which the wire is enclosed, and of the water in its immediate neighbourhood, have either changed their place or been affected? There is undoubtedly the exertion of a new power; but how innumerable are the powers in the universe of which we yet know nothing! We may not fully comprehend, but the analogies around us may at least bid us be silent.

2. It may be urged that, even if the general idea of such a body as that of which we have spoken be admitted, it is difficult, if not impossible, to think that the transition to it could have been effected in a moment. A gradual, not an instantaneous change to the new body, it may be said, is alone intelligible. Even those who may adopt this view, however, would be compelled to admit that the forty days between the Resurrection and the Ascension are the only period to which they can assign the change; and that period is far too short to be of the slightest use for such a purpose. If the process of change is to be thought of as gradual, ages upon ages are too little for its completion. In this respect, therefore, the suddenness of the change is in its favour rather than the reverse; for such suddenness is not without analogy in other parts of the history both of our Lord Himself, and of His people. What was the Incarnation? Was not the light which from "the beginning" had been shining in the darkness then embodied in an instant? Was not a "holy thing" then born into the world at once? and, if the idea of the perfect development of the race in its moral and spiritual aspects was thus suddenly realised, why may there not have been something equally sudden with the bodily development of Him who is the type of

the race, not only in its inward and spiritual, but also in its outward and material, aspects ? [1]  And then as to Christ's people.   The Apostle Paul tells us of those who shall be alive upon the earth at the Lord's Second Coming, that they shall be changed "in a moment, in the twinkling of an eye." [2]  What is possible in their case cannot have been impossible in their Lord's.   The transition from one great stage of being to another, from unconsciousness to consciousness, from death to life, must be always sudden. There may be long preparation ; the elements may be long ripening for what is to come ; but, when the hour does come, it must be with the rapidity of an electric stroke ; the gulf between the past and the present must be crossed at one bound.

3. It may be objected that the change spoken of is inconsistent with the preservation of personal identity. If our Lord did not rise with the very body with which He died, was He still the same Lord ?   The objection proceeds upon the supposition that personal identity depends upon the preservation of the same material and ponderable particles of the body, and that, too, in the same relation to each other.   Such a supposition is at variance with facts.   The particles of the human body, it is well known, undergo such continual change, that, in the body of the youth, there is probably not one that belonged to the body of the child ; in the body of the old man not one that belonged to the

---

[1] Note 17.                      [2] 1 Cor. xv. 52.

body of the youth. Yet personal identity is preserved through these different periods of life. The youth is the same personal individual being as the child, the old man the same as the youth. They know themselves, and we know them, to be so. The experiences of the earlier stages of our lives are, in their later stages, as truly ours, and ours alone, as at the moment when they were made. The memories of any one period of our existence belong to no one but ourselves, and do what we like we cannot transfer them to another. We are a part of all that we have seen, although now, when we look back, not one atom may be left of the old eye that saw. Nor is it thus only with man. It is the law of all existence. That which constitutes the identity of a grain of wheat is preserved, although the grain passes into the blade, the blade into the ear, the ear into the full corn in the ear. That which constitutes the identity of an insect is preserved, although the changes that take place in it are often so great that long-continued and patient tracing of its growth is necessary to establish a conclusion which would be rejected by every ordinary observer as incredible.[1] In neither of these cases is there the slightest resemblance between the beginning and the end; not one particle of matter is left in its old relations: yet identity is not destroyed. Upon what personal identity really depends is an altogether different question, and we are not called upon to answer it. We know too

[1] Note 18.

little either of the body or the soul, or of the particular law which, regulating their relation to one another, constitutes the personality of each individual, to be able to throw any light upon such a point. It is enough to urge that no change in the bodily frame, however sudden or complete, necessarily affects the identity of him in whom the change takes place. We can easily conceive our bodies to be endowed with properties altogether different from their present ones; to be under laws of limitation from which they are now free; to be free from laws of limitation by which they are now bound; to be independent of the means of sustenance now absolutely indispensable to continued life; to be possessed of organs of sensation elevated to a degree of accuracy and power of which we have no experience; to be delivered from all that hinders them from accompanying the soul in its loftiest or most distant flights,—while yet we ourselves shall remain the same beings as we are, in everything that makes existence either personal to us, or a worthy object of desire. Must it have been otherwise with Christ? We cannot too completely dispel the idea, ever apt to linger in the mind, that unless our Lord rose with the particles of His human body the same, and under the same laws, as when He died, He must be a different Lord, a different personality, from what He was.

These objections, then, may be dismissed, and we may return to the fundamental proposition of these

Lectures, that the body with which our Lord rose from the grave, though still a true body, was not the same as that with which He died.

If so, it cannot fail to be observed how absolutely unique is the fact with which we have to deal. Viewed even in its simplest form, indeed, the story of our Lord's Resurrection, as that of a rising from the grave, may be justly spoken of as unique. There have been stories of other so-called resurrections, when the popular mind, awed by the gigantic virtues or vices of heroes or of tyrants, has fancied to itself that those who had so deeply moved the world must return to this stage of life from which they had for the moment disappeared. But not one of whom such expectations were entertained was ever supposed to have actually died. It was not to death that the subjects of these popular legends succumbed; it was to sleep, only sleep prolonged for years or centuries.[1] If, however, even as compared with them, the Resurrection of our Lord, in any form in which it is possible to think of it, was unique, it possesses, when looked at in its true nature, a stamp of uniqueness wholly different and infinitely higher. They were, at the most, only resurrections to the old conditions of life, to be followed in due time by death. Here there was not only no more death; there was a total change. The Risen One was the same, yet not the same. A wonderful transition had taken place; and, although in the root

[1] Note 19.

of His Being, the Christ of the resurrection-morning was the same as formerly, His body was yet in many respects different from what it had been when He died on Calvary. The Lord Jesus rose, but not to His old condition :—that is the teaching of the New Testament, and the whole value of Christ's Resurrection is involved in it.

Such then is the fact with which we have to deal. Let us note two consequences which follow from it, the first connected with the Evidence, the second with the Effect that the evidence ought to produce on us.

1. As to the Evidence, we cannot expect it to be in all respects similar to that which proves the reality of the life of Jesus before His crucifixion. In point of fact we know that it is not. It is the evidence of believers *only;* and from the days of Celsus downwards, it has been urged that the Christian cause is weakened by this fact. Even now there is an impression upon many minds that our evidence would have been much stronger and more irresistible than it is, had it also been borne by the world; had Jesus showed Himself not to disciples only, witnesses chosen before of God, but to all the people,—to Pharisees and Sadducees, to the judges who condemned Him, and to the soldiers who nailed Him to the cross. What has been said ought completely to expose the fallacy of such reasoning. If our Lord's post-resurrection state was such as has been described, it was not possible

for Him to come in contact with the world again.
To have done so would have been to renew His
Passion. That Passion consisted in other things
besides sufferings deliberately inflicted upon Him by
the world. Mere intercourse with the world caused
no small part of it. To have His aims misunderstood, His motives misinterpreted, His invitations
scorned ; to have the very works in which the glory
of His Father most conspicuously appeared, traced
to a league on His part with Beelzebub; to find that
much of the Divine seed sown by Him fell upon the
hard wayside, and was taken away before it could
penetrate the heart; to come into hourly contact with
ignorance instead of knowledge, selfishness instead of
love, oppression instead of justice, formalism instead
of piety, truth perverted by its appointed guardians,
His Father's house turned into a den of thieves, consolation torn from the wretched, man living without
God and dying without hope,—all this was suffering
and sorrow ; it was His burden and His cup of woe.
No approach even to a fresh experience of a like kind
was possible after the burden had been borne, and the
cup drained to the dregs. From the very nature of
the case, the Risen Lord could come in contact only
with disciples,—with those in whom, instead of
finding cause for a renewal of His pain, He might
"see of the travail of His soul and be satisfied."
If His Resurrection was the beginning of His glory,
it would have been a reversal of the whole plan of

D

our redemption, a confounding of the different steps
of the economy of grace, had He " after His passion "[1]
presented Himself alive to any but disciples.

But that is not all. It was not only on His own
account that our Lord, having now entered upon His
Glorification, could no more show Himself to the
world,—it was also because the world could neither
have understood Him, nor borne true witness to Him.
The mere sensuous perceptions of men could not have
appreciated what He was ; and the impressions of
ordinary observers would have been false. Having
before known Him only as a man, with the limitations and wants of other men, what would they have
thought when they saw Him unconfined by these
limitations, unaffected by these wants, no longer
dependent upon food, and suddenly appearing and
disappearing as the inhabitant of some higher world,
but either that He was a spirit, or that He was not
the same Jesus as before ? We have no right therefore to ask for evidence from the world of the Resurrection of our Lord. It was not an arbitrary thing in
the Almighty to reject such evidence, nor was it part
of a judicial process, in order to deprive those who
had not turned their eyes to the Christ in His humiliation of the opportunity of beholding Him in His
exaltation. It was necessary ; it was an essential
part of that fitness of things which God never vio-
lates. The world could not have borne witness to

[1] Acts i. 3.

what Jesus had become ; and, because it could not, it had no opportunity of making the attempt.

2. As to the Effect which the evidence ought to have on us, it follows from what has been said, that we cannot have a true view of the Resurrection of our Lord until we have come within the circle of Christian truth, and have been spiritually prepared to apprehend it. The Resurrection is more than an outward fact ; it has a transcendental meaning. Proof of the outward fact men may have—such proof as has led many to believe that there is no fact of the past so well attested. But then the fact alone is of comparatively small importance. It is a miracle ;—so is the raising of Lazarus or of the widow's son at Nain. We cannot say of any one miracle that it is greater or smaller than another in respect of evidential power. It may be more or less striking, more or less calculated to impress the imagination or to touch the feelings,—but what passes in the least degree beyond human capability brings us at once into the presence of the Divine. It is not wrong then to say that the mere fact of our Lord's rising again is of comparatively small importance. Had He returned to a human state altogether similar to His former one, it would concern us little. Like any other miracle, it might help to convince us that Christianity is from God, but it would have no organic connexion with our own Christian life ; it would neither satisfy our wants nor appease our longings. What we care to believe is

that, after His Resurrection, our Lord entered on a new and spiritual stage of being ; that He moved in another region—in another world ; that He was no longer spirit dwelling in a tabernacle of clay, but spirit expressing itself in a form wholly suitable to its nature as pure spirit, and lifted above the conditions by which it had been formerly confined. This cannot be felt by those who are living outside the circle of Christian truth ; and only, therefore, when they come within that circle, can they acknowledge the full power of the evidence of the Resurrection of Christ, because only then can they comprehend its meaning.

It may indeed be said that the Apostles preached the Resurrection of their Lord to the Jews and to the world as a fundamental verity of the Christian faith, and that they expected the world to be convinced by the assertion that God had raised Him from the dead. Undoubtedly they did. But when they did so, they did not proclaim the Resurrection simply as a miracle. They proclaimed it in all the depth of its meaning, in all the vastness of its issues, as a part of the whole body of Christian truth, that it might thus touch the hearts of the susceptible, that it might stir the little spark of conscious relation to God which is by nature in the breast of every one, and which, when not suppressed or extinguished, is waiting to kindle into flame in the presence of the full brightness of the Truth. The preaching of the Resurrection of our Lord by His Apostles was not simply a display of evidence. It was that, but it was more. It was the assertion of a truth of Christianity, which, by its meaning, unified and irradiated all its other truths. The two things reacted on each other. The fact, resting on its appropriate evidence, invited to the consideration of its own transcendental meaning; the transcendental meaning, showing the place of the fact in the Divine economy of grace, gave probability and even confirmation to the fact. This is the sacred circle of truth, the thought of whose completeness somewhere is suggested to every one by the intimations of his own breast. When we catch a glimpse of the whole, we can best determine whether the small arc on which we are standing is a part of that whole, or whether it belongs to some other circle. In vain should we attempt to make the truth easier of acceptance, by insisting only upon single parts of it for a time. It is not by a mutilated, but by a whole gospel, that we best win men to the faith of Christ. First one part of it attracts them, then a second part is seen, and perhaps a third; as yet isolated, unconnected, but awakening the thought that there is the same measure of circularity in each; until, at last, the conviction forces itself upon the mind that they are really parts of the same circle, and the circle itself stands before the view in all its completeness, around Him as its centre who is the centre of all truth, the Life and the Light of men.

Thus, then, we have suggested to us the course

which ought to be taken in connexion with the subject of these Lectures. In the first instance we have to deal with history. The fact that the Lord did rise must rest upon a firm basis of historical evidence. No wants or longings of the heart of man, no moral or religious considerations of any kind whatever, can of themselves establish such a fact. The fact must precede the dogma, if dogma it can be called, not the dogma the fact. But we cannot pause there. We must try to ascertain the meaning of the fact, to assign to it its position in the arrangements of the Almighty for the human race, and to see if it be not a fitting step in some great process, a part of some great plan. Then we shall have fresh evidence confirmatory of the historical, and the historical evidence will possess fresh power. Until the whole case, therefore, has been looked at, those perplexed with difficulties ought to suspend their judgment; and let it be the earnest prayer of each of us that, upon a matter involving such momentous issues, we may all be guided into all the truth.

# LECTURE II.

" This Jesus hath God raised up, whereof we all are witnesses."
ACTS ii. 32.

FROM the general considerations mentioned in my
last Lecture in connexion with the Resurrection of
our Lord, I proceed to the evidence for the fact. Yet
it is only a brief summary of this evidence that can be
now attempted. We must hasten onwards, with as
little delay as possible, to the theories which have
been brought forward to destroy its force, and to the
dogmatic and practical value of the fact itself.

## I.

I begin with the evidence of St. Paul; partly
because of its clearness and the weight of the circumstances attending it; partly because it is that
of which we possess the earliest record; for, to say
nothing of its other sources, it is contained in the
First Epistle to the Corinthians, written before either
the Apocalypse or the Gospels. It is not necessary
to dwell in detail upon the particulars given us of
that occasion on which St. Paul believed that he

beheld the Risen Lord, and of which we have no fewer than three accounts in the Acts of the Apostles,— one by the author of that book, the other two from the lips of St. Paul himself.[1] These particulars are familiar to every one.

It has indeed been urged that there are variations in the narratives which destroy their value, and which indicate either a mythical origin, or a tendency of the writer so to frame his story on each particular occasion as to adapt it to the circumstances in which he was introducing the Apostle at the time. But the differences are not greater than will always be found in accounts of the same event, given by different actors or even by the same actor at different periods of his life. Through them all the statement stands prominently forth, that Saul, on his way to Damascus, and in the circumstances described, beheld the Risen and Glorified Lord.

The passages, 1 Cor. ix. 1 and xv. 8, are to the same effect. The first of these, " Am I not an Apostle ? Have I not seen Jesus our Lord ? "[2] derives its whole force from the fact that St. Paul had actually seen the Lord after His Resurrection, and had received his apostolical commission from Him in the same way as his fellow-apostles. In the second, " And, last of all, as unto one born out of due time, He appeared to me also," the thought of a bodily appearance of the Risen Saviour is rendered necessary

---

[1] Acts ix. 1-30 ; xxii. 1-21 ; xxvi. 2-23.          [2] Note 20.

by the whole argument of the chapter, which unquestionably refers to a bodily resurrection of believers.

But it is not enough to dwell on passages such as
these, in which St. Paul directly asserts that he had
seen the Risen Lord. We have to remember the effect
produced upon him by what he saw. That effect
is indeed no sufficient proof that his impressions were
well founded, but it is a proof how deeply he was himself convinced that the sight had been real and not
imaginary. It changed the whole current of his life.
It is the key at once to his future labours, and to his
system of Christian thought. His belief in the Resurrection of his Lord filled his life with all that made
life worth living for, led him to accept his sufferings
not merely with patience but with joy, and taught
him to welcome the hour of his departure, though it
might be amidst the pains of martyrdom, as a king
waiting to be crowned welcomes the approach of his
coronation.[1]

To all this we have the most ample testimony
from his own lips. In the case of the Gospel
witnesses of the Resurrection of Jesus, we have
for the most part nothing except brief statements
of what they saw of their Risen Master; and we can
only infer that that sight roused them from their
despondency to the new and vigorous life of the
early Church. In the case of St. Paul, upwards of
twenty years of unparalleled labours are before us,

[1] 2 Tim. iv. 6-8.

with Epistles of his own, laying open, at every stage
of that long period, the inmost feelings of his heart,
revealing often in the most incidental manner the
motives by which he was animated, enabling us to
study him with the most minute analysis, showing us
the whole secret of his life and work.   And what was
that secret ?   It has been said by the great leader of
the negative school of criticism on the Continent that
it was the impressiveness with which the death of
Jesus came all at once to stand before his soul, and
that " from the moment of the revelation in which the
Son of God was revealed in him, he lives only in the
contemplation of the Crucified One ; his whole system
of thought turns upon this one fact." [1]   The same
idea, though not used for the same purpose, probably
prevails in much wider circles.   But it is not correct.
The importance attached by St. Paul to the death of
Christ depends not simply on the fact that Jesus
died, but on the fact that He who so died was afterwards the Risen One.   It was not by the thought
of the death of Christ as a sacrifice for sin that St.
Paul was led to the thought of His Resurrection.
The process in his mind was the reverse.   It was the
thought of His Resurrection, the thought that by it
He had been proved to be the Son of God with
power, which showed the peculiarity and importance
of His death.   Christ Himself, the second Adam, the
" Man from heaven," is the centre of the Pauline

[1] Baur, " History of the First Three Centuries," p. 47.

Theology; and it was as the Risen Lord that He
appeared to him in that character. Even were we to
accept Baur's view, we should still have to explain
how that death upon the cross, which in the eyes of
a Jew was fatal to Messianic claims, not only lost
its shame to the Apostle, but became to him the
germinating principle of a new order of things by
which the world was to be transfigured and glorified.
There would be only one solution of the difficulty,
and that solution the Resurrection.[1] Hence it is that
in many a passage in which St. Paul speaks of Jesus,
His Resurrection, although it may not be expressed,
is implied. The title " Lord," in particular, so often
used by him, always carries us to His heavenly not
merely to His earthly glory ;[2] while the general tone
of the Apostle's language, both in his addresses in the
Acts and in his own letters, shows us that faith in a
risen and living Christ is the undercurrent by the
force of which he is irresistibly borne along, whatever
at any particular moment are his feelings or purposes or aims. It is not conceivable that so powerful
an effect should have been produced upon him, had
he not himself been thoroughly satisfied as to the fact
to which alone it can be traced. It is certainly out of
a conviction as clearly formed and as firmly held as
human conviction can be that he speaks. Let us
suppose for a moment that he was wrong, it would
evidently have been a hopeless task to try to convince

[1] Note 21.  [2] Note 22.

him that he was so.   We may listen to him or not ;
his testimony will never change.

All this is the more remarkable when we consider
that St. Paul was thoroughly alive to the extraordinary
nature of the fact, and that he gives his testimony as one
who is aware that it needs confirmation by others, and
who is under a solemn sense of his own responsibility to
be faithful.   We see the first of these points in his summary of witnesses in the opening verses of 1 Cor. xv.,
and in the expression which comes in so incidentally
at verse 6, when, mentioning the five hundred brethren,
he adds, "of whom the greater part remain unto this
present, but some are fallen asleep."   We see the second
in verse 15 of the same chapter, in the horror with
which he shrinks from being " found " a false witness
of God, because he has " testified of God that He raised
up Christ ; " for the word " found " shows us that he
is thinking of Divine not human judgment, that he
is witnessing at the bar of God and not of man.

In circumstances such as these, St. Paul gives his
testimony to the Resurrection of our Lord ; and he so
gives it that the most skilful counsel in a modern
court of law will scarcely venture to think that it
would be in his power to shake it by any cross-
examination he could conduct were the Apostle now
before him.   Even Dr. Baur abandoned the attempt
to explain it fully.   " It is true," he says, " that no
analysis, whether psychological or dialectical, can
detect the inner secret of the act in which God

revealed His Son in him;"[1] in other words, the
miracle being impossible, and the inner process in the
Apostle's mind inexplicable, all that we can do is to
ask as to any step which prepared the way for his
transition to the Christian faith. Such a statement
cannot satisfy inquirers; and it has not done so.
Baur's own disciples have been dissatisfied, and have
resorted to the theory of visions. The value of that
theory must remain for consideration in my next
Lecture. In the meantime it is clear that we have,
in the Apostle of the Gentiles, not only a witness for
a bodily Resurrection of our Lord, but one whose
evidence is confirmed and strengthened by every consideration that can lend it weight.

## II.

We have not only the evidence of St. Paul, but also
that of others of the Apostles. It is true that writings
of only two or three of their number have come down
to us, so that we cannot, in the case of all of them,
refer to actual words which they employed. But,
when we can do so, nothing can be more explicit than
their statements. We have the witness of St. Peter,
so often given both in the Acts of the Apostles and
in his own First Epistle, that it seems hardly necessary to quote any special passage.[2] St. John, in the

---

[1] *u. s.*, p. 47.

[2] Acts i. 22 ; ii. 24-33; iii. 13-15; iv. 10 ; v. 31, 32 ; x. 40-42 ;
1 Peter i. 3-21 ; iii. 18-21.

Apocalypse, speaks of Jesus Christ as the "first begotten of the dead."[1]   And the writer of the Epistle
to the Hebrews, while implying throughout his whole
argument as to the High Priesthood of Christ that the
Lord is risen, draws his Epistle to a close with prayer,
on behalf of his readers, to the God of peace "who
brought again from the dead our Lord Jesus."[2]

We are not, however, left to such words as these.
Both in the case of those who wrote them, and in
that of the other Apostles, we have something more
powerful than words : we have their lives.  We can
compare what they were immediately after the Resurrection with what they were before it.  The change is
marked and striking.  The men who, but a few days
previously, had been so timorous that they had shut
themselves up in an apartment with closed doors, for
fear of the Jews, now hasten to the most public places
in Jerusalem, that they may testify to the innocence of
their Master and to the guilt of those who crucified
Him.  The men who had not only quailed before the
authorities when their Lord was seized, but had forsaken Him in His hour of utmost need, now face
without hesitation the highest tribunal of the land,
and openly defy it.  The men who shrank from suffering to such a degree that the boldest of them dis-
owned his Master's allusion to its coming, now glory
in affliction, persecution, and death.  Weakness has
given place to strength, sadness to joy, despair to

[1] Rev. i. 5.                    [2] Heb. xiii. 20.

hope. Above all, the narrow prejudices of their time
have been overcome ; and they rise to the thought of
a whole world gathered into one family of God, each
nation equally dear to Him, each equally fitted to
serve Him in its own place. Things like these are the
tokens of a change so great that we seem to move in a
region of fiction when we speak of it. Yet it is not
denied that it was real. How is it to be explained?
It needs explanation, and no explanation is even
attempted except one. The Apostles believed that
they had seen the Risen and Glorified Lord : whether
they deceived themselves is not the question now.
It is enough for us at present that they did believe,
and that these results can be traced to nothing but
that faith.

Nay, further, we ought not to overlook the fact
that the very office of Apostle which they held, was
much more intimately associated in their minds
with the Resurrection of Christ than we commonly
suppose. We have seen how closely the two things
were connected in the case of St. Paul. He felt that
his apostleship depended on his having seen the
Risen Lord. But this was not because to have seen
Him was a mere matter of Christian privilege, by
which he was placed upon an equality with the eleven
who had been in Christ before him. Both in their
case and his, the connexion with the Resurrection of
Jesus was of a much deeper kind ; and it lay in the
very nature of the apostolic office that the person

clothed with it must be a " witness " of the truth out
of which it sprang.[1]    Every apostolic work or suffering leads, therefore, directly to the thought of the
Risen Saviour.  The more faithfully the work was
done, the more patiently the suffering was met, the
more is each a testimony to Jesus, not simply as
He died, but as He rose again.

### III.

In addition to the evidence of St. Paul and of
other Apostles, we have also that of many of the
first disciples of Christ.   Putting out of view the
appearance to St. Paul, ten different appearances of
the Risen Saviour are recorded in the New Testament.[2]
It is by no means certain, indeed, that even these are
the only ones, for the language of St. Luke, when he
says that " unto the apostles whom He had chosen
He showed himself alive after His passion by many
infallible proofs, appearing unto them by the space of
forty days, and speaking of the things concerning the
kingdom of God," [3] would seem to imply that there
may have been other occasions when the Apostles
enjoyed the opportunity of beholding and conversing
with their Master.   But, whether absolutely all or
not, ten appearances are those of which alone we have
positive information, and to them we must confine
ourselves.   Even the evidence connected with them,

---

[1] Acts i. 22.   For a fuller statement on the point see Lecture VI.
[2] Note 23.                              [3] Acts i. 3.

indeed, there is no time to consider in detail; but it
is so well impressed on every memory that, without
attempting this, some of its general characteristics
may be noted.   Let us mark,—

1. The variety of circumstances under which the
Risen Saviour appeared.  It was not simply to one
person or set of persons that He manifested Himself at
different times; nor was it only to persons whose frame
of mind at the moment may be supposed to have been
the same.  The women in a company; the two disciples
on the way to Emmaus; the Apostles assembled without the doubting Thomas; the same Apostles assembled with Thomas in their midst; the five hundred
brethren; the seven Apostles by the Sea of Tiberias;
the eleven who were present at the Ascension; Mary
Magdalene, Peter, James,—each of these last alone,
—how different are the groups which witnessed the
stupendous fact!   Nor were the feelings of these
different groups, at the instant when the manifestations were made to them, less various than the groups
themselves.  The women departing quickly from the
sepulchre with fear and great joy; Mary Magdalene
standing without the sepulchre weeping; the two disciples talking in sadness of all the things which had
happened; the Apostles assembled with shut doors for
fear of the Jews; the same Apostles again assembled,
with the addition of one who was resolved to put any
appearance which they might witness to the strictest
proof; the brethren in Galilee gathered together in

E

obedience to Christ's command, and in wondering expectation of what was to happen ; the seven engaged in their old occupation as fishermen ; the eleven at Mount Olivet already convinced, their incredulity over, and rejoicing in the presence of their Lord with the full assurance that it was indeed Himself ;—is it possible to conceive a greater variety of moods than those in which *they* were, to whom Christ showed Himself alive ?   On many of these occasions, too, our Lord did not appear only for a moment, striking them with a sudden astonishment, and then disappearing from their sight.   He spoke to them, and they were able to treasure up His words.   He gave them in many particulars their commission to the world, and in the spirit of it they spent their whole future life. He encouraged them by His promises, and they found in them their stay amidst all the persecutions even unto death which they afterwards endured.   It is hardly possible to think of a greater variety of circumstances calculated to test the reality of the impression made on them.

2. While the opportunities of observation enjoyed by the Gospel witnesses were thus favourable, the characteristics of their evidence itself are not less worthy of our regard.   It exhibits a minuteness and circumstantiality which it is difficult to connect with anything but the position of eyewitnesses in perfect possession of every faculty for forming a sound and healthy judgment,—with eyes to see, and ears to

hear, and hands to handle, able to give attention to
whatever happened in their presence, and with the
power of memory to retain it. It is distinguished by
a simplicity which avoids all exaggeration, makes no
boast of enthusiastic feeling, and frankly confesses a
large measure of ignorance and blindness; whereas,
had it been the result of either conscious or uncon-
scious invention, it could hardly have failed to bear
marks of the excitement which gave rise to it. At the
same time it is presented with a gravity and serious-
ness, showing how fully alive the witnesses are to the
nature of the fact to which they testify. There is no
lightness of sentiment in regard to it, but rather a
deep and solemn sense of its supreme importance—
such a sense as leads them to communicate it with
eager haste to one another; and not only to speak of
it amongst themselves, but to proclaim it in the most
public and open, in the boldest and most decisive,
manner,—in the Temple, in the synagogues, before
the people, before their rulers, before Gentiles as well
as Jews, " in Jerusalem and in Judea, and in Samaria,
and unto the uttermost part of the earth."[1]

The Resurrection of their Lord was the very kernel
of their message to mankind—that without which it
seemed to them that their preaching would have been
vain, and the faith of their hearers also vain. We
may sometimes think that even without it they had
enough to tell the world. Could they not have spoken

[1] Acts i. 8.

only of the love of Jesus, of His life for man, of His death upon the cross, of His holy example, of the good hope which He had given of a happier home than earth ? It is unnecessary to make such a supposition. The more we magnify the other truths of Christianity, the more must it seem strange to us that the Resurrection of our Lord should hold the place it does in the Christian testimony of the early disciples, unless they were convinced of its unparalleled importance.

3. We ought not to forget that the evidence was published to the world on the very spot *where*, and at the very time *when*, the event was said to have happened, and that no one was able to controvert it. Forty days indeed passed during which there was little occasion for contradiction, because the disciples, in obedience to their Master's own command,[1] made no proclamation of the fact. Ten days more followed, while they waited in silence and seclusion for the promised Spirit. During that period they had ample opportunity for reflexion, alike upon what they were to preach, and upon the reception which, in preaching it, would in all probability await them. We cannot suppose that they did not think of these things ; yet, no sooner were the ten days over, than they at once came forth announcing the Resurrection of Jesus as a leading part of their message to men.[2] At a moment when it was yet possible to test every incident, to examine every witness, to expose every trace of

[1] Luke xxiv. 49 ; Acts i. 8.        [2] Acts ii. 24.

fraud,—the Apostles openly and unhesitatingly proclaimed the fact.[1]　And all this liability to exposure,
if the witness was false, continued upwards of twenty
years, until at least the first Epistle of St. Paul to
the Corinthians was written.[2]　Nor does any serious
effort seem to have been made by rulers or Pharisees
to contradict the testimony.　Among the people, indeed, the story—spread abroad at the first moment
of alarm—that the disciples had stolen the body while
the soldiers of the guard slept long continued to
circulate.[3]　But no reliance appears to have been
placed upon it by any in authority.　In all the trials
recorded in the Acts of the Apostles, the charge was
not once repeated by those who had the first preachers
of the Gospel at their bar.　Yet this could not have
arisen from any idea that the story of the Resurrection was either unimportant or unworthy of refuta-
tion.　The most striking proof of the contrary is
indeed afforded by the singular contrast presented by
the Sadducees in their eager opposition to the first
preachers of the Gospel, and their general indifference
to the preaching of our Lord Himself.　The preaching
of the Resurrection, not of the general resurrection,
but of that of Jesus as an actually accomplished fact,
roused within them a spirit of persecution from which
they had hitherto been free.[4]　Even before the event
took place, the chief priests had been desirous to

[1] Acts iii. 15 ; iv. 10-33.　　[2] 1 Cor. xv. 6.　　[3] Matt. xxviii. 15.
[4] Note 24.

anticipate it.[1]   It was indeed the most urgent interest of all, whether Pharisees or Sadducees, to refute the fact.   The Church which they so much dreaded was rising around them by the preaching of the Resurrection of its Founder.   Thousands were converted by the tidings that One whom they had crucified as a malefactor had been brought back by the Almighty from the grave.   If this statement was true, they, and not the Christians, were in opposition to that God in the knowledge of whom they gloried,—they, and not their victims, were contending against the most signal manifestations of His will.   They were certainly not blind to this ; their whole conduct proves the contrary.   It is not that of men indifferent or scornful, but of men who, desirous to convict an adversary, have no argument sufficient for the purpose.   They resort neither to evidence nor reason, but to violence—the last argument of despair.   They threaten, they imprison, they rouse popular prejudice against the witnesses of the fact ; the fact itself they do not touch.

Is there any defect in all this evidence ?   We are told that there are two.

1. In the first place, it is said that we have no eye-witness of the Resurrection itself ; no one beheld the Saviour rise.[2]   But what of that ?   A friend has been absent on a journey, and no one witnessed his return. Would any member of his family dream for a moment

[1] Matt. xxviii. 13-15.          [2] Note 25.

of urging, when he is found in his own room, that
it was not himself? There might be an emotion of
joyful surprise, and an inquiry when and how he
came ; but it would never even occur to the wildest
scepticism to question his identity upon a ground so
trifling as that he had not roused the household when
he entered. So also in the case before us. The whole
question turns upon the fact that our witnesses
recognised their Lord after He rose to be the same
Lord whom they had known before He died. They
might have been mistaken ; but that consideration
the objection does not touch. It relates solely to the
fact that they did not behold Him in the act of
rising ; and, so far, it is absolutely valueless if they
afterwards knew Him to be the same. He had died,
He had been buried, He was now beside them ; and
He could not have been so if He had not risen. Or
suppose that they had actually seen Him come forth
from the tomb on the Resurrection morning, and had
proclaimed to the world that they had done so, does
any one imagine that their evidence would have been
strengthened by such a statement? Their recognition of Him would have had no more legitimate
grounds than those upon which it rested at a later
date ; and theories to account for their delusion
would have been as easily multiplied as they are now.

2. It is urged, as a second defect in our evidence,
that our different witnesses are inconsistent with each
other, thus confirming the suspicion that their accounts

are not historical, but mythical or legendary. One
or two general observations may be made on this.

There must always be a certain allowance for
divergences when we have before us narratives of
the same event by different persons. No two men
see the same thing exactly in the same way, or receive
from it precisely similar impressions. If they are
faithful to themselves, they must differ from one
another,[1] and it is the province of the impartial judge
to disentangle the different statements, and to determine whether the fact as a whole, or how much of it,
is true. This general principle is as fully applicable
to Scripture as it is to legal processes. However
miraculous any fact there related may be, nothing
is more certain than that the record is given us
through the same laws as those which regulate all
history; and that we are thus entitled to apply this
principle to it with the same precision, and to the
same extent, as in every other case. Statements
directly and positively contradictory as to the main
point at issue would undoubtedly justify our reject-
ing it; but where the main point is admitted by
every witness, slighter differences are not only perfectly consistent with its truth, but are of the utmost
importance for establishing it. This is precisely the
state of matters with which we have now to deal. It
is denied by no one that through all the evidence
afforded by our witnesses there runs the one decided

[1] Note 26.

conviction that their Risen Lord had manifested Himself to them or others. They thoroughly believed that ; they wished to give expression to their belief. Unless it can be shown that the differences are such as to lead us to the thought of mythical or legendary exaggeration, we are bound to give them the benefit of a principle of universal application.

It is further to be observed, therefore, that the divergences of our Gospel narratives bespeak an origin wholly different from that of the legend or the myth. Accretions springing from such sources are unregulated and loose. They bear upon them the marks of the popular imagination, and they are connected with hopes cherished by a united people, rather than with obligations to a moral and religious state, which different classes of a community must see in a light peculiar to themselves. It is with the latter that we have to do. In the case of our Evangelists we mark no working of a general fancy heaping up various particulars, but special aims in accordance with their special circumstances and work. We do the Evangelists injustice when we regard them as witnesses in a court of law, who have been appointed to prove a fact, and who have deliberately taken it in hand to do so. Such is not their position. In those days men did not need to have every great fact of the Christian faith proved to them by historical narrative before they believed. They did not wait for one witness after another to come forward and demon-

strate the truth of the varied doings and sufferings of
their Lord. The first stirrings of faith were awakened
by the general tradition of the Church. Men were
attracted to her by the sight of her blessed and
glorious life ; and then they were gradually, within
the bosom of her family, made more and more
acquainted with the fulness of the facts from which
that life sprang, and by which it was sustained. So
far as their faith was at first concerned they could
have done, and they actually did, without the Gospels
altogether. But they naturally desired to hear more
of the life of Jesus; those who had been eyewitnesses
of His majesty were as eager to write what they had
seen ; and thus, with a view mainly to the satisfaction of present wants, and with little, if any, thought
of affording for the benefit of future generations a
contemporaneous history of events, our Gospels came
into existence.[1]

If this be so, it will be at once seen that the point
of view from which the different accounts of the life
of Christ given in the Gospels, and, amongst others,
the different accounts of His Resurrection, sprang,
could not fail to exercise a material influence upon
the structure of the narratives. It is not the relation
of simple objective facts that will occupy the thoughts
of the writers ; it is these facts in the light in which
they are of special interest to themselves, and to
those for whom they write. Each writer will select

[1] Note 27.

what is most appropriate to his object ; he will be
to a certain extent indifferent to its bond of connexion
with what he is not concerned to relate ; he will
pass suddenly into that for which he cares ; and, while
he will not depart from historical truthfulness, he will
yet so handle his materials, that in order to understand them we must keep distinctly before us his
special aim.

Godet, in a short essay on the Resurrection of
Christ, has touched upon this point. He compares
the different narratives of the Resurrection to the
different pieces of a child's map which, when taken
down, a little care can reconstruct.[1] The comparison
leads the reader to expect too much. We are not
dealing with the solid pieces of a child's map, each
of which fits in exactly to its proper place in the
whole. We are dealing with facts capable of being
differently viewed, and certain to be so, when brought
into contact with minds interested in different aspects
of the truth.

In point of fact, when we turn to the narratives
of the Resurrection in the four Gospels, we find them
distinguished in a marked degree by this characteristic. The purpose of the different Evangelists is
simply to present the Resurrection of their Lord in
a light corresponding to that in which they had
treated His whole previous life. Thus it is that St.
Matthew, having been occupied with the Galilean

[1] " Conférences Apologétiques," i. p. 15.

ministry, as that in which he beheld the fulfilment
of Old Testament prophecy,[1] and having throughout
the whole of his Gospel set forth Jesus as the Bringer
in of a true righteousness, as the great Lawgiver of
the New Testament Economy, has these thoughts
mainly in his mind when he comes to the Resurrection. The appearances in Galilee assume supreme
importance in his eyes, and the idea of the Lawgiver
may be traced in those words of the Risen Lord which
He alone has preserved, "Go ye therefore, and make
disciples of all the nations, teaching them to observe
all things whatsoever I commanded you."[2] Thus it
is that in the closing verses of St. Mark's Gospel, in
which the early Christian Church recognised a narrative corresponding to the Gospel to which they were
added, we find particulars and words of the Risen Lord
which at once recall to us that mighty march of His
power with which we have been made familiar by the
Gospel as a whole.[3] Thus it is that St. Luke, who
had especially set forth the human Saviour and the
universality of His mission of forgiveness, seizes upon
those things in connexion with the Resurrection
which illustrate the same points. He alone tells us[4]
of the broiled fish eaten by the Risen Jesus for the
purpose of showing that He was still what He had
always been, the human Friend.[5] He alone speaks,
not as St. Matthew, of teaching all the nations, but

---

[1] Matt. iv. 12-17.        [2] Matt. xxviii. 7, 10, 16-20.
[3] Mark xvi. 9-20.        [4] Luke xxiv. 41-43.        [5] Note 28.

of repentance and remission of sins to be preached
to all;[1] and he alone tells us of the consolatory
blessing with which, lifting up His hands, the Lord
blessed His disciples when He ascended to heaven.[2]
Finally, it is thus that St. John, to whom Jesus is the
prophet, not so much of Galilee as of Judea, and who
had been occupied throughout all his Gospel with the
manifestation of His glory, and with the triumph of
faith over unbelief, fixes upon those particulars connected with the Risen Lord which illustrate the same
truths.   The "manifestations" of which he speaks
are mainly those in Jerusalem; and even these are
related, less for the purpose of convincing us that the
Lord had risen, than for the sake of pointing out the
*nature of His resurrection-state*, and the manner in
which the loftiest confession of the Gospel was drawn
forth by it, "My Lord and my God."

These differences not only presuppose the existence
of the same belief; they are inexplicable without it.
The streams are slightly coloured by the different
soils through which they have passed, but they conduct us to the same fountain-head; and that is
enough for our present purpose.

The alleged defects in our evidence, therefore, fail
to establish the point for the sake of which they are
urged; and we are entitled to fall back upon our early
Christian witnesses, as witnesses whose evidence is
marked by all the characteristics that can lend it force.

[1] Luke xxiv. 47.          [2] Note 29.

## IV.

A fourth branch of direct evidence is to be found in the rise and continued existence of the Christian Church, with her life and institutions.  It is admitted in the fullest manner by those who reject the fact of the Resurrection, that the belief of it was absolutely necessary to disperse those doubts of the early followers of Christ which had been occasioned by His death.[1]  Let us consider for a moment the importance of this admission.  The origin of the Christian Church cannot be explained without the belief in the Resurrection of her Head.  Then it must be impossible to show that Christianity and the Church were a mere stage of human development, a mere product of natural forces working at the moment, unless it can also be shown that not only the idea of a resurrection, but of *such* a resurrection as that of our Lord, was one of these forces, and that at least the germs of the belief already existed in the preparatory stage. We must be able to educe from the ideas of the time preceding something that approaches to the conception of a risen and glorified human body.  Natural development of ideas admits of no sudden break—of no introduction of anything entirely new.  It may well be doubted whether more is not lost than gained by the admission before us to the cause for which it is alleged.  But, apart from that, it only throws us a

[1] Note 30.

step further back.　If there was no Resurrection of
our Lord, how did men come so to believe in it as to
form themselves into a Christian Church; to separate
themselves at great cost from the community around
them; to constitute themselves into a distinct body,
with rules, principles, aims, and hopes, which were
both a new thing on the earth and peculiar to themselves?　Either the fact must have taken place by
Divine interposition, or the culminating moment of
a long process of preparation for it in the natural
education of the world must have come.　Our opponents hardly meet us here in a perfectly straight-
forward spirit.　When it is their object to discredit
the testimony upon which we rest, all those expressions of the Evangelists which illustrate the mysterious and apparently unnatural character of the body
of the Risen Lord are brought prominently forward:
when it is their object to show that a conception of
immortality, or even of a bodily resurrection, existed
in the ideas of the age, the thought of these peculiarities is dropped, and Christ's resurrection-body is
referred to as if it were simply the body which He
had possessed before.　Such a change of meaning is
unfair.　The peculiarities of the Lord's resurrection-
body must be kept distinctly in view; and when
they are so, it is impossible to produce the faintest
shadow of evidence that before the Christian Church
came into existence there was any preparation for
such an idea in the minds of men.　Even after it was

received, no attempt was made to bring into harmony
its apparently discordant elements. St. Luke, by
whom both classes of facts bearing on the nature of
our Lord's resurrection-body are so distinctly mentioned in the 24th chapter of his Gospel, simply
states them. The same remark is applicable to St.
John in the 20th chapter of his Gospel; and it is
only in the writings of St. Paul that we meet with
that conception of a "spiritual body" in which both
are blended into one. Such, however, could not have
been the case had the idea grown up gradually, and
according to those laws of order which produce in the
course of ages all the harmonious relations of the
universe. Time smooths the edges of things that pass
down its stream side by side. It mingles gently
into one the waters that, flowing from different
sources, were discordant at the first.

Whence then, if the Resurrection of our Lord was
not a fact, did the Church obtain a conception of it,
which, while embracing such peculiar elements as
those now spoken of, was at the same time so clear
and powerful that by the confession of our adversaries, it alone accounts for her existence? Baur says
that we are not bound to answer such a question;
that it is unnecessary to account for the belief; that
it is enough for us to know that it was there.
But Strauss has justly rebuked his master for so far
departing from the province of the historian;[1] and

[1] Note 31.

Strauss is right. We must account for it. The
Church of Christ has been too important an institution, and her beginning falls too much within historic
times, to permit us to be indifferent to the rise of a
belief without which she would have been extinguished at the moment of her birth.

If, therefore, an account of this belief must be
given, and if everything is against the supposition
that it was simply due to the natural growth of
thought, we are thrown back upon the only other
explanation possible. The first Christians must have
been satisfied that those who proclaimed the Resurrection of Jesus had ample evidence of it. They
must have questioned them regarding it to a much
greater extent than has been told us. In Palestine,
beyond Jerusalem, still more in foreign cities, there
must have been eager discussion concerning all the
facts which constituted the substance of the first
proclamation of the Gospel. Can we imagine that
among these the Resurrection of Jesus would not be
a main point of inquiry? Would it be accepted more
easily than the story of His life or of His death?
We are apt to think that we have the whole process
that led to the formation of the Church set before us
in the Acts of the Apostles, instead of which we have
the most meagre and imperfect outlines of it. Yet
the disputings, the questionings, the long-continued
meetings, that are there alluded to,[1] are enough to

---

[1] Note 32.

F

show us how the first preachers of the Gospel would be examined and cross-examined as to what they related. If these things did not generally awaken faith, they were at least necessary to confirm it. The Church must have had, what she certainly supposed herself to have, intelligible reasons for her faith. Belief in the Resurrection of her Lord was no subordinate element in her views. The place occupied by it in the mind of St. Paul has its perfect parallel and analogue in the place which it occupied in her mind. The Epistles of the great Apostle, which testify to his own feelings, also testify to hers. He writes not only as a teacher, but as a partaker with the Church of a "mutual faith;"[1] and as we often learn from a letter less of the writer than of his correspondent, we can judge from the way in which the Apostle speaks of the Resurrection of his Lord, how deeply the life and mind of the Church also were penetrated and pervaded by it. The Church, in fact, was reconstructed on the basis of this belief.[2] As it was the special fact to which the Apostles witnessed, so also it was the special point upon which the faith of their converts was fixed. It is no disparagement to the death of Christ to say so. That death is in reality the foundation of the whole Christian system, and it was not because the Resurrection was more

---

[1] Rom. i. 12.

[2] See this point fully brought out in Row's "Bampton Lectures," p. 323 and elsewhere.

important in itself that it received its prominence.
We have to recall to mind the circumstances of the
time. Men had not yet learned, like us, to glory in
the cross of Christ. It was the main difficulty in
their way. To the Jew it was a stumbling-block, and
to the Greek foolishness. The Resurrection dissi-
pated the shame, and threw light on what was otherwise unintelligible. From the Exaltation, therefore,
men were to reason back to the Humiliation, and
in the Christ risen were to understand the Christ
crucified. Without the one, the other would simply
have prostrated those who had been awakening to a
sense of Christ's moral and spiritual power, and the
smiting of the Shepherd would have been the scat-
tering of the sheep.

If we turn to other facts bearing upon the life of
the early Church, we find all that has now been said
confirmed.

We have the institution of the Lord's day, of
which there are traces within a week of the Resurrection, and which no one will dream of denying was expressly designed to commemorate that event. Surely
there must have been a depth of conviction as well as
an amount of power difficult to estimate, in a belief
that could lead to such an institution. Nor do we see
the full force of this until we remember the totally
different conceptions which the Sabbath and the
Lord's day expressed,—the one the last day of the
week, when man, weary of the work of the world,

desired rest; the other, the first day of the week,
when, about to enter upon the work of the world, he
sought the joyful strength of God in which to face it;
the one commemorating the close of the old creation,
the other, the beginning of the new. A whole world
of the most Divine ideas lies in our drawing aright the
distinction between the Sabbath and the Lord's day;
and yet that great distinction came in a moment.
How? Because it was believed that Jesus rose from
the grave on that first morning of the week. It was
this fact that made the difference, and a more powerful testimony to men's conviction of the truth of the
event within a week after it is said to have happened,
it would be impossible to produce.

Akin to the institution of the Lord's day was
that of Easter day,—that one day in the year when,
in the commemoration successively of the great facts
of the Lord's life, the Church commemorated His
Resurrection. That Easter feast was the culminating
point in the series of festivals which expressed the
truly Christian and exquisitely beautiful idea of the
Christian year. It was styled the Queen of Days and
the Festival of Festivals.[1] To it all the months from
Advent rolled on, gradually swelling up to Easter's
burst of praise. For it the Church waited, that on
that day she might break into all the heavenly joy of
her new creation; among the finest hymns of her
poets are Easter hymns; and so keenly did she feel

[1] Bingham, Book xx. chap. 5, 5.

in regard to it that a controversy in the second half of the second century, as to the particular day on which Easter should be celebrated, nearly rent in twain the Eastern and Western Church, which took different views upon the point.   The testimony of the institution of Easter is like that of the institution of Sunday, a testimony to the deep and powerful hold which the belief in the Resurrection of her Lord had over the Church's mind.

We trace the same fact, further, in the Liturgies of the Church, for in the very earliest forms—handed down from still earlier times—they speak of our lifting up our hearts unto the Lord, that is, unto the Risen, Living Lord.

Once more, we have the language of secular as well as sacred life to appeal to, for it is a well-known fact that, in the first ages of the Church, a frequent salutation of Christians to one another, when they met, was " Christ is risen."

It thus appears that from the dawn of her history the Christian Church not only believed in the Resurrection of her Lord, but that her belief upon the point was interwoven with her whole existence.   Her institutions and forms of worship were moulded, the very language of her daily life was coloured, by it. The stream leaps all at once, like the streams of Syria, from its fountain-head ; and that which lends to it its volume, its impetus, and its colour, is faith not in the death only, but in the Resurrection of the Christ.

Whence came this faith, at once so powerful and universal, upon a point so hard to credit as the rising from the grave of one who had died and been buried? There is nothing to fall back upon except the fact that the Lord actually rose.

## V.

While speaking of the positive evidence of the Resurrection of our Lord, it may be further urged that the fact, if true, harmonizes all the other facts of His history. This argument, indeed, cannot be urged with those who deny at once His superhuman origin and His superhuman life; but it may be urged with propriety in the case of all who, admitting these, have doubts in regard to His Resurrection. If the latter be true, all else that is made known to us regarding Him falls into harmony and order. The light shed into the tomb when the stone was rolled away becomes an emblem of that light which is reflected along His whole previous life, with its mingled elements of greater than human grandeur, and yet greater than human sorrow. We can understand the miraculous conception, the God manifest in the flesh, the miracles of Divine power and love, the teaching whose depth of meaning all the centuries that have passed since then have not been able to exhaust. We can understand, also, the sufferings so much greater than those of ordinary men,—the sorrow of which it was said, "Was ever sorrow like unto my sorrow?" With the

Resurrection of our Lord everything else that has been revealed of Him assumes proportion, order, harmony ; without it all is mystery,—a lock without a key, a labyrinth without a clue, a beginning without a corresponding end.

## VI.

There is yet another point to be spoken of for a moment, though the evidence afforded by it may be said to be rather negative than positive,—the empty grave. That on the Resurrection morning the grave was empty is hardly denied. Some even of the most zealous opponents of a bodily resurrection look upon the fact that the grave was empty as one of the most settled in connexion with this whole inquiry.[1] But if it was so, while yet there was no Resurrection, the body must have been taken away either by friends or foes. Had it been taken by the latter, it would certainly have been produced as the most effectual way of silencing for ever those who roused so much indignation by their preaching of the Risen Lord. Had it been taken by the former, the Church of Christ would have rested not so much upon delusion as upon fraud — upon fraud springing from motives perfectly inexplicable, and leading to results totally different from any that could have been either intended or looked for. Nor can it be said that, without inquiring into this particular point at all, we may easily regard it as one of the

[1] See Schenkel in his " Charakter-Bild Jesu," p. 331.

legendary accretions of a later date; for in that case
our Gospels would surely have mentioned the appearances of the Risen Lord first, and the emptiness of
the grave would have been noted only as a subsequent and subsidiary circumstance.    But the singular
thing is, that this procedure is reversed.    In all our
narratives the emptiness of the grave is mentioned
first, and the appearances of the Risen One follow.
Nothing could better establish the fact that the grave
was empty when it was first visited on the Resurrection
morning; and if it was, we must either take refuge,
like Strauss, in the wholly untenable idea that Jesus
was never buried there, or we must find in the fact
a strong corroborative testimony of the truth of His
Resurrection.

It is impossible to enter further into the historical
evidence for the Resurrection of our Lord, but one
remark must still be made.    The evidence hitherto
adduced has been exclusively historical, and it was
necessary that it should be so.    Other evidence connected with the meaning of the fact with which we deal
will meet us as we proceed.    But it is in the fact first,
in the idea afterwards, that the vast importance of the
Resurrection of our Lord is to be found.    Before we
can be influenced by it we must be convinced by distinct historical evidence that it actually took place.    It
may have a deep foundation in human nature; it may
satisfy what seem to be inextinguishable longings and
aspirations of the human heart; it may be the point

to which the aims of all those other religions point
that have exerted, or that still exert sway, over millions
of our race ; it may reconcile the contradictions of these
religions, and may blend into one harmonious whole
the antitheses which they present.   Considerations
such as these can never be despised by one who would
study the history of man ; and they may lend a
powerful subsidiary weight to that evidence of the
fact which we are able to produce.[1]  But unless the
Resurrection of our Lord be first established as a
historical fact, its value even for these purposes is
destroyed.  It then takes its place in a series of
human speculations, which, though they may have
been so far pervaded by the Divine Spirit, and may
be "broken parts" of Him without whom "was not
anything made," and in whom what "was made was
life,"[2] have yet nothing in them of a definite or a final
character.  It becomes a speculation, which, as it was
the result only of a long evolution in the past, must
be followed by a long and unknown evolution in the
future.  It can come to us with no force of certainty ;
and though, even when it rests upon such grounds
alone, we may not feel entitled to accept it or to dismiss
it as we please, yet the considerations leading to its
acceptance will come home to us with a much slighter
sense of our responsibility to yield to them.  The

---

[1] Comp. the valuable Essay by R. H. Hutton on " The Incarnation
and Principles of Evidence," in his volume of Theological Essays.

[2] John i. 3, 4.  For the rendering here adopted see the Commentary on St. John spoken of in Note 5.

thoughts of the allegiance which we owe to the demands of our own nature does not affect us so powerfully as the thought of the allegiance which we owe to an external fact. Not that these demands are less important, but the difficulty is often to be so certain what they are as to feel that we are without excuse in resisting them. It is otherwise with an external fact. If we refuse to bow to it when sufficiently vouched for, we overturn the very foundation upon which our existence rests. Therefore it is that the historical evidence of the Resurrection of our Lord must hold the first place in our regard; and it is because of my deliberate conviction that it ought to do so, that I have placed it first.

# LECTURE III.

"But he said, I am not mad, most noble Festus ; but speak forth the words of truth and soberness."—ACTS XXVI. 25.

IF the evidence for the Resurrection of our Lord be such as we have seen it to be, the question immediately arises, By what means is the force of it evaded? Is there any other reasonable explanation of that belief of the early Church, which we have found to be not only so essential but so powerful an element of her life? Three theories of explanation require to be noticed, although for the first two a very few sentences will suffice.

1. There is the theory of those who assert that our Lord did not really die upon the cross, that His supposed death was no more than a temporary swoon, and that His Resurrection was simply His return to consciousness.[1]　In defence of this theory are urged— the rapidity of His death, in contrast with the slowness with which death by crucifixion generally took place ;[2] the fact that persons are known to have

---

[1] Note 33.

[2] An elaborate discussion upon this point will be found in Paulus, " Exegetisches Handbuch," 1842, iii. p. 929.

recovered who had been crucified and taken down from the cross as dead; the effect that would be produced by the cool air of the rock-hewn sepulchre, as well as by the aromatic spices with which the body had been prepared for burial;—and the conclusion is drawn that the apparent restoration to life is thus sufficiently and easily accounted for.

To all this it is replied, and replied with force, that the impression produced upon the disciples by their Risen Lord was wholly different from what would have been the case in the circumstances supposed.[1] When their first fears were dispelled, it was one of joy, of boldness, and of enthusiasm; we see none of those feelings of pity, of sympathy with suffering, of desire to render help, that must have been called forth by the appearance of a person who had swooned away through weariness and agony, who had continued in unconsciousness from a Friday afternoon to a Sunday morning, and who was now only in the first moments of recovery. The signs around us are not those of a sick chamber, but of health and strength and busy preparation for a great work to be immediately engaged in. Despondency has given place to hope, despair to triumph, prostration of all energy to sustained and vigorous exertion. No wonder that later critics of the Resurrection, like Strauss, have heaped contempt upon the old theory of a swoon.

Much more, however, may be said. Let us sup-

[1] Note 34.

pose the theory to be correct, and how equivocal
is the relation in which we place the Redeemer to
His early followers. They thought that He had died;
He knew that He had not, and that the ideas entertained by them upon the point,—filling them with
so much wonder, remoulding the whole character of
their lives, supplying them with a chief part of the
message with which they were to convert the world,—
were nothing more than a delusion; yet He did not
interpose to save them from being the miserable
victims of their love and loyalty to Himself! Surely
such a supposition, looked at in the light of the
whole life of Jesus, is too monstrous to be for a
moment entertained.

Again, What reason could our Lord have to expect
that His disciples, when they made His Resurrection
the foundation of their Gospel, would in such circumstances be listened to? He must have seen that
a message with no reality to rest on, centring in
a statement so incredible, and admitting of an explanation which would at once occur to any keen-eyed
observer, would prove more a hindrance than a help
to His cause. It is not consistent with His usual
calmness of judgment, with His knowledge of men,
with His expectations of universal empire, to think
that He would have suffered His disciples to proclaim
Him risen, when He had only swooned, and recovered
from His swoon. He knew too well the feelings both
of Jews and Gentiles upon the point, to have risked

everything upon such a chance. It would have proved Him to be simply an excited enthusiast if He had.

Still further, if the Resurrection of our Lord was only recovery from a swoon, what became of Him for the remainder of His days? There can be no more thought of Resurrection or Ascension into heaven. He must have retired to some solitary retreat unknown even to the most attached of His disciples. While His Church was rising around Him, shaking the old world to its foundations, and introducing everywhere amidst many difficulties a new order of things,—while it was torn by controversies, surrounded by temptations, exposed to trials, placed in short in the very circumstances that made it most dependent on His aid,—He was absent from it, and spending the remainder of His days, whether few or many, in what we can describe by no other term than ignoble solitude. And then at last He must have died—no one can say either where, or when, or how! There is not a ray of light to penetrate the darkness, and these early Christians, so fertile, we are told, in legends, have not a single legend to give us help.

What has been said is a sufficient answer to the theory we are dealing with. But there is another still more conclusive. If the Risen Jesus was thus Jesus recovered from a swoon, He must have been exactly the same as He was before He died upon the cross, He must have had the same body of flesh and blood, with members and limitations in every respect the same as then. But we have already seen that this was not the fact, and that it is neither what the Church believed, nor what is given us to contend for.

Finally, it may be observed upon this point, that the most determined modern opponents of the Resurrection of our Lord are those who most decidedly reject the theory we have been considering. It is essential to their treatment of the subject that the death upon the cross shall have been real. The idea of recovery from a swoon has been exploded quite as much by their efforts as by those of the defenders of our faith; but it is not an unnatural explanation; it is ever apt to rise before our minds when we doubt a real Resurrection, and it was therefore necessary to speak of it.

2. A second theory meets us. The disciples, it is said, practised a deliberate imposition on the world. They stole the body from the grave, and then proclaimed to men that their Lord had risen. The theory is an old one. It was anticipated by the Jews when "they gave large money unto the soldiers, saying, Say ye, His disciples came by night, and stole Him away while we slept."[1] It was urged, though with some difference of detail, by Celsus.[2] But by whomsoever anticipated or urged, a more incredible supposition could not be made. To imagine

---

[1] Matt. xxviii. 13.　　[2] Comp. Orig. "Contr. Celsum," Book II. chap. 56.

that the disciples of our Lord, with a burden of this kind upon their consciences, could have gone out into the world as they did,—could have preached a kingdom of truth and righteousness as the one great effort of their lives,—and that for the sake of that kingdom they could have suffered even unto death,—is to imagine one of those moral impossibilities which may be accepted for a moment when men are hard pressed in controversy, but which, in the cool hour of reflexion, is at once dismissed. It is not necessary to discuss the theory. It has been abandoned by every inquirer to whom a moment's attention is due.

Both these theories may be set aside; and this much may be regarded as established,—that the early disciples of our Lord were thoroughly and honestly convinced that their Master had risen from the dead. The Apostles and the whole Church believed that such was the fact, and the most determined opponents of the Resurrection make no attempt to deny the sincerity of their belief. We are thus brought to the third theory to be considered; and as upon it, in one or other of its forms, modern unbelief rests, it will be necessary to give it fuller consideration than was required by the other two.

3. The theory of visions. Let us understand distinctly what it means. Different ideas may be attached to it; some holders of the theory being even disposed to allow that the visions of the Risen Saviour may have been real, and that they were

actually vouchsafed by the Almighty in order to convince men of the continued life and glory of His Son.    It may be doubted if anything is gained by this for the removal of difficulties.    We have in it an immediate Divine interposition; and, when once we accept such interposition, we need not hesitate to proceed further, so long as we do not ascribe to God anything inconsistent either with His character or with our own responsibilities.    If we believe that the Almighty directly favoured the disciples with visions of the Glorified Lord, we may as well believe, so far as principles are concerned, that He raised Him from the dead.    The ablest defenders of the vision theory are alive to this, and are resolutely opposed to all modifications of the theory which admit the Divine interposition to any extent or in any form.    The visions with which we have to do can only be the product of human agencies.

Nor is it difficult, we are told, to discover in the present instance how a belief in visions originated and spread.    The idea of a resurrection from the grave was already familiar to the disciples of Jesus in their Jewish faith; their state of mind was one of great excitement; they treasured the memory of their Master with a fondness which made it almost impossible for them to believe that He was gone.    It was one of those critical moments when decisive steps are taken; when all our hopes and all the "fears that kindle hope" are either for ever extinguished, or when they burst forth to a height of daring of which they who have cherished them would be the last to think; when faith must either give way to despair, or "must break through the barrier of death itself, and force its way from death to life."[1]     Then, too, they had vague intimations in the Old Testament to appeal to, and the words of Jesus Himself, who had foretold His death but had always associated His Resurrection with it, must have returned to their minds with a new power. Their whole mental condition, in short, was such that it needed only the application of a spark to kindle the flame.

That spark was applied by Mary Magdalene—a sensitive and nervous woman; and no sooner was it applied than the flame was kindled.   Her story that she had seen the Lord was eagerly embraced; it spread with the rapidity and force of an epidemic.   As has happened on innumerable occasions of a like kind, what she believed that she had seen others immediately believed that they too must see.   Their expectations were fulfilled, and in a space of time by no means incredibly short the conviction seized all the members of the early Church that their Lord had really risen from the grave.

Such is the theory.   In considering how far it is applicable to our witnesses, we again begin with St. Paul.   It is adduced in his case partly on the ground of certain expressions of his own, partly on account of

[1] Baur, "Hist. of First Three Centuries," p. 42.

the estimate which his writings in general teach us to form of his character. Let us first look at the particular expressions.

The most important of them is Galatians i. 15, 16; "But when it pleased God, who separated me *even* from my mother's womb, and called me by His grace, to reveal His Son in me that I might preach Him among the Gentiles." It is urged that in these words St. Paul expressly resolves the whole manifestation of the Risen Lord that had been granted him into an internal revelation, and that this meaning must, in consequence, be applied to all other passages in his writings where the point is spoken of. The argument is greatly relied on,[1] and we must consider it for a moment. It might be enough to say that an internal does not exclude an external revelation, but more may be said. Two things are obviously mentioned by St. Paul as distinct and independent steps of a process which *preceded* the revelation in him of the Son of God— his "separation" from before his birth to the apostleship (for he is not speaking of Christian faith in general), and his "call" to it by the grace of God. This call can thus be no other than that on the way to Damascus, and it is distinguished from the inner revelation of the Son which followed it—a revelation by the *contents* of which he learned to know the Son as the Redeemer of Gentile as well as Jew.[2]

---

[1] See Schenkel in his "Bibel-Lexicon, Auferstehung Jesu."

[2] Note 35.

Nor is this all; for it is impossible to think of the "Son" mentioned in the words as any other than that Son of the Father of whom we are told, in the first verse of the chapter, that the Father "raised Him from the dead." The thought of the Resurrection is thus included in the word "Son." "It pleased God to reveal his Son in me" is equivalent to—"it pleased God to reveal His Son whom He had raised from the dead in me," and the internal revelation of the Son distinctly implies that the Son is contemplated as risen.

The second passage to be spoken of is 2 Corinthians xii. 1-3—especially verses 2, 3—in which St. Paul declares that he could not tell whether he was in the body or out of the body when, on one occasion, he was caught up into the third heaven. Here, it is said, we have the Apostle's own declaration that he was familiar with visions, and that he did not know the difference between a manifestation of the Lord to his senses and a vision presented to him when he was in an ecstatic state.

But, if we attend to the first verse of the chapter, we shall at once see that the "visions and revelations" of this passage were of a character entirely different from the manifestation near Damascus. The latter was a vision of the Lord, and it proved that He was exalted. The former were visions "*from*" Him (for that is the force of the original in verse 1),[1] and they presuppose His exaltation. However frequently, too,

---

[1] Comp. Hofmann *in loc.*

the Apostle had referred to the Damascus vision, it would have been impossible for him at any time to say of it, as he says of his other visions in the eleventh verse, that he had become a fool in glorying, for that vision constituted in his eyes the whole ground of his right to the apostolic office; nor could he have imagined that "a thorn in the flesh" was needed to prevent his being exalted above measure by an occurrence, the thought of which, so far from exalting him, always filled him with humility and shame. It belonged, therefore, to a class of manifestations entirely different from those here referred to.

Then, as to the statement that in the second and third verses of the chapter he confesses his inability to distinguish whether what was shown him was in vision or in reality, the words of these verses, when contrasted with his language upon other occasions, prove exactly the reverse. Let two things, which will be at once admitted, be kept in view—first, that the description here given us by the Apostle of his state is designed to magnify the greatness of the vision or revelation mentioned; and secondly, that if the manifestation at Damascus belonged to this class of visions at all, it was, as having produced the most wonderful results, the greatest that he ever had—the one that he would be most constrained to magnify. Does he then on any single occasion refer to it in terms similar to those that he employs here? Not certainly in his address from the stairs of the castle at Jerusalem, when he details every particular of the scene with such minuteness, and even distinguishes it from another appearance of the same Lord with which he was shortly afterwards favoured as he prayed in the Temple, *and was in a trance;*[1] not in his speech before Agrippa, when he introduces his account of it with the words, " Why should it be thought a thing incredible with you that God should raise the dead ? "[2]; and certainly not in any of his Epistles.   Never once does he even hint at the idea that, at the time of this vision, he did not know whether he was in the body or out of the body.   He rather always speaks of it as one who felt that, when it occurred, he could both clearly note the circumstances, and appreciate their real significance.

His language in one passage, indeed, is absolutely conclusive upon the point that he drew the most decided line of demarcation between his sight of the Risen Lord on the way to Damascus, and every vision of Him, or from Him, at other times.   In 1 Corinthians xv. 8, he says, "And last of all He appeared to me also." These words do not mean only that St. Paul was the last of the particular series of persons named in the previous verses, leaving it possible to think that such appearances might have been afterwards renewed to them or others.   They imply also that this was the final appearance of the Risen Lord in the particular form and way that had just been spoken of.   We

---

[1] Acts xxii. 17.          [2] Acts xxvi. 8.

know that St. Paul had many visions and revelations of the Lord after this;[1] and he could not, therefore, tell us more distinctly than he does by this expression "last of all," how fully and clearly he distinguished between his Damascus vision and every other vision of the Risen Saviour that followed it.[2]

It is further alleged, however, that, apart from these particular expressions, his own writings as a whole lead us to think of him as a visionary, weak, even epileptic, unable to distinguish between facts and delusions springing from his own heated imagination. Little need be said to show how entirely mistaken is such an estimate of the great Apostle. Could he have toiled for upwards of twenty years as he did "in labours more abundant" than all the other Apostles, if this were a true description? Or let us look at even but a few of the qualities displayed by him in carrying on these labours—at his profound sense of his own weakness, and his absolute dependence upon the grace of God;[3] at his wonderful skill in the guidance of those controversies by which the early Church was nearly torn asunder;[4] at the wisdom of his rules for the regulation of those extraordinary gifts of the Spirit, which, to a fanatic, would have seemed far beyond human control;[5] at his large-hearted charity for those who differed from him;[6] at his respect for

[1] Comp. Acts xviii. 9; xxiii. 11.  [2] Note 36.
[3] 1 Cor. xv. 10.  [4] Rom. xiv; 1 Cor. viii.  [5] 1 Cor. xii. xiv.
[6] Rom. xiv. 3, 4, 5, 6, 13, 15.

established customs; [1] at his faith in the general
principles of order and propriety in the conduct of
public worship; [2] at the manner in which he won the
confidence of the Churches—a confidence which he
met by taking upon himself all their cares; [3]—or let us
further mark his practical work in founding and
building up young Christian communities in different
lands, and in so presenting to them the great facts of
the Christian revelation, in a manner adapted to their
particular necessities, as to lay the foundations of
Christian theology in the true sense of the term;—
these and such-like qualities are not those of a visionary, but of a keen, clear intellect, accompanied by a
knowledge of men, and a sympathy with them such
as no visionary has.

Even St. Paul's enemies felt all this at the time.
They never dreamt of trying to prove by a reference
to his visions that he was a visionary in any sense
n which the thought of weakness can be associated
with the word.   In this respect the passage already
alluded to in 2 Corinthians xii. is full of interest, for it
shows us that in Corinth the visions and revelations
experienced by the Apostle would be regarded as a
proof of his Divine commission, and as a reproach to
those who did not receive him as they ought.   His
enemies cannot have considered visions a proof of
weakness.   They must have remembered that under
the Old Testament Dispensation it had been one of

[1] 1 Cor. xi. 16.            [2] 1 Cor. xiv. 40.            [3] 2 Cor. xi. 28.

the signs of a prophet that the Lord should make
Himself known to him by "visions and dreams."[1]
They could not have forgotten the promise fulfilled
in the Pentecostal gift of the Spirit, that the Church's
young men should see visions, and her old men dream
dreams.[2]  They must, accordingly, have argued against
St. Paul on the ground that he had too few rather
than too many visions; and they thus constrained
him, however unwillingly, to show in self - defence
that he was favoured with these manifestations of
Divine favour and support.[3]  There can be no doubt
that St. Paul was regarded by adversaries who spared
no reproach or even calumny, if it promised to be
effective, as the very opposite of a visionary.

If there be thus nothing either in particular
expressions of the Apostle, or in the general strain of
his writings, to favour the application of the vision
theory to his case, the difficulty of doing so is
increased when we ask, When and how he obtained
that faith in a Risen Lord which found expression in
his Damascus vision.  We are told that he had been
passing through a mental conflict of the most painful
kind; that his heart had been tossed with anxious
fears lest, in his enmity to the Christian cause, he
might be found to be fighting against God; that the
simple faith and unresisting submission of the pious
women whom he was haling to prison and to cruel
judgment - seats had touched him with tenderness,

[1] Numb. xii. 6.　　　[2] Acts ii. 17.　　　[3] Note 37.

even in the midst of his fierce intolerance ; above all, that the language and upward look of the dying martyr whose clothes were laid at his feet had created such a tumult in his breast, that before he set out on his memorable journey he was already more than half converted. It is difficult to speak positively upon these points, so little information has been given us as to the actual facts. St. Paul's own statement that, down to the moment of his conversion, he " verily thought within himself that he ought to do many things contrary to the name of Jesus of Naza- reth,"[1] rather implies that the representation is not correct. But, even if we allow its probability, one thing seems clear,—that we must go much further back than the date of his conversion, both for the existence of his Christian convictions and for the struggle in his mind to put them down by force. At the date of the journey to Damascus, a vision of the Risen Lord was not so simple and natural a consequence of believing in His Resurrection as we may at first suppose. Such manifestations had long ceased. Several years had passed since any Christian claimed to have beheld the Risen Christ. The state of the Church was in this respect very different from what it had been before the Ascension. If, therefore, Saul's mental struggle was recent, it is in the highest degree unlikely that it would have led to such a vision as he actually had— a vision expected by no Christian at the time. The

[1] Acts xxii. 4, 5 ; xxvi. 9-12 ; Gal. i. 13.

struggle must have been an old one.　Only a conviction deliberately resisted for a length of time could have produced, by the power of its reaction, an effect which there was nothing in the expectations of the moment to suggest.　There must have been in the persecutor's mind a deep sense of guilt *long* incurred, remonstrances of conscience *long* silenced, the thought of injury *long* done to the Redeemer against his own better judgment, before his revulsion from his former self could have produced the result which actually followed.　But we are not left to conjecture here; we know that there was nothing of the kind.　We have his own account of his feelings at the time when he was persecuting the Church; he tells us that he obtained mercy because he did it "ignorantly in unbelief."[1]

Even if we admit, however, all that is said of the struggle in Saul's mind—and it is not at all impossible that there may have been some struggle — another question has to be answered: What becomes of the vision theory?　That theory has to account for the rise of Christianity by showing that visions of a Risen Saviour produced Christian faith.　By its own confession this cannot be done in the case of that Apostle who played a more important part in establishing and propagating the Christian Church than any other member of the apostolic circle.　He believed first, and saw afterwards.　The vision which was to account for the faith has to discover the faith in

[1] 1 Tim. i. 13.

order to be itself accounted for. We are as far as
ever from clearly understanding the process by which
one to whom we are told that Christianity owes more
than it does to Jesus was led to Christian conviction.
Whether applicable to others or not, the vision theory
is certainly not applicable to St. Paul.

Is it then applicable to others—to our other witnesses—to the early Church at large? We have to
contend that it is not.

1. It is inconsistent with the mental state of the
disciples previous to the manifestations. Before we
can account on natural principles for the occurrence
of a vision, two things at least must mark the subject
of it—belief in the idea that it expresses, and excited
expectation that the idea will somehow be realised.
The first is necessary, for a vision is simply a trans-
ference to supposed realities of what has already possession of the mind. A particular idea so powerfully
affects the visionary that it is constantly before him
as a fact. He so sees it with the mental eye that all
doubts as to the existence of a corresponding reality
vanish. It becomes the centre of his thoughts, the
light by which he reads both himself and the world.
The second is not less necessary, for mere belief that
an object exists will not of itself bring along with it
a manifestation of that object to the eye. We believe
in the existence of innumerable beings connected
alike with this world and the next, whom we never
see because we never expect to see them. There is

no power even in the firmest faith, as faith alone, to translate the unseen into the seen. Faith in its normal condition is rather the opposite of sight, and is accompanied by the conviction that while we live by faith we shall not see. It is only in cases where expectancy is awakened in the mind that the bodily senses cease to discharge their functions with sufficient accuracy to guide us, and that the expected object may suddenly take shape before them as one which they can recognise. Belief and Expectancy are thus two factors absolutely essential to the production of visions.

In the subject with which we are dealing both these factors are awanting.

We know from the whole of the New Testament, as well as from every other source that throws light upon the feelings of the time, that there then existed no belief in the resurrection of any individual from the dead before the last great day, at which all should rise.[1] The Old Testament had given no countenance to any such idea, for Enoch and Elijah had not died; and even Martha, who believed that had Jesus been present during the last illness of her brother He would have warded off the stroke of death, could not at first allow the thought of a present resurrection to enter into her mind. "Thy brother shall rise again," said the Redeemer to her, in tones, we may well believe, intended to convey an intimation that he might

[1] Note 38.

rise then.   I know that he shall rise again," was the reply, " in the resurrection at the last day." [1]

Nor is it possible to show that prophecy supplied at once the fact and the details.[2]   There is nothing in it that could supply them.   The fact is indicated; but in such a way that only after it occurred could the predictions referring to it be understood;[3] not one single part of the narratives can be shown to be taken from the Old Testament.   Even our Lord's own intimations that He would rise again, frequently as they were given,[4] seem to have made no impression upon the disciples; the thought was so strange to them that they were unable to take it in.

With what has now been said the facts as related by the Evangelists strictly correspond.   The women who went on the third morning to the tomb went to anoint a dead body, not to behold a Risen Lord; and on the way they perplexed themselves with the question, "Who shall roll us away the stone from the door of the sepulchre?"   Mary Magdalene came to the grave, and found not only that the stone had been rolled away but that the body was not there.   Yet it never occurred to her that a resurrection had taken place; and the only tidings that she could bear to the two disciples to whom she desired to communicate what had happened were, "They have taken away

---

[1] John xi. 23, 24.          [2] " Sup. Rel.," iii. p. 486, etc.
[3] Comp. on this point the words of the fourth Evangelist in John ii. 22.          [4] Matt. xvi. 21 ; xvii. 9 ; xx. 19 ; xxvi. 32, etc.

the Lord out of the sepulchre, and we know not where
they have laid Him." [1]    Even when she returned to
the sepulchre, and when Jesus first spoke to her, she
was so far from having any idea that her Master could
have risen, that she supposed Him to be the gardener ;
and she needed all the power of the tender recollections awakened by His passing from the word "Woman" to the word "Mary" to convince her that it
was indeed her Lord.    The two disciples on the way
to Emmaus spoke to the stranger who joined them
upon the road of nothing but disappointed hopes ;
and there is a sad pathos in their last words, as they
described what had happened in the Christian community that morning—"but Him they saw not." [2]
Finally, the eleven were gathered together in an
upper room at Jerusalem, with no expectation that
their Lord would appear to them again ; and, when
He did appear, instead of eagerly grasping at the fulfilment of hope, they were "terrified and affrighted,
and supposed that they had seen a spirit." [3]

All this is incompatible with the vision theory.
The visionary mind sees the object of its expectation
at once, and the distinctness of its impression leaves
no room for the slightest doubt.    Its visions are only
as the stamp of the soul upon the outward world.
How can the soul, in the very moment of tracing the
sharp lines of the stamp, hesitate to recognise them ?

[1] John xx. 2.                    [2] Luke xxiv. 24.
[3] Luke xxiv. 37.

If it does—and it did so in the instances now mentioned—we have a proof that the state of mind out of
which visions spring had no existence.

But if there was then no thought of even an
ordinary resurrection, how much less was there any
thought of such a resurrection as our Lord's. There
had been raisings to life in the Old Testament, and
miracles of the same kind had been performed by
Jesus; but the peculiarity here is that the idea of
the Resurrection of our Lord which took hold of the
Church's mind had no one bond of connexion with
these except that of death overcome. They were
raisings of the man as he had been: this was the
raising of One in an entirely different condition. In
them, the dead came forth to an existence as much
as ever subject to the law of mortality—"Dust thou
art, and unto dust shalt thou return;" in this, our
Lord left behind Him in the grave all that connected
Him with a passing world, and entered upon a state
which was never again to know either interruption
or end. Let it be granted that prophecy had so
clearly taught the Resurrection of the Messiah as
to lead to the expectation of it, it will hardly be
denied that between the expectation and the event,
in the light in which the latter must be viewed,
there was as great a difference as that between the
expectation of the first coming of our Lord and
the occurrence itself. In both cases what happened
was wholly different from what had been thought

of. When it is urged, therefore, that the "strong subjective impression that Jesus would rise would create a vision of Him,"[1] it is exactly this impression, so far at least as we must suppose a correspondence between it and the event, that is awanting.[2] Nor is it possible to say that the idea of the *glorified* Lord was a later addition to the earlier and simpler form of the story; for, from first to last, the narratives in the Gospels and Acts of the Apostles, and the statements in the Epistles, have the same double colouring,—the Risen Lord is the same as He had been, yet He is glorified. The Christian tradition could not have been moulded from foregone conclusions which had no existence; and, at a time when there was absolutely no idea such as that which found expression in the Resurrection, the Resurrection could not have been beheld in vision. What has now been said may be illustrated by the case of the Second Coming. Probably no belief was stronger in the early Church than that this event was immediately to take place, yet the belief led to no vision. No Christian, or company of Christians, ever proclaimed that the signs of the Lord's approach had either been heard or beheld by them in heaven.[3]

We have already seen, however, that it is not enough that the idea found in a vision shall have been firmly believed in; the mind must have been

---

[1] "Sup. Rel.," p. 545.　　[2] Note 39.　　[3] Note 40.

H

excited by it, and so filled with expectation as to
need only a favourable combination of circumstances
in order to change the expectation into accomplishment. Men do not see visions in calm moments,
nor unless they are dwelling eagerly upon the truth
which is thus to take shape before them. The opponents of the Resurrection of Christ are thoroughly
alive to this; and they show their sense of it in their
analysis of the mind of Saul of Tarsus at the moment
when he was converted. But spiritual tension of the
kind is wholly awanting in the case before us. There
was no excitement. The Christian community was
depressed rather than excited. The minds of its
members were in a great measure prostrated by the
events of the last few days. In the words, "We
hoped that it was he who should redeem Israel,"[1]
they bade farewell to all expectation of beholding
their Lord again. The first imperative condition of
the vision theory was wholly awanting in the early
Christian community.

2. The vision theory is inconsistent with the
nature of the manifestations themselves. Two suppositions are possible. Our Lord might have been
thought of as One returning from a heavenly world,
where He had spent the interval between His dying
and rising again. In that case, there ought to have
been about Him some symptom of that glorious light
which filled the presence-chamber of the Most High,

[1] Luke xxiv. 21.

and the influence of which had once lightened with
unearthly light the face of Moses when he spoke
with God upon the Mount.   Certainly there ought
not to have been less of the light of heaven around
Him than there was around Moses and Elias upon
the Mount of Transfiguration ; for that scene, being
also by the supposition the product of the imagination, shows us the manner in which *they* were
thought to be changed who were admitted even to
the outskirts of the " excellent glory." [1]

But we have every reason to believe that there
was nothing of the kind visible in the Risen Lord.
There is no ground for thinking that His appearance
after He rose was, to the outward eye, different from
what it had been before.   We do not even read such
a statement as that made upon one occasion by St.
Mark regarding Jesus during His earthly life, "And
they were in the way going up to Jerusalem ; and
Jesus went before them : and they were amazed ; and
they that followed were afraid." [2]   A state of excitement would certainly have produced traits of a
more striking nature than those that we actually
possess.

On the other hand, if the imagination of the
disciples did not lead them to think of a heavenly
abode to which their Lord might have retired during
the interval of three days, but simply of the fact that
their beloved Master and Friend was again in the

[1] 2 Peter i. 17.          [2] Mark x. 32.

midst of them, would not that condition of excited and enthusiastic love which alone could produce a vision, have made it necessary to imagine Jesus also meeting them with an eagerness and fondness equal to that with which they met Him? But again there is nothing of the kind. There is rather something almost repellent in His words to Mary Magdalene, "Touch Me not." At the very moment when the two disciples recognised Him at Emmaus, and would have their hearts most open to Him, He vanishes out of their sight.[1] When Peter was restored to the apostleship, it was only at the third question, "Lovest thou Me?" that He met the Apostle's expression of warm and friendly love,—such love as that with which he had loved his Master upon earth,—with the same word as that which St. Peter himself had used. When He asked the eleven on one occasion whether they had any meat, and having taken fish before them ate, there is no evidence that they were asked to join in the meal;[2] and when, at the Sea of Galilee, He prepared a banquet for them on the shore, it does not appear that He partook of it. In all His manifestations of Himself, in short, which are said to be the mere reflexion of the love and devotion of the disciples, He appears in quite another character from that in which love and devotion would have fancied Him. He is distant, reserved, the Master and Teacher rather than the old familiar

[1] Luke xxiv. 31.　　　　[2] Luke xxiv. 43.

Friend. We can hardly think that Mary would now have had courage to sit at His feet, or that the beloved disciple would have ventured to lean upon His bosom. It was not thus that He would have appeared had He appeared in vision.

3. The vision theory is inconsistent with the state of matters in the Christian community after the manifestations. Had excited expectation led to these, the excitement could not fail to have been increased by their actual occurrence. A single visionary may perhaps be calm and collected; may perhaps, notwithstanding his excitement, display a clear perception of the future, and make skilful preparation for its needs. A community can hardly do so. The general feeling will be too high, too hopeful, and too daring. Having seen the fulfilment of its most extraordinary, even of its most extravagant, expectations, it will not be cool enough to anticipate difficulties, to calculate consequences, to think of arrangements suitable for quickening the ordinary slowness of human apprehension, and overcoming the ordinary stubbornness of the human will. Yet this was exactly what the Apostles, with the concurrence of the whole Christian community, did immediately after the manifestations of Himself by the Risen Lord, and during the very time that they were taking place. The history of the forty days between the Resurrection and the Ascension is peculiarly interesting when considered in this point of view. Let us think of these days for an instant,

and what should we naturally expect? Ever and again during their course the Risen Lord was reported to have shown Himself from time to time in the midst of His disciples—now to one, now to several, now for a moment only, and now for more lengthened intercourse. In circumstances like these, is it not natural to think that the disciples would be unfit for all deliberate planning as to the future, for all dwelling on the task before them, for all thought of the best means of carrying home to others, by argument and reason, a conviction impressed upon themselves by the immediate interposition of God? Is it not natural to think that they would rather live either in constant expectation of some fresh manifestation of their Lord, or under the influence of the powerful emotions which those already given must have awakened? Yet such an impression would be wholly incorrect. In point of fact, the forty days during which the manifestations are said to have continued seem to have been far less days of emotion than days of training and instruction for the hardest task ever undertaken by man. At first, no doubt, there was great emotion:—Mary "running to bring the disciples word;" St. Peter and St. John "running" to the grave; the two disciples at Emmaus "rising up the same hour" in which Jesus made Himself known to them, and returning "in haste" to Jerusalem; while, amidst all the simplicity of the Gospel narrative, we hear the weeping and see the joy. But that time passes away; and when St.

Luke afterwards sums up the nature of the intercourse which the disciples, during that time, had with
their Lord, he describes Jesus as "speaking the things
concerning the kingdom of God," and as charging
them not to depart from Jerusalem, but "to wait
for the promise of the Father, which they had heard
of Him."[1]    The greatest commissions given to the
disciples were given during these days; and among
them was at least one commission —"that they should
make disciples of all nations,"[2]—which they were not
till a considerable time afterwards even able to comprehend, and which therefore could not possibly have
proceeded from their own state of Christian feeling
at the time.    No sooner, too, were these days over
than what seems to have been the whole number of
disciples at Jerusalem met together in an upper room
for prayer and supplication, and, as appears from
the address of St. Peter on the occasion, for mutual
counsel.[3]   Nor can we fail to be struck with the quiet
wisdom of those words in which that Apostle pointed
out the course that it seemed proper in the circumstances to pursue, as well as with the readiness with
which his advice was adopted by the whole assembly.
There is not the slightest trace of excitement in his
language.    Not the slightest indication is conveyed
to us that we are in the midst of a company of
visionaries who have wrought themselves up to such
a pitch of expectation as to be able to persuade them-

[1] Acts i. 3, 4.        [2] Matt. xxviii. 19.        [3] Acts i. 14.

selves that one of the wildest fancies ever entertained
by men had been an actual reality.   Even the Resurrection itself, though the point most of all to be
witnessed to, is on that occasion not the only object of
the Apostle's thoughts.  He goes back to the whole
ministry of Christ, and advises that a witness of the
Resurrection should be chosen from among those who
had companied with them all the time that the Lord
Jesus went in and out among them, "beginning from
the baptism of John until that same day when He was
taken up from them."   They all gave heed to what
was said, prayed to Him who knew the heart to point
out which of the two named by them He had chosen,
and determined the matter by the customary method
of casting lots.[1]   Never did the infant Church display
more of the spirit of a sound mind than at the very
moment when, upon the theory of visions, she should
have been least self-possessed and calm.

It was the same in the years immediately following, and before the enthusiastic impressions in which
the theory of visions supposes her to have originated
had had time to die away.   Everything recorded of
the Church at that time betokens a state of mind the
very opposite of the unregulated or fanatical.   She is
deeply convinced of the reality of her faith, desirous
to enjoy it in peace, glad when others are persuaded
to cast in their lot along with her.   We read of her
continuing in the "Apostles' teaching and fellow-

[1] Acts i. 21-26.

ship, in the breaking of bread and the prayers."[1]
Her members seem still to have combined the worship
of the Temple and the synagogue with their own more
peculiar rites, as if either they did not themselves see
the issue involved in their new faith, or were desirous
not to break hastily with the past. As necessity
called for it, they appointed new offices in the Church,
and, with a singular delicacy of perception as to what
was fitting, they chose the first deacons from among
the Hellenistic Jews ; doubtless, because it was widows
of that class who had complained that the widows of
the Hebrew Jews were favoured in the daily minis-
trations. When they were persecuted, they bore their
trials without a murmur. When they had rest, they
walked in the fear of the Lord and in the comfort of
the Holy Ghost.

All this, too, is of the more avail for our present
purpose when we bear in mind that the Christian-
ising power of the early Christian Church lay not so
much in teaching as in the transmission of a certain
spirit from one generation or community or person to
another. A convert was of course led to views of
Divine truth which he did not previously hold ; but
what especially made him a Christian was his imbib-
ing the spirit of the existing Church: and the spirit of
the Church at any one point of her existence in these
primitive times leads us back with much more confi-

---

[1] Acts ii. 42.   On the state of the Church at this time compare
Keim, "Jesus von Nazara," iii., pp. 594-600.

dence than would be the case now to what must have
been her spirit in the immediately preceding stage of
her history. When, accordingly, we find the Church
of the latter half of the first century exhibiting the
calm, clear confidence in the power of her Risen Lord
which actually distinguishes her, it is impossible to
think that she could have sprung out of impressions
which, if not correct, could only have been as wild a
hallucination as ever occupied or excited the mind of
man.

4. The theory of visions is inconsistent with
various subordinate circumstances marking the manifestations of Himself by the Risen Lord.

(1.) It is inconsistent with the length of time
during which the manifestations often lasted. It is
true that they were occasionally brief, but they were
very far from being always so. The walk to Emmaus
must have occupied a considerable time, and during
it there was not only conversation between Jesus and
the two disciples, but a lengthened explanation from
the lips of the former, when, "beginning at Moses
and all the prophets, He expounded unto them in all
the scriptures the things concerning Himself."[1] The
appearances to the Apostles on two successive Sunday
evenings were certainly not appearances lasting only
for an instant; and the teachings granted during
the forty days concerning the kingdom of God undoubtedly imply not only long but patient inter-

[1] Luke xxiv. 27.

course on the part of Jesus. Visions, however, have
never been known to last in this way. They are
flashes of sudden conviction, and are over in a
moment.

(2.) The theory is not less inconsistent with the
fact that the manifestations were made to numbers
at the same instant. There is indeed a kind of
electric sympathy in numbers wrought up into the
same state of lively expectation, by means of which
an impression made on one is often conveyed with
remarkable rapidity to the rest. But such simultane-
ousness of conviction is never produced at the very
first. A point of departure must be afforded for it,
and one alone must give the word, which may then
pass with lightning speed throughout the company.
We have nothing of this kind to deal with in the
case before us. When the Risen Saviour appeared to
the assembled Apostles, He addressed Himself immediately and directly to them all, "Peace be unto
you." There was no cry on that occasion, as there
was at the Sea of Galilee, on the part of any one of
them, "It is the Lord." Our narratives bear distinctly on their face that the whole company was
instantaneously affected in the same way.[1] Similar
observations apply still more to the number of "above
five hundred brethren at once," spoken of by St.
Paul.[2] It is utterly impossible to think that upwards
of five hundred persons could, without previous pre-

---

[1] Luke xxiv. 37 ; John xx. 20.          [2] 1 Cor. xv. 6.

paration (and the word "appeared" implies that there was none), persuade themselves by the mere power of the visionary faculty that they beheld the Risen Lord before them when they did not; or, if we imagine that they did, some of so large a number must afterwards, in cooler moments, have reflected upon what had passed, must have recalled the means by which their state of excitement was brought about, and must have suspected the reality of what they had seen. But no second thoughts of this kind can have existed, or St. Paul would not have felt himself entitled to appeal so calmly to the impression produced upon that whole number, " of whom the greater part remained unto that present, but some were fallen asleep."

(3.) The theory is inconsistent with the place where the chief manifestations were made. Strauss has endeavoured to discredit the appearances to the Apostles in Jerusalem,[1] and has urged that they cannot have taken place there, because the first message of the angel to the women was, "Behold, He goeth before you into Galilee; there shall ye see Him;"[2] and because Jesus Himself in His first manifestation gave His sanction to the message, "Go tell My brethren that they go into Galilee, and there shall they see Me."[3] Strauss's purpose is an obvious one. Visionary appearances were much less likely to

---

[1] "Leben Jesu f. d. D. V." p. 313, etc.

[2] Matt. xxviii. 7.　　　　　　　[3] Matt. xxviii. 10.

be seen in Jerusalem than in Galilee.   In the one the
prevailing  tone  was  selfishness,  coldness,  hardness,
bitter opposition to  the  claims  of  the  Messiah, while
the disciples were few in number and overwhelmed
with dread of the authorities of the land ; in the other
there was a spirit freer, bolder, not so wedded by
selfish interest to existing institutions, ever ready to
catch at new and promising ideas ; while, at the same
time, its lake, its towns, its hills, and fields had been
far more associated with the life of Jesus than Jerusalem had been.   There, therefore, was the natural
soil for visions, and there the Gospel narrative itself
leads us to believe that they were to take place.   On
grounds like these it is urged that we cannot attach
value to the reported appearances in Jerusalem :
Galilee alone could be their scene.   Let us not attach
value to them : it is enough for our present purpose
that they are related, and that, so related, they are to
be regarded as the mere product of the visionary
faculty.   But, if so, how came the very same mental
state of the early disciples to indicate, by means of
the messages of the angels and of Jesus, that Galilee
was to be the scene of the manifestations, and then
to attach so many of them to Jerusalem ?   These
messages were of course parts of visions.   There was
certainly no more reality in them than in any special
appearance of the Risen Lord.   How came the early
Church to be in such confusion and self-contradiction
upon the point ?   It was believed with a belief, the

firmness and liveliness of which are the fundamental
requisites of the vision theory, that the Risen Saviour
was to be seen in Galilee ; yet, instead of being seen
there either alone or first, the earliest and most
important visions are connected with Jerusalem.   On
the third day after the crucifixion tidings pass like
wildfire through the small Christian community of
the capital : " An angel has appeared ; the Lord has
appeared ; and the message of both is that if we go
into Galilee we shall see our Master again, amidst the
scenes where we have so often met Him ; " and lo !
that very night He makes Himself manifest at
Jerusalem,—in that very place with which, according
to the negative school of criticism, He had no associations, where He had never laboured, which He had
visited after His ministry began for the first time
that very week in which He died.   The vision theory
must be more in harmony with itself before it can
take the place of the Church's faith.

(4.) Once more, the theory is inconsistent with
the fact that the visions came so suddenly to an end.[1]
We have already seen cause to believe that during
forty days appearances of the Risen Lord must have
been more frequent than those actually recorded.
The whole bearing indeed of the earlier verses of the
first chapter of the Acts of the Apostles would almost
lead to the inference that a continual process of intercourse had gone on, which, at the close of the forty

---

[1] Comp. Keim, "Jesus von Nazara," iii., p. 597.

days, came suddenly to an end. After that time no appearance of the Risen Lord is recorded except that to St. Paul, the circumstances and object of which were altogether exceptional. But it is not thus that enthusiasm works, and especially when all the intimations given by the Lord Himself of His future presence with His people had seemed to infer a continuous presence with them rather than one of such short duration. No promise of His rising again had been connected with the mention of forty days. On the contrary, in the Gospel of St. John He had spoken of seeing them after a little while, when their heart would rejoice with a joy that no man should take from them;[1] and in the Gospel of St. Matthew His promise had been, "Lo, I am with you alway, even unto the consummation of the age."[2] We can understand words like these of the presence of His Spirit; but the infant Church could hardly apply them in that way. It was much more natural for her to think of continually repeated manifestations, which should rather grow in brightness and in number in proportion as she needed them. These, however, did not take place; and days of trial and persecution, when they came, did not witness even one example of a fresh manifestation of her Risen Lord.

Nor is even this all that may be said. The vision theory supposes a high state of excitement and enthusiasm on the part of the disciples. That state reached

---

[1] John xvi. 22.    [2] Matt. xxviii. 20.

its culminating point at Pentecost, when the gift of the
Spirit put not only the Church but the whole city in
a stir, and when St. Peter filled his first sermon to the
people with thoughts of the Risen Lord.   Still, there
was no new manifestation of Him.   Ten days before
the manifestations had ceased ; and from that moment
onward there is not a whisper that any of them had
been repeated.   The fact is remarkable ; and it helps
to illustrate the imperfection of the theory we have
been examining.

Thus, then, it appears that the attempt to explain
the alleged Resurrection of our Lord by the vision
theory is attended with difficulties which may be
fairly pronounced to be insuperable.   There is no
theory at the present time so confidently relied on
by those who are unable to accept the Resurrection as
a fact.   It is in substance urged by Strauss[1] and
Renan ;[2] it is defended with great acuteness of in-
vestigation by Holsten ;[3] it is accepted by the author
of "Supernatural Religion."[4]   Yet, from whatever
point of view we look at the circumstances of the
early Christian Church, at the same time taking into
account well-known laws of the human mind which
must have been the same then as they are now, we
find them incompatible with the supposition that the
appearances of the Risen Saviour proceeded only from

[1] See "Das Leben Jesu f. d. D. V.," p. 304.       [2] Note 41.
[3] See Holsten's work, "Zum Evangelium des Paulus und Petrus."
[4] Vol. iii., p. 526.

that excited and expectant imagination of His followers
which might have given rise to visions. The theory
is contradicted by the condition of our Lord's disciples at the moment of His death, by the nature of
the manifestations themselves—even though they were
no more than pictures of the fancy—by the after life
of the Church, and by different subordinate circumstances, such as their duration, the numbers who
witnessed them at the same instant, the place where
they occurred, and their cessation when they might
have been expected to increase. The vision theory
is a deeply interesting one. If true, it would undoubtedly overthrow the fact of a bodily resurrection
of our Lord, and with it the existence of the Christian faith in any sense worthy of the name. But it
cannot for that reason alone be summarily dismissed.
The chapter of human history involved in the literal
Resurrection of our Lord is of unrivalled importance;
and we are bound to inquire with as much calmness
as possible into both the fact and the objections to it.
Of these objections the vision theory is undoubtedly
the most formidable; but it, as well as the others
that have been mentioned, fails to satisfy the indispensable conditions of inquiry.[1] It also, therefore,
must be rejected, and we have no legitimate resource
but to accept the fact. We may be thankful that it
should be so. We may believe that the Church of
Christ has not grounded her life and hope for

[1] Note 42.

I

eighteen centuries upon a delusion ; and, in the face of either denial or scorn, we may assert that our words are those of truth and soberness, when we proclaim that He who died upon the cross rose on the third morning from the grave.

# LECTURE IV.

"Behold, I cast out devils, and I do cures to day and to morrow, and the third day I shall be perfected."—LUKE xiii. 32.

"THE LORD is risen indeed." We have satisfied ourselves as to the fact that the Redeemer who died upon the cross, and was buried, came forth upon the third morning from the grave; and that, after having for forty days from time to time appeared upon the earth, He ascended, in the glorified condition in which He rose, to His Father and our Father, to His God and our God. The fact is one of so stupendous a nature as to demand inquiry into its purpose and effect. The Almighty does nothing in vain; He wastes no strength; His means are always in just proportion to His ends. A fact like this, therefore, can hardly fail to have a place among the great facts belonging to the scheme of our redemption. Is it so? and if so, what is that place? are the questions that we have now to ask.

It has indeed been alleged by one of the most eminent theologians of the Church of Christ, whose labours contributed more than those of any other that can be named to the revival of religion in the early

part of the present century—the distinguished Schleiermacher—that the Christian consciousness is wholly
independent of the Resurrection of our Lord. That
Resurrection is a matter of Scripture statement, and
must be accepted by those who can satisfy themselves
that the evidence is good; but it is no part of the
convictions that make the Christian what he is; and,
altogether apart from it, we may have a complete
impression of everything that Jesus was as our Redeemer, and a complete experience in ourselves of the
blessings of His redemption.[1] The same view has been
advocated by theologians of later date;[2] and there
can be no doubt that at this moment it is more or
less adopted by many members of the Christian
Church. Important advantages are thought to be
connected with it. It seems to leave us the substance of our faith, while at the same time it affords
a means of escape from the reception of its greatest
miracle. The life of our Lord is supposed to be
untouched, except in so far as the view may affect
the credibility of the Evangelists. We may still
speak, it is imagined, of the risen life, of a life above
the world, of a life to which we can apply the
Apostle's words, "It is not I that live, but Christ
liveth in me;" and what more do we require?

　　Even in this country, where such an extreme
view is probably seldom adopted by professing
Christians, there is a mode of looking at the Resur-

[1] "Glaubenslehre," vol. ii. § 99.　　[2] Note 43.

rection of our Lord which is hardly less fatal to what
we have yet to speak of as its real place and power.
It is regarded mainly in its evidential value.  It is
dwelt upon as a fulfilment of prophecies either found
in the Old Testament, or uttered by the lips of Jesus
Himself; as an attestation of the truth of His doctrine and claims; as a solemn guarantee that His
atonement has been accepted by the Father; as the
pledge and earnest of our own resurrection at the
great day of account.[1]  It is treated less as an
essential and integral part of the work which the
Lord Jesus Christ had been sent into the world to
accomplish, than as something following that work;
as the visible and glorious reward bestowed by the
Father upon the Son of His love, who had been faithful unto death and had finished the work given Him
to do.  This is the view of the Resurrection almost
exclusively presented to us, both in the teaching of
our pulpits, and in the writings of our divines.  Few
members of the Christian Church seem to think of
more.  It is not without great value.  The Resurrection of our Lord does include alike the inferences
that have been spoken of, and others of a similar
kind; yet it is obvious that all of them may be
accepted by us, without the Risen Lord having any
*immediate* place in our Christian consciousness or
any *immediate* influence on our Christian life.  They
may only lead us back again, though with quickened

[1] Note 44.

gratitude and deepened interest, to His death.   The
cross may still be in our eyes the grand termination
of His redeeming work.   But the view thus taken,
even if so far correct, is as a whole in a high degree
imperfect ; and the teaching of the New Testament
distinctly shows us that it is so.

Thus, in John x. 17, 18 we read, " Therefore doth
the Father love Me, because I lay down My life, that I
may take it again.   No one taketh it away from Me,
but I lay it down of Myself.   I have power to lay it
down, and I have power to take it again.   This commandment I received of My Father."   It is the whole
" commandment " of the Father, the whole charge or
commission of the Father, as given to the Son in the
counsels of eternity, that is here referred to ; and that
commandment extends not only to the laying down
of His life by the Son, but to His *taking it again.*"
The latter, as well as the former, was a part of that
doing of the Father's will in which the free and
perfect submission of the Son to the Father was so
conspicuously exhibited as to form the very foundation of the eternal love with which the Father loved
the Son : the two parts of the statement cannot be
separated from one another.   Nay, not only so ; the
taking of His life again is here spoken of by our Lord
as the *ultimate act* in which both the will of the
Father and the free adoption of that will by the Son
are manifested.   It is not a mere consequence of His
laying down His life : it is the end for which the life

is laid down,—" Therefore do I lay down My life, that
I may take it again." The words of our Lord Himself thus teach us that in the original commandment
of His Father, not death, but resurrection from the
power of death, was the true goal of that race which
He was to run, the true completing of that obedience which in the scheme of redemption He was to
render.

Again, in John xii. 27 we have an expression of
the feelings with which our Lord contemplated His
own work in its most trying hour, " Now is My soul
troubled ; and what shall I say ? Father, save Me
out of this hour : but for this cause came I unto this
hour." The true rendering of this passage is not
that of our English Bibles, Father, save Me "*from*,"
but Father, save Me "*out of*" this hour;[1] and, when we
observe this, the whole aspect of the prayer is changed.
It is no longer a prayer on the part of Jesus that He
may be spared the bitterness of drinking to the
very dregs the cup of wrath. We know indeed
that He did shrink from the draught, although in a
manner so entirely in submission to His Father's will
that the shrinking cannot be associated with any
thought of sin, " O My Father, if it be possible, let
this cup pass from Me : nevertheless not as I will,
but as Thou wilt."[2] These words, however, do not
express the whole of His mental state ; and the
record of St. John supplies what the earlier Evan-

[1] Note 45.　　　[2] Matt. xxvi. 39; Mark xiv. 35; Luke xxii. 42.

gelists have left unnoticed. Our Lord prayed not merely that He might be saved *from* that hour, but *out of* that hour; not merely that, if possible, He might escape suffering, but that, if it was impossible for Him to escape it, He might pass through it to a glorious deliverance,—that through death He might be conducted to that life beyond death in which the purpose of His coming was to be reached. At the moment when He uttered the prayer before us He felt that He was the corn of wheat about to be cast into the ground to die,[1] but He did not think of dying as the end for which the great Sower scattered Him from His hand. Wheat is sown not for death but for the harvest; and for the sake of the harvest, for the sake of the life through death, Jesus came to that hour.

Again, it is upon this principle that we are to explain the remarkable word used by St. Luke in his account of the Transfiguration, when, telling us of the subject upon which Jesus then conversed with the representatives of the law and the prophets, he says that they spake of the *exodus*, not of the " decease," which He should accomplish at Jerusalem.[2] *Exodus* is more than " decease; " it is a going forth from a state of humiliation and suffering to a glorious rest.[3]

*departure*

But it is not only in passages such as these, in which we have the words either of Jesus or of an

[1] Verse 24.        [2] Luke ix. 31.        [3] Note 46.

Evangelist, that we find a pre-eminence attached to the Resurrection of our Lord which the Church too often fails to recognise ; the same point is brought before us elsewhere in the New Testament, both in special texts and in the whole strain of the sacred writers' thoughts.

Thus, in the Epistle to the Hebrews we find on one occasion words exactly similar to those that have already met us in the 12th chapter of the Gospel of St. John, although the sense of them is again marred in our English Bibles by the substitution of the preposition "from" for the preposition "out of :" "Who, in the days of His flesh, having with a strong cry and tears offered up prayers and supplications unto Him that was able to save Him out of death, and having been heard for His reverent fear, though He was a Son, yet learned obedience by the things which He suffered." [1] In that prayer which he selects as the strongest evidence afforded in the life of Jesus of His reverent fear, the sacred writer tells us that He prayed not that He might be delivered "from" death, but that He might be delivered "out of" it. Or take such passages as the following from St. Paul : "If thou shalt confess with thy mouth the Lord Jesus, and shalt believe in thine heart that God hath raised Him from the dead, thou shalt be saved ;" [2] "Wherefore God also hath highly exalted Him, and given Him a name that is above every

---

[1] Heb. v. 7.　　　　　[2] Rom. x. 9.

name : that every one should confess that Jesus
Christ is Lord" (that is, the Risen and Glorified
Lord) "to the glory of God the Father;"[1] "For if,
when we were enemies, we were reconciled to God
by the death of His Son, much more, being now reconciled, we shall be saved by His life;"[2] "Who
is he that condemneth? It is Christ that died, yea
rather, that is risen again, who is also at the right
hand of God, who also maketh intercession for us;"[3]
while it is unnecessary to quote the many passages
in which the Resurrection of our Lord is mentioned,
along with His death, as one of the two great facts
which are essentially and equally necessary to the
accomplishment of our salvation.[4] It is worthy of
notice indeed that "salvation," in the full meaning
of the word, is never connected in the New Testament with the death of Christ alone. Pardon of sin,
redemption, and reconciliation are, but not salvation.
Salvation includes life ; and though the seed must
be dissolved, it is from the living germ in the seed,
and not from the surrounding death, that the life
springs up.[5]

Once more, it will repay the attentive reader
of the word of God to study in this point of view
the combination of ideas presented to us in the Gospel
of St. John, and in the Epistle to the Hebrews. He
will find that the leading theme of the Gospel,—one

---

[1] Phil. ii. 9, 11.    [2] Rom. v. 10.    [3] Rom. viii. 34.    [4] Note 47.
[5] See further remarks on this point in Appendix to Note 53.

appearing both in its general structure and in the
structure of particular passages,[1] both in the words
of Jesus which it preserves, and in the scenes from
His life which it describes,[2]—is not suffering and death
upon the one hand, or glory upon the other; nor
is it a theme with two separate parts, life *and* death,
or death *and* life. The main thought of the Gospel
is single, though compound. It is glory won through
shame, triumph through apparent defeat, life through
death. The two things come constantly together.
Both are included in the remarkable expression
"lifted on high," so characteristic of St. John; [3] and
we do not catch the idea contained in the expression by saying that Jesus dies *and* is glorified, but
by saying that Jesus passes through death the first
stage of glory to a still higher and more perfect stage
of glory.

The same thing is not less strikingly apparent
in the Epistle to the Hebrews. Only one text in
that Epistle makes direct mention of the Resurrection of our Lord,[4] and even there it is incidentally
introduced; but the whole Epistle presupposes His
Resurrection. It is the Risen and Ascended Lord
who is its great theme throughout, the High Priest
after the order of Melchizedec, both Priest and King
"for ever." [5]

The Resurrection of our Lord, in short, according

---

[1] Note 48.          [2] Note 49.          [3] Note 50.
[4] Heb. xiii. 20.              [5] Note 51.

to the invariable teaching of Scripture, is not something consequent upon His redemptive work; it is a part of the work itself. It is not something merely designed to prove to us that that death upon the cross which the world scorned is " the power of God and the wisdom of God unto salvation." It is itself " power " and " wisdom ; " it is one of the great redemptive acts of Jesus. Let us consider it,

I. In relation to His own Person. It is unnecessary to repeat what was said in a previous Lecture as to the condition of our Lord at the moment when He rose, or to dwell again upon the fact that what He was when He ascended to His Father in heaven, He was when He came forth from the tomb ; that what He is now in His glorified state, He was during the forty days when He showed Himself from time to time to His disciples. If the observations then made were correct, the point which now claims our attention is, that in our Lord's resurrection-state there was, so far as regarded the constitution of His Person, an advance upon what it had been during His previous life. The body now possessed by Him was not His old body, with whatever amount of outward glory we suppose it to have been glorified ; but rather that old body changed, transfigured from within, so that it might be the fitting and perfectly adequate expression of pure spirit. A body of that kind our Lord could not

have possessed before. Not at the Incarnation ; for
even in Paradise, before the Fall, man's body was
" natural," not " spiritual ; " and if our Lord's body,
at the time when He became incarnate, had been
the latter instead of the former, it would have been
different from ours. He would not have been " made
of the seed of David according to the flesh," and
the assurance so necessary to faith would have been
awanting, that " inasmuch as the children are partakers of flesh and blood He also Himself likewise
took part of the same." Nor could our Lord's body
have become " spiritual " through the transforming
influence of the Spirit at any stage of His earthly
life subsequent to the Incarnation. All along, indeed, the Spirit in His fulness dwelt in Him. He
was conceived in the Spirit's power ; [1] at His Baptism
the Spirit not only descended, but " abode " upon
Him ; [2] and it was in the power of the Spirit that He
began His ministry.[3] But up to the time of the
Resurrection He was not free to let the Spirit produce His natural and proper effects upon His bodily
frame. He was still continuing, as it was necessary
that He should continue, that " emptying Himself
of His glory " which was essential to the carrying
out of His great work. The first purpose of His coming had not yet been answered. Standing in our
room and stead, He had not yet wrought out, in
the very nature that had sinned, His victory of love.

[1] Matt. i. 18.　　　　[2] John i. 32.　　　　[3] Luke iv. 14.

Had His body been changed before this was done,
He would have failed to be our Representative and
Substitute at the very moment when that love had
reached its point of highest intensity ; [1] when it was
most pleasing to the Father ; [2] and when it had
achieved its most glorious results. [3]   At the Resurrection it was different.   The suffering for our sake to
which love led Him to submit had culminated in
death ; the sacrifice rendered necessary by the relations between a holy God and sinful man had been
presented ; the corn of wheat, having fallen into the
ground and died, was ready to produce much fruit.
No hindrance existed now to the passing onward of
our Lord's body to its perfection ; and in such a
body—a distinct advance upon that with which He
had formerly lived and died—Jesus rose.

Not only so.   It is of peculiar importance to
observe that the advance thus made was in conformity with principles which the Almighty had stamped
upon the constitution of things, and with the design
which He had originally formed.   " Howbeit, "
says St. Paul, as he reasons on the subject, "that
is not first which is spiritual, but that which is
natural ; afterward that which is spiritual.   The first
man is of the earth earthy : the second man is of
heaven." [4]   It is of no moment whether the Apostle
is here thinking only of the two kinds of bodies of

---

[1] John xiii. 1.      [2] John x. 17.      [3] John xii. 32.
[4] 1 Cor. xv. 46, 47.   Note 52.

which he had just spoken,—the one so frail and
corruptible, the other so powerful and incorruptible ;
or whether he has in his eye a universal law of history.　In either case the lesson for our present
purpose is the same.　We learn that, in the relation
of the resurrection-body of our Lord to His body
as it was before He died upon the cross, we have the
operation of a great law which may be traced both
in the record of creation and in God's providential
dealings with our race.　There is nothing final in
the universe except God.　Everything comes from
Him ; everything tends to Him.　There is a constant
aspiration through the long ages on the part of all
that exists towards something higher, better, nobler
than itself,—towards something liker its source,—
that, is liker God, liker spirit.　This progress is,
without doubt, through much humiliation and suffering, even through an amount of sacrifice and death
at the thought of which we often stand appalled.
It would be foreign to our subject to show that there
again the Lord Jesus Christ fulfils the great law
of our humanity ;　and it is enough to say that,
however trying the means may be which are indispensable to purge us from the influences of sense,
and to bring us under the one and absolute dominion of spirit, the latter is the end to which our
nature points.　To draw indefinitely nearer God is
the glorious destiny of man.　But man cannot effect
this by shaking off the body altogether.　He would

then be no longer man. His body can never be
wholly changed into spirit. Had we to think of a
time when man shall be nothing but a Divine spirit,
and when there shall be no outward expression of
that spirit in what is perceptible to the senses, then
man would be as God, instead of being only a manifestation of God.

In this path of bodily change, therefore, the Lord
Jesus Christ precedes us. He is the Archetype in
which the idea of the Divine mind is realised. In
the two facts of His Incarnation and Resurrection He
sums up the purpose of the great Creator. From the
moment that He resolved to become our Leader and
" Captain" in the path of life, it became necessary that
the words should be fulfilled in Him as well as us,
"Howbeit that was not first which is spiritual, but that
which is natural; afterward that which is spiritual."

Keeping in view, then, the nature of that body
with which our Lord rose, it follows, from all that
has been said, that His Resurrection was the perfecting in His Person—and that too according to God's
own eternal plan—of a humanity which even our first
parents had received only in its rudimentary and
initial not its ultimate stage, and the upward progress of which had been interrupted by the Fall. It
was the culmination of a great development for which
man was always destined, and which would have
been accomplished for him in some other way, even
if he had never sinned. It was the bringing about

of a result aimed at in fundamental and essential impulses of our nature, and towards which, therefore, that nature must always point, as what alone can satisfy its desires, fulfil its hopes, and complete its glory.

Such is the perfecting of our Lord's Person by His Resurrection. Not as Divine only, but as human He was perfected. He did not return, when He rose, to absolute Divinity; He is not simply spirit now; nor is He possessed of only an angelic nature, although in that nature He might be exalted above the brightest angel that is before the face of the Most High.[1]

As man, He rose, ascended into heaven, sat down upon His throne,—as man, with our human nature not less real and true than ever because it has been perfected,—as man, with an eye to look in love upon His own; with a voice to speak to them in its old tender tones; with a hand to lay upon the heads of children taken away before their sorrowing parents to His own gentle presence. O glorious consummation of all His toils ! O meet reward of all His sufferings ! O happy tidings for those who know that what their Lord is they shall in due time be !—that they shall be like Him who is not only true God but perfect man, no more needing to groan in this earthly house of their tabernacle being burdened, but being clothed upon, with what is mortal swallowed up of life.

One remark may be permitted before we pass on.

----

[1] Heb. ii. 5-9.

K

It will be seen that, looked at in this light, the Resurrection of our Lord is no longer an isolated miracle,
no longer a fact which simply guarantees another fact
embraced in the scheme of our redemption. It is
taken up into the great redemptive process. It is
a step—the highest and the final step—in a grand
development of humanity contemplated by the Creator
from the very first. It is the crowning act of a series
of events which was begun when all things " were
created " in Christ ; was carried on when all things
" consisted " in Him ; and was in its principle completed when He who had been " the first born of all
creation " became again " the beginning, the first
born from the dead, that in all things He might have
the pre-eminence." Then the human, not in " the
likeness of sinful flesh," but in the condition
originally designed for it, was united to the Divine
in one perfect unity for ever. Any one, therefore,
who accepts the Incarnation ought to have no
difficulty in accepting the Resurrection of our Lord.
The latter is only the completing of that humanity
which had been assumed in the former ; the perfecting
of a process which, without it, would have stopped
short of the only goal that we can regard as final.

II. From the Person of our Lord we have now to
turn to His Work, that we may ask how His Resurrection bears on it ? An answer to this question may
be given in two particulars—His Resurrection was the

completing of His work, and the Divine attestation
to its acceptance by the Almighty.

1. It was the completing of His work. For we
are not to imagine that that work was accomplished
either by His life on earth, or by His death. It is
true that the fundamental office which our Lord came
into the world to discharge was that of Priest, and
that His fundamental commission was to present the
one perfect offering for sin by which God might be
reconciled to man, and man to God. But the question immediately arises, How much did that priesthood and offering include? We know that they included His humiliation, and sorrows, and sufferings,
and death; for these were not merely what a good
man cannot escape in his conflict with the world.
They were in their own nature expiatory,—a true and
proper sacrifice for sin. "Christ our Passover is sacrificed for us;" "God hath made Him to be sin for us
who knew no sin, that we might be made the righteousness of God in Him;" "In Him we have redemption through His blood, even the forgiveness of sins;"
"The blood of Jesus Christ cleanseth us from all sin."[1]
But the point now before us is, whether our Lord's
offering for sin did not go beyond His death, whether
it did not also embrace His Resurrection and presentation of Himself to the Father in the heavenly Sanctuary.

In considering this it will be well to call to mind

[1] 1 Cor. v. 7 ; 2 Cor. v. 21 ; Ephes. i. 7 ; 1 John i. 7.

a part of the ritual of the law too frequently lost sight of,—the double procedure with the blood of the victim sacrificed; for, upon the great Day of Atonement (to say nothing at present of the ordinary sin-offerings), the High Priest's offering for sin was not completed by the mere slaughtering of the victim, and the pouring out of its blood at the bottom of the brazen altar in the Court. It was not when the High Priest *killed* the bullock of the sin-offering, and the goat of the sin-offering, that the atonement was accomplished; but then only when, putting some of the blood into a basin, he took it within the veil, and sprinkled it upon the Mercy Seat. There were thus two parts of the offering; there was a double procedure with the blood; and the two parts in the double procedure were not a simple repetition of the same idea,—a symbolical setting forth of the same relation between the Almighty upon the one hand, and the sinner upon the other. Confusion seems to have been introduced into this subject by the failure of inquirers to observe that, in both parts of the ceremonial which, while distinct, were closely related to one another, the blood was still the same blood, and that, considered simply by itself, it represented in both the same thing. In neither case was it dead; in both cases it was warm and living blood. The language of Lev. xvii. 11 is express, "For the life of the flesh is in the blood; and I have given it to you upon the altar to make an atonement for your souls." It is the blood as *life* that is there "given upon the altar," not the blood as death. Throughout the whole ritual, therefore, up to the moment when all the actings with it were over, the blood of the victim was its life, as much alive when it was sprinkled, only that then it had passed through death, as when it was first drawn forth by the knife of the offerer. But while the blood was thus itself the same, the procedure with it seems to have had a different meaning at the two different stages of the offering. At the one it bore along with it the life of the offerer sacrificed in the person of the victim to Him who had said, "The soul that sinneth shall die." At the other it bore along with it the same life of the offerer *saved in death and through death,* and now surrendered upon that "Propitiatory" or Mercy Seat which God had Himself provided as the covering of the ark of His testimony. In the first act, that of the slaughtering, there was death, although death only as the way to life. The people died in the sacrifice; and the high priest, as their representative, acknowledged that they deserved to die. In the second act, that of the sprinkling, there was life. The people had accepted, and passed through, death; and the high priest, as their representative, laid their life in its new aspect as an offering before God, expressing their reunion to Him who had redeemed them, and their willing surrender of themselves in the bond and on the conditions of His covenant. Then only, when all this had been done, could it be said that the covenant relation had been re-established between God and Israel. Then only was the high priest's work as the representative of Israel finished; and then only could he come forth from the inmost part of the sanctuary as the representative of God to proclaim that the offering was complete, that Israel was both a pardoned and a holy people, and that its sins might be sent away into that darkness and desolation to which sin belongs. But, before this proclamation could be made, both the actions with the blood that have been spoken of were necessary; and, had the high priest, in addition to setting forth the death of Israel at the Altar in the Court, not also laid Israel for a new life upon the Mercy Seat, he would not have accomplished the service of the day.

Still further, it can hardly fail to be seen that it was in the second part of the service that the whole ceremonial culminated. All inquirers are agreed upon this point, and it is unnecessary to discuss it. Life laid upon the altar of God, to be His for ever, must always be a higher thing than life yielded up to death because of sin; and the words of the Almighty by His prophet sounded throughout the whole of the Old Testament Dispensation, "As I live, saith the Lord, I have no pleasure in the death of the wicked; but that the wicked turn from his way and live: turn ye, turn ye from your evil ways; for why will ye die, O house of Israel?" [1]   In the second part of the

[1] Ezek. xxxiii. 11.

service the people were not only ransomed, but
dedicated; not only pardoned, but consecrated. A
separation had been made between them and the
power not less than the punishment of sin.[1]

Let us pass from the type to the Antitype. The
writer of the Epistle to the Hebrews has left us in no
doubt as to the manner in which all this was fulfilled
in our Lord. The lesson constantly enforced in that
Epistle is that the high priesthood of Christ is "fulfilled" by His work in heaven; that only after His
Resurrection is He in a position to exhaust the
functions of that office; and that His offering is not
completed until, within the heavenly sanctuary, He
presents Himself to the Father in all that perfection
of service which the Father claims. The meaning of
our Lord's presentation of Himself in heaven is thus
different from that of His death upon the cross. Both
are indeed parts of one whole; but they are not on
that account to be confounded with one another, or
to be regarded as the expression, in different ways, of
one and the same thought. There is a distinct difference between them. In the one our great Representative and Substitute bears the penalty of our sins,
submitting Himself to death, the first demand of the
Divine law upon the sinner,—yet doing this, not
simply that He may die, but that He may pass
through death to life. In the other He who is still
our Representative and Substitute presents Himself to

[1] Note 53.

His Heavenly Father, as One who has passed through
death to life, and whose life, redeemed from the
power of death, is now to be presented for ever to
the Father in joyful gratitude and praise. Were it
not for the first act, our Lord, and we in Him, would
approach into the Divine presence without that free
acceptance of penalty which must be the very first
step in our return from evil. Were it not for the
second, actual return to God would not take place.
Without the former, that death would be awanting
out of which alone the corn of wheat can spring up
in life.[1] Without the latter, there would be no
springing up of the corn of wheat at all. Neither
act is sufficient without the other ; and both must be
accomplished before the work of the Heavenly High
Priest can be regarded as complete.

It conveys, therefore, a false idea of the work of
our Lord when we say that it was finished on the
cross, and that His Glorification was only His reward,
and the guarantee to us of His acceptance with God.
He Himself indeed had cried on the cross, " It is
finished." But what was finished ? His groans and
tears, and agonies and cries ; His submission to the
pains and sufferings and death appointed for Him ;
His struggle with the world and its prince ;—these
were finished, but not His offering. That was not
finished until, as One who had died and risen again,
He went, perfected through death, into the Holiest of

[1] John xii. 24.

all, and there devoted Himself, and His people in
Him, to the perpetual service of the Eternal Father.

The Resurrection of our Lord, instead of being a
mere consequence of His work, is thus a part of the
work itself.   Without it He would have left that
work unfinished.   As our Representative He might
have led us to the sacrifice of death rendered necessary by the fact that we had sinned.   But He would
not have led us into the higher life,—the life in God,
—for which we were created, and in which the end of
our existence is attained.   It is only by the continued
offering of Himself in the new life of His resurrection-
state that His people are taken "in Him" beyond
death into heavenly and eternal life.

Two other parts of the priestly work of Christ might
still have been spoken of had time permitted—Intercession and Benediction.   It is enough to say that
without our Lord's Resurrection neither of them could
have been realised, and that He could not, in consequence, have been a perfect Priest.

If the work of Christ as the High Priest of His
people would thus have been unfinished without His
Resurrection, the same thing may next be said of the
other offices discharged by Him for His people's good.

Thus, *e.g.*, the message of salvation which He
reveals as Prophet would not have been complete.
That message is founded upon what He has done as
Priest.   It is the glad tidings of an atoning work
which is not only begun but finished, of a salvation

which includes not only the death of the old man, but
the quickening into life of the new man within us, of a
change which involves our dying unto sin in order that
we may live unto righteousness.   This is " the will of
God for our salvation,"—not simply fresh discoveries
of the power or wisdom or goodness of the great
Creator ; not simply the inculcation of moral precepts
more comprehensive and beautiful than the world had
yet possessed or could have reached by speculations of
its own, but a union in love with the Father through
the Son as Priest.   Such a will of God could only be
revealed after Christ had risen.   His Resurrection was
a part of the revelation ; and without it the very
word to be proclaimed could not be perfected.

But there is more than this to be said upon the
point before us.   To assert only that the Resurrection of our Lord is necessary to the fulfilment of His
prophetical office, because His Resurrection is a necessary part of the revelation to be proclaimed, is to
look at the matter in a more outward light than that
in which it is presented to us in the word of God.
There is not less an inner bond between the fact of the
Resurrection of Christ and the execution of His work
as Prophet ; for, in that work, our Lord was to do more
than simply reveal the truth once for all, and then
leave it as a legacy to the world, in the fixed and
definite form which is implied by its being written in
a book.   The Gospel message was not to be in word
only but in " power," so that in whatever age it might

be proclaimed, it should bring with it the freshness
of a new morning.   In order to this, however, the
word of life required to be accompanied by the
quickening agency of a living personality, from
whom it might pass as a spirit into the spirits of
its hearers.   The word itself might be the same,
but it was necessary that it should be seen in the
new light which every generation needs, and that
it should be adapted to the new experiences which
every generation makes.  This could only be done
by the Living Spirit of the Lord, and the gift of
that Living Spirit could only be bestowed by a
Living, and therefore a Risen, Saviour.   If the
Spirit is to bestow life, is to clothe the word with a
present and a living energy, He must come to us from
a Living Lord, and not from the mere recollection,
however lively, of One who had lived and died.
Such is the lesson taught us by our Lord Himself,
in words which contain some of the deepest and
most important truths of His kingdom.   "I have
yet many things," He said, "to say unto you, but
ye cannot bear them now ; but when He, the Spirit
of the truth, is come, He will guide you into all
the truth : for He will not speak from Himself ; but
whatsoever things He shall hear He will speak; and He
will declare unto you the things that are coming." And
again, "These things have I spoken unto you in proverbs : an hour cometh when I shall no longer speak
unto you in proverbs, but I shall tell you plainly con-

cerning the Father." [1]  We must be careful not to
mistake the meaning of these words.   Our Lord
neither refers in them to *new* truths to be taught
after His departure to the disciples, in addition to
those which they had been taught already ; nor
has He in view a manner of teaching which, while
it was formerly indirect and enigmatical, was now
to become direct and clear.   He had Himself taught
them " all things " necessary for the salvation of
the world, and for the edification of His Church to
the very end of time.[2]   Any idea of a development of truth beyond what was contained in His
own words, rests upon an exegetical misunderstand-
ing of this great passage in His last discourse to
His disciples.   Again, He had taught with a simplicity and lucidity of statement that had nothing in
common with the darker side of either parable or
proverb ; and the effect had corresponded to his
teaching,—" The people were astonished at His
teaching ; " " the publicans and sinners drew near
unto Him for to hear Him ; " the officers sent to
take Him exclaimed,—" Never man spake like this
man ; " " Grace was poured into His lips." [3]   In the
future, therefore, now stretching before His disciples,
He was to teach them neither new truths nor old
truths more plainly.   He was to make them take
up again the *whole* revelation which they had already

---

[1] John xvi. 12, 13, 25.          [2] John xiv. 26.
[3] Matt. vii. 28 ; Luke xv. 1 ; John vii. 46 ; Psalm xlv. 2.

received, and to learn it in a different way. Hitherto
He had taught as a Master who moved in a sphere
of thought superior to theirs : He had spoken of
the "heavenly things" that He alone had "seen ;"
and He had come before them as One, of the deep
meaning of whose instructions they were only able
from time to time to catch a distant glimpse. His
lessons had been enforced by His outward authority,
and had been listened to with wondering awe. It
was mainly because He spoke them that they were
accepted as true. They had not yet commended
themselves to the inward experience of the heart,
nor had the full divineness of their wisdom been
recognised by the spiritually enlightened mind.

Now, however, all this was to be changed. With
the Resurrection and Glorification of our Lord the
ministry of the Spirit bestowed by Him was to begin.
Up to that time "the Spirit," that is, the Spirit in
His power, "was not."[1] He had indeed existed from
everlasting as one of the Persons of the Trinity : He
had moved upon the face of the waters when order
was produced out of chaos :[2] He had "striven" with
men before the Flood :[3] and down to the moment of
the Resurrection He had more or less comforted the
pious, and inspired the prophets, of Israel.[4] But He
had not yet become an indwelling power in man ; He
had not yet been given "without measure ;"[5] and our

---

[1] John vii. 39.　Note 54.　　　[2] Gen. i. 2.　　　[3] Gen. vi. 3.
[4] Ps. li. 11, 12 ; 1 Peter i. 11.　　　[5] John iii. 34.　Note 55.

Lord testified, "It is expedient for you that I go away: for if I go not away, the Advocate will not come unto you; but if I go, I will send him unto you."[1] With the Resurrection, accordingly, the time for that sending came. One of the very first acts of the Risen Lord of which we read was that in which He "breathed on" His disciples and said unto them, "Receive ye holy spirit;"[2] and from that time onward,—through Pentecost, through all the varied seasons, whether of depression or of triumph, that have marked the history of the Church, as well as through all the more private experiences of the people of God,—that Spirit whom it is the province of the Glorified Redeemer to bestow has descended into believing hearts and dwelt there, to lead them into all the truth in a manner in which they had not been led into it before. Enlightened by His influences they not only know what the truth is; they learn also to know that it is the truth. It commends itself in the sight of God to their consciences and their hearts. It has its answer from within. The word itself is no doubt necessary, for the Spirit acts by and with the word. But the Spirit is also necessary, for without Him the word will be no more than a letter which kills. The word brought home to us by the Spirit is the end of the prophetic teaching of our Lord; and inasmuch as He could not bestow that Spirit when He was on earth, His prophetic

[1] John xvi. 7.        [2] John xx. 22.

office was not then "fulfilled;" it is fulfilled only now when He is risen and glorified.

Once more, similar remarks apply to our Lord's kingly office.  No doubt, even during His life on earth He gave occasional indications of His royal dignity.  At the very time when He was despised and rejected of men He laid His commands upon the wind and the sea, and they obeyed Him; disease of every kind yielded to His word; and the very demons were constrained to listen to Him.  Nay, there was at least one occasion on which He Himself distinctly proclaimed that He was a King, though in a sense in which men had not yet learned to understand the word.  " Pilate therefore said unto Him, A King art Thou, then?  Jesus answered, Thou sayest that I am a King.  To this end have I been born, and to this end have I come into the world, that I should bear witness unto the truth : every one that is of the truth heareth My voice."[1]  How strange a kingdom, yet how real in comparison with the kingdoms of this world!  The absolute kingdom at the bottom of all existence, and ruling all existence, is that of truth ; and the more we can witness as humble ministers to that truth, the more does our power increase.  He who in the kingdom of nature is nature's most willing servant and most faithful interpreter has the highest rule.  It is not otherwise in the kingdom of grace.  Jesus, therefore, the only perfect witness to

[1] John xviii. 37.

the eternal verities of that kingdom, was always by
right the only King in it.   His work as a "witness"
and His dignity as a "King" went hand in hand.
But precisely because it was so He could not be
fully King before His death; for the death upon the
cross was the full witness to that truth of the love of
God to sinful men, which it was His commission
especially to proclaim.   It is with His Resurrection
accordingly, that His Kingship is closely connected in
the New Testament.   Then the kingdom which had
always been His by inheritance, but His own personal
claim to which He had been working out during the
whole course of His life, was actually received by
Him.   Thus it is that St. Peter, in his first sermon
to the people, speaking of the fulfilment in Jesus of
that prophecy which had said, "Thou wilt not leave
My soul in hell, neither wilt Thou suffer Thine Holy
One to see corruption," connected it with His Kingship, and His Kingship with His Resurrection,—
"Being therefore a prophet, and knowing that God
had sworn with an oath to him that of the fruit of
his loins He would set one upon his throne; he fore-
seeing this, spake of the resurrection of the Christ."[1]
Thus it is that St. Paul, in his address at Antioch in
Pisidia, associates the same great event with God's
setting His Son as King upon Zion His own holy
hill,—"God hath fulfilled the promise made unto the
fathers in that He raised up Jesus; as also it is

[1] Acts ii. 30, 31.

written in the second Psalm, Thou art My Son, this
day have I begotten Thee;"[1] and that again, in his
Epistle to the Ephesians, the same Apostle speaks of
the working of the might of God's strength, "which
He wrought in Christ when He raised Him from the
dead, and made Him to sit at His right hand in the
heavenly places, far above every principality, and
authority, and power, and dominion, and every name
that is named, not only in this world, but also in that
which is to come;"[2] while the writer of the Epistle to
the Hebrews sees the two Messianic predictions of
Psalms ii. and cx. fulfilled in Him at the time when
He "sat down at the right hand of the throne of the
Majesty in the heavens."[3]   Nothing indeed can be
clearer than the teaching of Scripture upon the point
before us.   The fulness of that kingly office which
our Lord exercises on our behalf begins with His
Resurrection.   The kingly power that He exerts, the
kingly protection that He affords, the kingly grace
that He displays, the kingly honours that He bestows
—all, in short, that most intimately affects the position and privileges of the Christian in their most exalted form,—comes from Christ as the Risen Lord.   It
is on Him, too, in that capacity, that the great work
of carrying on the contest with the world depends.
The words spoken to Him were,—"Sit Thou on My
right hand until I make Thine enemies Thy footstool."
The subduing of evil, and the establishing in its place

[1] Acts xiii. 33.          [2] Ephes. i. 20, 21.          [3] Heb. viii. 1.

L

of that righteousness and peace, the prospect of which constitutes to so large an extent the burden of ancient prophecy, is associated not with the thought only of a Saviour who died, but with that of One who reigns with a sceptre that is right. Hence the explanation of the difficult words of the Apostle Paul in 1 Corinthians xv.—"Then cometh the end, when He shall deliver up the kingdom to God, even the Father, when He shall have abolished all rule and all authority and power. For He must reign, till He hath put all His enemies under His feet."[1] The "kingdom" there is obviously the kingdom wielded by the Risen and Exalted Lord for the purpose of establishing righteousness in the hearts of men, and of putting down all sin. *That* kingdom must close when its purpose is accomplished. In that sense, but in that only, in which a king puts down his enemies, and has then no more opposition to contend with, there is the prospect of a time when our Lord can be no longer King.

Thus, then, it appears that the Resurrection of our Lord is the completing of His work; for it is the completing of the different offices by which that work is accomplished. It is an essential part of the work which He left the mansions of His Father's glory to perform. If He did not rise from the dead and return to His Father, He is neither Priest, Prophet, nor King, in the full sense of any of

---

[1] 1 Cor. xv. 24, 25.

these terms. He may present us along with Himself as a sacrifice when He dies upon the cross,
but we shall have no part in that new life of dedication to the Father, for the sake of which it is well
that the old man should die. He may teach us
the letter of His word, but the Spirit will be wanting,
through whom alone that word can be made "a
fountain of springing water" "within ourselves." He
may lead us onward in a path of "witnessing," but
while we witness, we shall be "of all men most
miserable." His work without His Resurrection is
no interrupted, broken work, with no result able
to throw light upon its mystery, with no termination sufficient to explain either its beginning, its
course, or its close.

Now, however, by His Resurrection, that work
has been accomplished, and as Prophet, Priest, and
King, He lives at the right hand of God, to provide
for us the powerful and gracious influences of which
we stand in need, and which it is His in these
offices to supply. In the unity of His Person is found
every function needed for the guidance of His people
through the different stages of their mortal pilgrim-
age; in Him they have a Redeemer "mighty to
save." What He laboured and died to purchase, He
rose to complete, and is now living to bestow.

2. The Resurrection of our Lord is not only
the completion of His Work; it is God's own at-

testation to the Work itself, and that in two
respects,—(1), to the *manner* in which it had been
accomplished ; (2), to the *fact* that by it sin had
been for ever blotted out, and the foundation of
the new life laid. Let us look at these two particulars for a moment.

(1.) The Resurrection of Christ attested God's
own approbation of the manner in which His work
had been accomplished. In His Resurrection Christ
was " justified." We have to bear in mind that
the sacred writers draw no such distinction as is
often drawn by theologians between the active and
passive obedience of our Lord. To them His whole
work is one. Hence His Resurrection is the Father's
testimony to it all. In the Epistle to the Philippians
His Exaltation is connected not only with His death
upon the cross, but with His making Himself of
no reputation, and taking upon Him the form of
a servant.[1] In the Epistle to the Romans it is
in contrast with His having been made of the seed
of David according to the flesh, that He is said to
have been declared to be the Son of God with
power, according to the spirit of holiness, by the
resurrection of the dead.[2] In the First Epistle to
Timothy, in like manner, Christ's being justified
in spirit is contrasted with His having been manifested in flesh ;[3] and a similar lesson is conveyed
by the words of Jesus Himself in the Gospel of

[1] Phil. ii. 6-11.          [2] Rom. i. 4.          [3] 1 Tim. iii. 16.

St. John, when He says that one of the three
parts in which He sums up the work of the
Advocate to be sent after His departure, shall
be to convict the world of righteousness, because
He goes to the Father, and they see Him no more.[1]
No one can doubt that these and other similar
passages present the Resurrection of our Lord as
a proof of the Father's approbation of His work
in itself, and of the manner in which He had
accomplished it.   There is a great law written upon
the very nature of things, although we continually
rebel against it,—the law that self-sacrifice is the
foundation of all right relations to God, and therefore the beginning of all good, the law of love
declared by the Apostle to be the fulfilling of all
law,[2] the law of God Himself, for God is love.   To
that great law, Jesus, standing in our room and
stead, had accommodated Himself.   Men thought
that when the Messiah came with a redemption
that had formed the theme of type and prophecy
for two thousand years, He would come with outward glory, with worldly pomp and power.   He
had come in a manner the very opposite.   His life
had been one of humiliation, of ministering, of self-
denial, of suffering for the sake of others,—had been
in short one continued sacrifice,—until at last the
culminating point of sacrifice was reached in death.
We "glory" in this; but when the events actually

[1] John xvi. 10.                    [2] Rom. xiii. 10.

occurred, the life was despised rather than honoured;
the death drew down scorn rather than applause.
It is difficult for us even to conceive the facts
when we read of them; most difficult to think
that the world misapprehended and misinterpreted
them as it did; that it preferred a robber and a
murderer to the holy Lord; and that, when at last
it had what it deemed the false Preacher of righteousness within its power, it was roused into an
agony of excitement to destroy Him.

Jesus needed to be "justified;" and His Resurrection was His justification. God Himself then
came forth to vindicate the righteousness of One
whom the world had rejected, and to show that
the Searcher of hearts, who estimates all things as
they really are, and who weighs the "works" of
men in the balances of a perfectly righteous and
unerring judgment, had another than the world's
sentence to pronounce. Then it was seen that while
the world had scorned the Son of God, the Father
had been watching over Him with unceasing love;
that while the world had placed Him at its bar
as a malefactor and blasphemer, the Father had
been making ready a seat for Him at His own
right hand; that while the world nailed Him to
the cross, the Father had been preparing for Him
"many crowns," and a name that is above every
name; that while the world had gone to the grave
in the garden, setting a watch and sealing the

stone, and had then returned to its feasting and
merriment, because the Preacher of righteousness
was no longer there to trouble it, the Father had
waited for the third morning in order to bring
Him forth in triumph from the grave.

The Resurrection of our Lord was a testimony to
God's approbation of the whole course that had been
pursued by Him, and of the whole spirit of His work.
But in being this it was also more, for—

(2.) It attested the fact that by it sin had been
blotted out, and the foundation of the new life laid.
There is one text upon this point so emphatic that it
is unnecessary to quote others, while it is all the more
proper to quote this one, because it seems to have
been so often and so strangely misunderstood. The
text is in Rom. iv. 25, where we read of Him " who
was delivered up because of our trespasses, and raised
because of our justification." It is not stated in these
important words either that our salvation begins in
Christ's death but is perfected in His Resurrection, or
that our offences were the *ground* on account of which
Jesus was offered, but His Resurrection the *end* for
which God raised Him from the dead. The object of
the Apostle is to set forth in two contrasted but precisely parallel clauses the manifestation which God had
made of Himself in Christ; and in doing so he tells
us that God had delivered Him up *because of* our
offences, and had raised Him *because of* our justification. In other words, God gave up His Son to death

because we had sinned, and that pardon might be
possible.    He raised Him again because He had
procured the pardon of our sins, and had thus, by
justifying us, made the new life possible.    A work
was to be done ; Christ died and did it.    The work
was done ; Christ was raised, and His Resurrection
established the fact that He had done it.[1]    In raising
His Son from the dead, the Father gave a decisive
testimony to the fact that He was well pleased for His
righteousness' sake, that He accepted the sacrifice that
had been offered for sin, and that He rejoiced in beholding those great principles of law and justice and
truth vindicated, which are essential to the order
and happiness of His creatures.    The Resurrection of
our Lord is thus the assurance to us that in the plan
of our redemption mercy and truth have met together,
righteousness and peace have embraced each other.
The burden of sin which He bore has been cast off ;
and He Himself, and we in Him, are free.

Therefore it was that our Lord as He looked forward to His Resurrection, and to that Glorification
which was then to begin, prayed, " Father, glorify Thy
Son ;" " And now, O Father, glorify Thou Me with
Thine own Self with the glory which I had with Thee
before the world was." [2]    It was not for outward glory,
such as a throne and a sceptre and crowds of ministering angels, that He thus prayed.    He prayed for a glory
which should consist in a demonstration to the world,

[1] Note 56.                [2] John xvii. 1, 5.

first, that He whom the world had persecuted to death
because of His meekness and lowliness and self-deny-
ing love, was the object of the highest approbation
and love of God Himself; and secondly, that the
lowly and crucified Redeemer was, in His one perfect
offering for sin, the sure foundation of our peace and
joy and hope and life.

And God heard the prayer. He glorified His Son
Jesus; and in that Glorification we now rejoice, not
simply for the sake of what it brings to us, but for
the sake of what it brought to Him, and because it is
the Divine testimony to an order of things which the
world scorns, but which we know to be the order of
eternal truth and righteousness. Therefore we follow
the Risen Lord; and, dismissing every thought of
sacrifice accepted or atonement made for us, we cry,—
" Gird Thy sword upon Thy thigh, O Most Mighty,
with Thy glory and Thy majesty. And in Thy majesty
ride prosperously because of truth and meekness and
righteousness. . . . Thy throne, O God, is for ever
and ever: the sceptre of Thy kingdom is a right
sceptre. Thou lovest righteousness and hatest wicked-
ness: therefore God, Thy God, hath anointed Thee
with the oil of gladness above Thy fellows;"[1] " Lift
up your heads, O ye gates; and be ye lift up, ye everlasting doors; and the King of glory shall come in.
Who is this King of glory? The Lord strong and
mighty, the Lord mighty in battle. Lift up your

[1] Ps. xlv. 3, 4, 6, 7.

heads, O ye gates; even lift them up, ye everlasting
doors; and the King of glory shall come in.   Who is
this King of glory?   The Lord of Hosts, He is the
King of glory;"[1] " Bless the Lord, ye His angels, that
excel in strength, that do His commandments, hearken-
ing unto the voice of His word.   Bless ye the Lord,
all ye His hosts; ye ministers of His, that do His
pleasure.   Bless the Lord, all His works in all places
of His dominion: bless the Lord, O my soul." [2]

[1] Ps. xxiv. 7-10.      [2] Ps. ciii. 20-22.

# LECTURE V.

"That I may know him, and the power of his resurrection."
Philip. iii. 10.

We have considered the bearing of the Resurrection
of our Lord upon His own Person and Work; and
we proceed now to the bearing of the same great
fact upon ourselves.  In no part of His work does
the Lord Jesus Christ stand alone; and in His Resurrection, therefore, as well as in all its other parts, He
takes along with Him the members of His body.
Here, as elsewhere, He is the head of that new humanity which He has formed for Himself.  He is the
Representative and Life of His people; and what He
is determines the nature of their position, and duties,
and privileges.  He is not merely the object of their
faith; in that faith they are one with Him.  He is
more than their type and model; in Him they inhere
as living stones of the temple of which He is the
foundation—as branches of the vine of which He is
the stem—as members of the body of which He is
the head.  Whatever befalls Him befalls them.  They
live in His life; they work His work; they suffer in
His sufferings; they die in His death; they rise in

His Resurrection ; they ascend to the heavenly places
in His Ascension ; they sit with Him upon His throne ;
they accompany Him as His assessors when He comes
to judge the world at the last day ; they reign there-
after as kings and priests with Him, the King and
Priest of the new creation, for ever and ever.  This
doctrine of the union between the Lord Jesus Christ
and His people is the central doctrine of the New
Testament.  It may well be doubted whether it is as
much before the mind of the Church in our day as it
ought to be.  Our forefathers dwelt more upon it than
we do.  The mystical union, as they called it, held a
far more prominent place in their thoughts than it
holds in ours.  We speak in popular language of justification, adoption, and sanctification, together with
the benefits that accompany or flow from them, as if
these were the several parts of a process by which we
are brought near to Christ, and in which we are united
to Him.  But that is not the order of things either in
Scripture or in the Standards of our own Church.  In
the former Christ comes first, and the blessings enu-
merated follow.  They are not steps that lead us to
Him ; they are deductions from what we have in Him.
"Come unto Me, all ye that labour and are heavy laden,
and I will give you rest ;" "This is the eternal life,
that they may learn to know Thee the only true God
and Him whom Thou didst send, Jesus, as Christ."[1]  In
that eternal life we possess all ; we only do not know

---

[1] Matt. xi. 28 ; John xvii. 3.

what we possess until we have analysed its parts, traced their relation to one another, and distinguished them by their different names. Such, indeed, is the character of all the doctrinal teaching of the New Testament. It comes after, and not before, a Divine life already in existence.

But union with Christ is not only the centre of the New Testament; it occupies the same position in the authoritative teaching of our Church. When the questions of our Shorter Catechism relating to the work of Christ are finished, and those relating to the application of His redemption begin, we are at once told that " the Spirit applies to us the redemption purchased by Christ by working faith in us, and thereby uniting us to Christ in our effectual calling." After this, effectual calling is itself explained as a persuading and enabling us " to embrace Jesus Christ freely offered to us in the Gospel." Then follow the questions relating to Justification, Adoption, Sanctification, and their benefits; and they describe, not the path by which we come to Jesus, but the blessings which we enjoy in Him. Such is the true order of Christian experience. To make us one with Himself, and in Himself one with the Father, is the supreme and final purpose of our Lord's work. And He Himself, in His own words, expressed that purpose both in its character and extent, when He prayed on behalf of all who should yet believe in His name, " that they all may be one; even as Thou, Father, art in Me, and I in Thee,

that they also may be in Us : that the world may believe that Thou didst send Me.    And the glory which
Thou hast given Me I have given them; that they may
be one, even as We are one : I in them, and Thou in
Me, that they may be perfected into one ; that the
world may learn to know that Thou didst send Me, and
lovedst them even as Thou lovedst Me."[1]    Our union to
the Son, in the Son to the Father, in the Son and in the
Father to one another, and all in the love which is at
once the fundamental element of the Divine existence
and the most essential constituent of human happiness,—that is the end of our Lord's work, and the
glorious hope in which we are saved.    What we have
now to do, therefore, is to examine the bearing of the
Resurrection of our Lord upon that new life, the most
important conception of which is, that it is union
with Christ, that it is life given to believers not so
much by Him as in Him.    It will be well also, in
doing this, to keep distinctly in view the light in
which we learned to look at the Resurrection of our
Lord when we considered its bearing on His own
Person and Work : it is the complement, the filling up,
of His Incarnation.

1. In the Risen Lord we have the source of that new
life of union with God which Christians are to lead.
It is in Him as Risen that the Almighty continues
that revelation of Himself to us as a Father, upon
which the life of sonship rests.    To make such a

---

[1] John xvii. 21-23.    Note 57.

revelation at the first was the great aim of the Incarnation. It was not merely that He might be in a
position to fulfil the law or to endure its penalty, to
yield a perfect obedience to His Father's will, or to
die upon the cross, that the eternal Son of God became the Son of man. These purposes were no doubt
also contemplated by our Lord,—they may even be
said to have been the first steps in the course which
it was necessary for Him to take; but the main purpose of His coming lay much deeper. It was so to
bring the Divine and the human into union with one
another—two distinct natures into one Person for
ever—that the closest possible connexion might be
established between them. It was to bridge over that
gulf between the Almighty on the one hand and
His creatures on the other, which all religions and all
philosophies had tried, but had failed, to bridge over.
It was to reveal a fact fundamental to the very conception of a religious life in human beings,—that there
is in a certain sense a community of nature between
God and us, the human in the Divine and the Divine
in the human. Were it not so, it would be vain to
speak of union on our part with God. There must
be some community of nature between two beings
who are to be united. Love is otherwise impossible;
and it is in love that the union between God and man
is formed. The Incarnation effected this union; and
it was because it effected it in the most perfect way,
that the religion of Christ is the most perfect conceiv-

able religion ; that it is the fulness of a light which, however it might have shone partially in the world before, only reached its greatest brightness when the Word became flesh and dwelt among us. Then He who " by divers portions and in divers manners had of old time spoken unto the fathers in the prophets, spoke unto us in a Son," who was " the radiance of His glory and the very image of His substance." [1] The absolute Divinity of that Son was as necessary to His effecting of the end He had in view as His perfect humanity :—" No man hath seen God at any time ; an only begotten God, which is in the bosom of the Father,"—that is, one who is only begotten, who is God, who is in the bosom of the Father,—" He hath declared Him." [2] Again, His perfect humanity was as necessary as His absolute Divinity :—" The law was given through Moses ; the grace and the truth came through Jesus Christ." [3] Had not the union of the two been found in our Lord, He would have lived and died in vain.

Such is the teaching of the Bible, but not of the Bible only. Universal experience shows that man cannot hold close and affectionate intercourse with pure spirit ; and that when we try to direct our thoughts to One of whom we know only that He fills all space with His presence—that He is motionless, passionless, alone—we are lost in a sphere to which we

---

[1] Heb. i. 1, 3.        [2] John i. 18.   Note 58.
[3] John i. 17.

have no sufficient bond. The Incarnation of Christ was therefore necessary, if a true basis was to be laid for that fellowship between God and us in which the essence of religion lies.

But if the Incarnation was necessary at the moment when it took place, its continuance is not less necessary now. It would not be enough to tell us that at one time the Son of God became incarnate, if after a short sojourn of three and thirty years here below He laid aside His humanity and returned to that condition in which He existed before He came into the world. No revelation which the Almighty makes of Himself can be thus fleeting, if any permanent result is to be effected by it. He may indeed *gradually* reveal Himself, because men may not be able to bear at first the full brightness of His light. The partial revelation given at one stage may be taken up and absorbed into the fuller revelation given at another; but what God has once revealed of Himself can never pass away or be destroyed, without confounding all our notions of the Divine, without extinguishing that very adaptation between it and its effect which He intended to produce. The spirit of the Christian life, therefore, cannot spring from the thought of any merely past Incarnation of God. The Incarnation must be continued. If it was ever necessary, it is necessary now. For all ages a Personal Incarnate Lord is the only "way" to the Father; and for us an Incarnate Lord must be a Risen Lord. Take away

M

His Resurrection, and the very foundation of our spiritual life is removed.

In strict accordance with this is the teaching of Scripture with regard to the Second Adam. No one will doubt for a moment that it is through the Second Adam that the new life comes to us. The question thus immediately arises, At what point of His history did our Lord assume that relation to man which these words imply? In 1 Cor. xv. St. Paul has given us a full and clear answer to the question. The two Adams are in that chapter contrasted with one another; and the whole argument of the Apostle is based upon the view that our Lord, instead of being the Second Adam during His earthly life, then possessed (sin, which does not belong to our true nature, of course excepted) the nature of the first Adam as well as we. He had taken to Him a true body and a reasonable soul like ours. He had identified Himself with our position, and had entered into our circumstances, that, bearing the penalty of the law which we had incurred, and fulfilling the righteousness of which we had fallen short, He might afford a new starting-point for the human race, at which and from which men might share with Him the glorious results of His mission. That was the beginning of His work, but the work was not completed until His Resurrection. Therefore it was not at His Incarnation, when He only took the first step in the course by which we were to be redeemed, but at His Resurrection, when He had yielded His obedience, offered His sacrifice, and gained His victory, that He was really constituted the Second Adam. Hence such words of the chapter as these,—" If Christ hath not been raised, then is our proclamation (the subject of our teaching) vain, and your faith is also vain ; " [1] " If Christ hath not been raised, your faith is vain, ye are yet in your sins ; " [2] " Since by man came death, by man came also the resurrection of the dead." [3] Hence also the sowing and the raising up that are spoken of, for in these words the " sowing " is not the burial, and the " raising up " the bringing forth from the grave, of the same human body. The sowing has its primary reference to the body bestowed upon our first parent at his creation, and in due time assumed by our Lord ; the raising up refers to the body bestowed upon our Lord at His Resurrection. Hence, finally, the fact that the words of verse 47, " the second man is of heaven," apply not to the Christ on earth, but to the Christ in heaven, from which He will come at last, bringing all His people with Him.[4] The whole chapter, in short, is full of the Risen Lord, and of Him alone ; and He, therefore, as Risen, is the Second Adam.

Nor does the Apostle merely state the fact ; he shows us also that it could not be otherwise when, in direct connexion with what he had asserted of the corruptible and the incorruptible, of the natural and

[1] Ver. 14.          [2] Ver. 17.
[3] Ver. 21.          [4] Note 59.

the spiritual body, he says, "the first man Adam became a living soul, the last Adam became a life-giving spirit." [1] These words can have no meaning except one,—that it was only when our Lord's body passed into its final, its heavenly stage, that He could communicate to us out of His own fulness that power of the Spirit without which no child of the first Adam is born again.

The whole application of redemption thus belongs to our Lord in His ascended state. "The God of our Fathers," said the Apostles Peter and John before the council, "raised up Jesus. . . . Him did God exalt at His right hand to be a Prince and a Saviour, for to give repentance unto Israel, and remission of sins;" [2] and, on the day of Pentecost when the Church was constituted by the outpouring of the Holy Spirit, St. Peter cried before the people, "This Jesus did God raise up, of whom we all are witnesses. Being therefore exalted at the right hand of God, and having received of the Father the promise of the Holy Spirit, He hath poured forth this, which ye see and hear." [3] Everywhere the lesson is the same. When, therefore, we apprehend in faith that Second Adam from whom the new life comes, it is with the Redeemer as One who not only died but who rose again that we have to do; and the Church of Christ felt this with that wonderful instinct of which it is difficult to speak as if it

---

[1] 1 Cor. xv. 45.   [2] Acts v. 30, 31.   [3] Acts ii. 32, 33.

were less than inspiration. Why did her weekly day
of worship not commemorate the Incarnation or the
death upon the cross? Because neither was the beginning of her life. At neither of these points of His
history was her Lord in a position to give her life.
It was at His Resurrection that He became a "life-
giving spirit,"—a spirit clothed with a body entirely
conformed to His spiritual state, and able without let
or hindrance to dispense itself to man in all the fulness of its heavenly power. In the Risen Christ,
therefore, the new life of believers has its source.
But not only so,—

2. From Christ as thus risen it also derives its
character and scope. It will be at once admitted by
every Christian that the Lord Jesus Christ is Himself
the Alpha and the Omega, the Beginning and the
End, the Type and Model of that life which His followers are to lead in a present world. Yet it is possible to speak of this in a manner that falls short of
what is really contemplated in the New Testament.
We may take our standard from the human and
earthly aspect of our Lord, instead of fixing our eyes
mainly upon what He is as Divine and Heavenly.
One of the strongest and most alluring tendencies
of our time is, indeed, to do so. Everywhere there
are many who will consent to recognise in Jesus of
Nazareth the fairest and the noblest member of the
human family. They will compare Him with the
heroes of the past, only to show how far these have

fallen short of Him.  They will even kindle into enthusiasm as they gather together the varied traits of that wonderful life which has, for centuries, so powerfully influenced the history of the world.  One thing only they will demand, that we shall banish from our conception of Him everything supernatural and heavenly, all thought of God in Him, of a Divine Spirit resting upon Him, ruling in Him,—all, in short, that lies beyond the compass of our natural powers, or to which a simply natural development might not attain.

It may be said that this is an extreme case ; but the tendency is natural.  It takes away from the life of Christ what at first sight seems its single and isolated grandeur.  It may be urged that it brings it more within the sphere of our knowledge and the reach of our imitation.  It includes it in a series of the lives of men who are only like ourselves ; and it may even nourish a lofty pride that, by faithful and persistent effort, we may become the Christs that are to be.

Other and more worthy considerations often lead practically to the same result.  Most men who are advanced in life, and who have paid attention to these subjects, can remember the time when, after the formalism which ruled under the great name of Theology in the earlier part of this century, and the extravagant supernaturalism of the Evangelical School which was produced by the reaction, the doctrine of the human Jesus came upon them almost like a reve-

lation.　There was something in that human life so
beautiful and tender, that it filled their hearts with
emotions of loving wonder.　They could hang upon
the words of One who spake as never man spake;
they could linger around the footsteps of One who
wrought as never man wrought; they could cling to
the side of One who was such a friend as the world
had never seen; and yet, all the time, they might be
swayed by nothing higher than mere natural feeling.
Oh! they cried, let us only think of Jesus as the
perfect, as the pattern man, as the great head of our
humanity,—wise where we are ignorant, holy where we
are sinful, perfect where we are imperfect, yet nothing
more than man; then we can understand and love
and cleave to Him; then we can take Him to be our
Guide, Companion, and Friend.　Otherwise He is too
far away from us, too unknown, too unearthly, too
mysterious.　We are men, and only of things human
can we say that they are not strange to us.

Feelings such as these have been extremely common of late years; they are extremely common now;
and the whole tone of our Christian life is affected by
them.　What is more common than to hear Christian
men in all sincerity defending, nay even urging, from
the recollection of what Jesus was, a certain accommo-
dation to the world?　To be too separate from it, they
exclaim, is not only to put an undue strain upon
humanity; it is to awaken needless prejudice, and to
excite a degree of opposition which, for the sake of all

parties, had better be avoided. To stoop to the world is part of the wisdom that would raise it to our own higher level. Let us show the world that we can come down to it as our Master did, without being affected by its sinfulness; that we can adopt its manners and its ways without sacrificing our Christian character. The Lord whom we serve came "eating and drinking;" let us not forget that the Son of God was also the Son of man.

Now, whatever be the effect of this, and without asking at present whether the results aimed at are obtained or not, it is sufficient to observe that the New Testament presents a different teaching, and that the Lord in communion with whom it bids us find the standard of our Christian life is the Risen Lord. Thus it is that St. Paul speaks in one of the most remarkable passages of his writings, when his mind was full of the thought of that Redeemer who not only died for us but rose again: "Wherefore we henceforth know no man after the flesh; even though we have known Christ after the flesh, henceforth know we Him so no more. Wherefore if any man be in Christ, he is a new creature; the old things are passed away; behold, they are become new." [1] We cannot imagine for a moment that the Apostle means by these words that a time has come when he will forget the friends whom, in Epistles written long afterwards, he mentions in such loving terms. He means only that,

[1] 2 Cor. v. 16, 17.

much as he valued them, he will "henceforth" not
be influenced by them as men alone. He will feel
that they and he are to have views and aims and
principles of judgment different from those of mere
earthly friendship; that they are no longer natural
but spiritual men; and that they are to know each
other, not after the flesh but after the spirit. Thus
also, when he says that henceforth he will not know
Christ after the flesh, no one will imagine for a moment that he undervalued the human life of Jesus.
But he felt that, whatever amount of power or beauty
might have marked it, it did not express the full
ideal to which Christians were to be raised. Such an
ideal was to be found only in that glory of the Risen
Lord which Christians, like a mirror, were to reflect,
and into a full conformity with which they were to be
changed from glory to glory, even as from the Lord
the Spirit.[1]

What St. Paul thus says with regard to himself,
he often says substantially, although in more general
terms, with regard to all Christian men:—In the
Epistle to the Ephesians, "But God, being rich in
mercy, for His great love wherewith He loved us,
even when we were dead through our trespasses,
quickened us together with Christ (by grace are ye,—
saved men), and raised us up with Him, and made
us to sit with Him in the heavenly places, in Christ
Jesus."[2] Again to a similar effect in the Epistle to

---

[1] 2 Cor. iii. 18. Note 60.　　[2] Ephes. ii. 4-7.

the Colossians, " If then ye were raised together with Christ, seek the things that are above, where Christ sitteth on the right hand of God. Set your mind on the things that are above, not upon the things that are upon the earth. For ye died, and your life is hidden with Christ in God."[1] And once more in the Epistle to the Romans, " We were buried therefore with Him through baptism unto death : that like as Christ was raised from the dead through the glory of the Father, so we also might walk in newness of life. For if we have become united with the likeness of His death, we shall be also with the likeness of His Resurrection."[2]

In passages such as these the life of Christians is distinctly set before us as life in a Risen Saviour, as life deriving its character and colour not merely from what Jesus was, but from what He is—as life pervaded by the spirit of an entirely new world, and not by the spirit of the old world, however elevated and improved through the influence of the Christian faith.

It is true indeed that the individual graces of the Christian life can hardly differ in their essence, whatever be the aspect of our Lord from which we draw them. Even if formed in us after what they were in the Christ on earth, they must still, in their substance and main features, be the same as when formed in us after the Christ in heaven. He is the same "yesterday, to day, and for ever." Humility, gentleness,

[1] Col. iii. 1-3.　　　　[2] Rom. vi. 4, 5.

meekness, patience, forgiveness of injuries, and such
like, cannot be imagined more Divine than they were
in the human life of Him who " did no sin, and in
whose mouth there was found no guile." The difference lies less in these graces considered individually
than in the tone and spirit of the Christian life considered as a whole.

But there the difference is great; and it seems to
show itself chiefly in the three ideas of Separation
from the world, Consecration to God, and Freedom.

(1.) In Separation from the world: for in His
Resurrection our Lord separated Himself for ever
from the things of earth; and, in token that He did
so, He left behind Him in the grave the linen cloths
and the napkin in which He had been wrapped. He
rose as one who had entered a higher world, which
was thenceforward to be His only home. In like
manner a life in the Risen Lord is a life of separation
from the world. It may appear hard to say so, but
the words do not mean that we are to withdraw ourselves from all concern in the affairs of earth, to dis-
own its relationships, and to take up our abode in
some wilderness or monastic cell to which no sound
of busy life can penetrate. We, as well as others,
have to act our part amidst our fellows, and to discharge the duties upon which our own existence and
that of many dear to us depends. We have to occupy the position of husbands and wives, parents and
children, sons and daughters, friends and neighbours,

members of society and citizens of the State. Nor is an
interest forbidden us either in nature or in art. We
may still admire the beauty of creation, and rejoice in
the light that is upon the land and upon the sea. The
treasures of human genius may enrich us more than
they enrich those whose circle of thought is bounded
by them alone. Christian separation from the world
does not mean that we have nothing further to do
with these things. We still mingle with them as
before ; but we discover beneath their outward forms
what tells us of a higher world than the present ; they
have a voice which speaks of loftier aims than any
suggested by the fleeting shadows around us ; they
have their part not in any mere music of the spheres,
which must be as fleeting as all created things, but
in the melody of an everlasting chime. That is true
separation from the world,—to be in the world and
yet not of the world,—to work and suffer and rejoice
as members of a body whose ruling Head is a spiritual
and heavenly Lord.

(2.) In Consecration to God : for we have already
seen that this is the grand meaning of that Resurrection of our Lord which is to be viewed as the
completion of His offering rather than as a reward
for death endured,—as that step in which, taking
with Him those for whom He died, He presents them
in Himself to the Eternal Father, that they may
serve Him in cheerful obedience and in joyful submission of their wills to His will for ever and ever.

Out of this idea comes the whole consecration of
the Christian life to God,—the consecration of those
who are at once priests and offerings.  They accept
the consecration of the great High Priest as their
own, and in Him they become priests.  They accept
His offering as their own, and in Him they offer
up " a sacrifice of praise to God continually, that
is, the fruit of lips which make confession to His
name."[1]    And all this they do, and can do, only
in the power of the Holy Spirit whom the Lord
is exalted to bestow ; and whom He does bestow,
that, like the kings and priests of Israel—like the
tabernacle and all the vessels of the sanctuary—they
may be set apart from common to holy uses.   It is
greatly to be lamented that, except in two places to
neither of which it properly belongs, this word " consecrate " does not occur in our English New Testament,
though it occurs in the original Greek.[2]   It is more
than to dedicate, for that word does not bring out
the sacred change upon the object dedicated ; and it
is more than to sanctify, for that word connects our
thoughts with the human subject, instead of leading
us straight to the Divine Person to whom we are devoted.   Perhaps it is because we have lost the word
from our religious life, that we have so greatly lost
what is represented by it.   We speak of ourselves as
men more or less sanctified—how seldom do we speak
of ourselves as men consecrated !   We miss this con-

---

[1] Heb. xiii. 15.            [2] Note 61.

secration in the lives of many Christians. Even when they are separated from the world, it does not always appear that they are consecrated to God. They do not always bear about with them a fragrant " unction from the Holy One ;" they are not always " altogether lovely."

(3.) In Freedom : for it was when He entered on His heavenly life that our Lord, as not only Divine but human, was for the first time free. Here on earth He was limited and restrained by bounds inseparable from our humanity. He is delivered from all restrictions and limitations now. Here He was bowed down by the thought of the heavy burden He had undertaken in bearing the sins of men : " I have a baptism," He said, " to be baptized with, and how am I straitened until it be accomplished." That baptism has been accomplished, and He has risen out of it into a new and glorious life, over which death has no more dominion. Here the cup of His Father's wrath was put into His hands, of which He said, " Father, if it be possible, let this cup pass from me." It has now been drained to the very dregs, and instead of it He has received a cup full of the new wine of the kingdom of God. Here He was under the curse of the law—that law which to Him was so spiritual and just and good. The curse has now been endured, and the honour of the law has been for ever vindicated. Here He was oppressed by the sufferings and the sorrows which He had come to heal.

He has now healed His people by His stripes, and He continually presents Himself along with them before the throne of God, saying, "Behold, I and the children whom Thou hast given Me." What a mighty and glorious change is there in the freedom of His spirit when His work is over and His suffering borne,—when He has returned to His Father's presence, and has been welcomed with all the hallelujahs of heaven!

In Him therefore, as the Risen Lord, we are free. It is true that we have not yet attained to the full measure of our freedom. But even now in Him there is a freedom wherewith He maketh His people free. "Ye received not the spirit of bondage again unto fear; but ye received the spirit of adoption, whereby we cry, Abba, Father;" "The law of the spirit of life in Christ Jesus made me free from the law of sin and death."[1] We are free from the curse of the law, for He has borne it; from its condemning power, for He has fulfilled all righteousness; from the restraints of the letter, for the spirit of love is in our hearts, which knows no limit to its exertions, and is hemmed in by no restraint upon its energies. Even now we are the sons of God, no longer under a "schoolmaster," or under "tutors and governors until the time appointed of the Father;" but sons who have obtained access by faith into the grace wherein they stand, who are filled with

[1] Rom. viii. 15, 2.

the "law of liberty," and who know that the boundless love of God is the only measure of their happiness.

Such then is the character and scope of the new life given us in the Risen Lord; and we cannot fail to observe how great is the difference between that life thus looked at as flowing from Him in His exalted state in heaven, and what it would be, could we regard it only as the reproduction in us of the life which He lived on earth. If this last were all that, in communicating Himself, our Lord communicated to the members of His body, they would receive their new life only in the spirit in which it was led by the Redeemer during the days of His humiliation, and with the restrictions with which His own higher life was then restrained in Him. The conflicts and sufferings of His condition in His earthly body would then be a necessary part of the communication, for as the vine is so must the branches be. As it is, these are not directly communicated to us by the Risen Lord. No doubt they cannot be escaped, for they spring from weaknesses of the flesh, from which we are not yet delivered; from influences of a world in which we must still move; from the nature of our work, the time of resting from which has not yet come. But they do not belong to the idea of that position in which we are placed. The Head of the body is in heaven; and what we experience in virtue of our union with that Head is, not troubles of the world, but peace in the midst of them;[1] not tribulations like His own, but the cheerfulness with which, since they must be met, they may be faced and overcome;[2] not the toil of the seed-time, but the joy of the harvest field.[3] The whole character of the new life into which we are born would be changed if our Lord's earthly life alone, instead of His life in heaven, were made ours when we believe.

More particularly, it is here that the great New Testament doctrine of the consecration of the body finds its place. That our Lord did not simply live in the spirit after death, but that He rose from the grave in a human body, is the truth which most of all reminds us of the high destiny of our bodies, and most of all impresses upon us the importance of seeing that we discipline and train them now. Were it not in this respect for the lessons of the Resurrection of Christ, we should be involved in the same round of perplexity which has always marked men when they have either had no special revelation, or when revelation has been misunderstood. Every religion and every philosophy has tried, in its own way, to heal the breach which was felt to be in existence between the body and the soul. Of old, men sacrificed the body to the soul; now, they sacrifice the soul to the body; and at the end they are as far as ever from having solved the problem. The Resurrection of our Lord alone gives us the solution, teaching us, as it does, the sacredness of both.

[1] John xiv. 27.    [2] John xvi. 33.    [3] John iv. 38.   Note 62.

No mere doctrine of the immortality of the soul could do this; and no belief that the Lord Jesus Christ now reigns in a disembodied state upon the throne of universal empire could do it. It is done by the doctrine of the Risen Lord alone,—by that doctrine which tells us that He has still a body, but a body glorified. Animated by this thought, we learn to discipline not only the spirit but the body, and to train the one as we train the other for the time when He who has Himself been fashioned anew shall also fashion anew the body of our humiliation, that it may be conformed to the body of His glory, according to the working whereby He is able even to subdue all things unto Himself.[1]

3. In the Risen Lord the new life has its nourishment and strength. That life is a life of communion and fellowship with the Father through the Son; and in Scripture it is represented as led by the indwelling of the Son in us; "who," says St. Paul, writing to the Corinthians, and referring to our Lord, "to youward is not weak but is mighty in you, for indeed He was crucified through weakness, yet He liveth through the might of God;"[2] and again, writing to the Galatians, and speaking of himself, "I live, and yet no longer I, but Christ liveth in me;"[3] while the short and expressive formula used by our Lord Himself is, "Ye in Me, and I in you."[4] In the first two

[1] Phil. iii. 21.    [2] 2 Cor. xiii. 3, 4.    [3] Gal. ii. 20.
[4] John xiv. 20.

passages it is at once clear that the Apostle has in view the Risen Lord ; and attention to the context of the third will show that it is in the thought of Himself as glorified that Jesus speaks. How indeed can it be otherwise ? Living, present, communion can only be maintained with One who is Himself present and living ; it would otherwise be no more than a recollection of the past. We may thus remember the great men of history, or the friends now taken away who were wont to guide us amidst the perplexities, and to comfort us amidst the sorrows, of the world. We may recall their virtues, or may dwell in thought upon what was noble or pleasing in their characters. Although dead they may speak to us, and not a few of our most wholesome and touching memories may be kept green upon their graves. But all this is very different from that communion with Christ by which the spiritual life is maintained in vigour. It was not by recollection of what He had been during those eternal ages when He was the Father's delight, rejoicing always before Him, that our Lord Himself lived, when He was on earth ; it was by a present and uninterrupted communion with the Father. By a similar communion with Himself He teaches us that we must live,—" As the living Father sent Me, and I live because of the Father : so he that eateth Me, he also shall live because of Me."[1] In other parts of the same discourse He employs the

[1] John vi. 57.

strongest expressions to point out the need of our
continual dependence upon Himself for life. He tells
us that He is " the living bread which came down
out of heaven," and that " except we eat the flesh
and drink the blood of the Son of man, we have no
life in ourselves ;"¹ while these expressions are so
brought into connexion with the words " What then,
if ye should behold the Son of man ascending up
where He was before,"² as to show that, even after
He had returned to His Father, the very same sustenance must be still partaken of by His people. It
is by no mere imitation of our Lord's example when
He was on earth, by no mere listening to the teaching that then fell from His lips, by no mere trust in
anything then accomplished by Him, that we live, but
it is by abiding in Him, as the vine is in the branches
and the branches are in the vine. We live in a
Risen Saviour, and in Him our own life is a risen
life. We have neither to travel back over many
centuries, that in a distant past we may hold communion with Him as He was on earth ; nor forward
through an equally long period that, in a glorious
future, we may realise the hope of such communion
re-established for ever with Him as He is in heaven.
He is not less than He ever was, or will be, the present nourishment of His people. He is with them and
in them even now, communicating Himself to them
by means of that " other Advocate" through whom
He comes to them.

¹ John vi. 51, 53.  ² Verse 62.

Not only, however, is this the case.  It is necessary, in connexion with our present subject, to go further, and to add that the nourishment thus given to the spiritual life and the *bodily* Resurrection of our Lord have the closest relation to one another. For it will be at once admitted that the spirit bestowed by our Lord is *His own* Spirit.  He is not merely given as a rich and powerful friend might give us something external to himself; He is sent by the exalted Redeemer as the expression of His own Personality.  He is that Spirit who, according to the vital doctrine of the Western Church, proceedeth from the Son as well as from the Father, and who comes into our souls laden with the very breath of the quarter from which He comes.  The peace that our Lord gives is His own peace; the joy that He gives is His own joy;—the very peace, the very joy, with which His own breast is filled.  So here.  The Spirit that He gives is the Spirit of His own being; and He must, accordingly, bear the peculiar impress of what that being is.  But, again, this Spirit is to become our spirit; and we are men with a complex nature, with bodies as well as souls.  Unless, therefore, He be the spirit of one with a similar complex nature, He will not be completely and thoroughly adapted to us.  There will be a want of fitting in to the peculiarities of our state.  May not this, or something like this, be one of the reasons why, in the ages previous to the Incarnation, the Spirit was not given to be an indwelling spirit in man? He would not have been the spirit of one possessed of a human as well as of a Divine nature; and thus He would not have had that entire correspondence with our human necessities through which alone He can be really ours in the deepest and most intimate sense,—ours not simply as an outward gift bestowed upon us, but as a part of our regenerated " selves."[1] Whether this be the case or not, what has been said may help to show us that the Resurrection and Glorification of our Lord in the *body* were needed before He could so dwell in us by His Spirit as to satisfy every want of our compound nature.

There is indeed a large and devoted section of the Christian Church which, going still further than this, maintains that our Lord actually communicates His glorified humanity to His people. It is supposed that in some mysterious way, and especially in the sacrament of the Eucharist, His humanity, though locally present in heaven, is also present with believers, and that they actually eat His flesh and drink His blood in that holy ordinance. It is not easy to attach a definite idea to this language; and so far as it is possible to do so, it seems difficult to reconcile it with those words of our Lord's parting discourses to His disciples, in which He told them that He was going away, and that what He would send was " another " Advocate to be their strength. It seems enough to

[1] Note 63.

think that the " other " Advocate comes from that
Glorified Redeemer who is still possessed of a body
as well as of a soul. Because this is the source from
which the Spirit comes, He is able to communicate to
us who are in the body the things that we require in
a way in which they could not be given were our
Lord only exalted spirit.

Even if we rest here, what a truth is this, and
how little does it enter into our ordinary thoughts !
We think of the exalted body of the Lord as a part
of His reward, and as a pledge of what is prepared
for us. We lose sight of the fact that it is by means
of a Spirit coming from One who is not only spirit,
but who has at the same time an exalted body, that
we live. We have communications from Him not as
One who is spirit only, but as One who is still possessed of real and complete humanity. In a glorified
humanity He not only lives Himself, but He binds us
to Himself as One living in that state. The very
power that comes to us from heaven is pervaded by
human elements. It comes to us as men from One
who is not less truly man than we are, that it may
nourish us into the blessed life of the perfectly human
united to the perfectly Divine.

4. In the Risen Lord the new life has its consummation. For it is the Risen Lord who conveys to us
the blessed assurance not only that the life now
implanted in the soul shall never die, but that we
ourselves, in our individual personal existence, shall

survive the shock of death, and shall pass in triumph
through that dissolution of the grave from which all
the feelings of our nature shrink.  "If the Spirit of
Him that raised up Jesus from the dead dwelleth in
you, He that raised up Christ Jesus from the dead
shall quicken also your mortal bodies, because of His
Spirit that dwelleth in you ; "  "If we died with Christ,
we believe that we shall also live with Him: knowing
that Christ being raised from the dead dieth no more ;
death no more hath dominion over Him."[1]

There is more than the hope of immortality set
before us in such words.  There is the hope that we,
even as we are, with our present powers and faculties
and affections, with our present complex nature, with
our bodies as well as our souls, shall pass, like Israel
of old, through the swellings of Jordan into the land
of promise.

We shall not, indeed, be exactly what we are now.
When the Lord Himself arose, " the first fruits of
them that sleep," He was not the same as when committed to the grave.  Yet the change produced on
Him, however great, did not destroy His personality,
nor did it affect the individuality of that life with
which, during the years of His earthly ministry, He
had lived among His disciples.  He was still the same
Lord to them that He had always been, — not a
shadowy spirit, but the man Christ Jesus.  His form
stood before them in all the old clearness of its out-

[1] Rom. viii. 11 ; vi. 8, 9.

line ; they could touch His person and recognise His
voice. It is in a similar manner that our resurrection shall be perfected. We cannot, indeed, form
to ourselves a complete picture of the details, but we
can have no difficulty in accepting the general idea.
Even now we often behold gradual approaches to it.
The beauty of the inner life may change the very
features of the countenance. The thought of the
lofty destiny awaiting us may impart something of
its nobility to the outward frame. The voice, often
lifted up in private praise and prayer, may come to
speak in softer and more touching tones than those in
which it would otherwise find utterance. And thus
we have only to imagine our whole man penetrated
and pervaded by the Spirit of God, in order to believe
that all about us may be changed, yet so changed
that the essence of our personality and our difference
from other men shall be as distinct as ever. Nor
need any question be raised about the possibility of
the mutual recognition of the redeemed in the resurrection-state. The one fact that the Risen Lord, the
type of our own resurrection, was recognised by His
disciples dispels all hesitation or doubt upon the
point.

While, however, our individuality shall be continued in the future world, the Resurrection of our
Lord is not less the pledge of a great and glorious
change that we shall then experience. Here, at the
very best, the body comes far short of answering the

demands made upon it by one who would walk worthy of the kingdom and glory to which he is called. He would wish to serve God day and night in His temple, but the very alternations of day and night impose upon him the necessity of sleep. Like his Divine Master he would wish to go about continually doing good, but the feet refuse to carry him, and the hands that were raised to bless fall powerless by his side. At every step of his progress he would lift up his heart into the presence-chamber of the Great King, but the deeper the intensity of his feelings the sooner does the bodily constitution decline to endure the strain. Down to the last moment of our earthly existence we bear about with us a body which hampers the soul in its aspirations; and often, when the visions of heaven are just about to burst upon the eye and the ear, the one is blind to every sight and the other deaf to every sound. "There is a law in the members that warreth with the law of the mind;" "O wretched men that we are! who shall deliver us out of this body of death?"

The Resurrection of our Lord supplies the answer to the Apostle's question. It is the earnest of a time when the conflict between the soul and the body shall be for ever at an end; when the two parts of man's nature shall be in perfect accord and harmony with one another; when the flesh shall no longer struggle against the spirit or the spirit against the flesh; but when the body shall be a willing instrument in the

service of the spirit for that unchecked and uninterrupted performance of the will of God in which the
blessedness and glory of our nature must be found, if
they are found at all. Then we shall no more groan
within ourselves, waiting for the adoption, to wit, the
redemption of our body ; but, as we follow the Lamb
whithersoever He goeth, we shall send forth one song
of praise,—" We thank God through Jesus Christ our
Lord." The whole revelation of the New Testament
breaks down if that union with the Lord which is its
central principle is interrupted at any stage of His
eternal progress. " Yet a little while, and the world
beholdeth Me no more ; but ye behold Me, because I
shall live, and ye shall live."[1] Our union with Him is
not for a time only, but for ever.

Therefore it is that, in the hope of a full, personal,
undivided life beyond the grave, we lift up our heads
as the hour of our redemption draweth nigh. By the
great fact that Christ is risen the New Testament
teaches us that, if there be a future life at all, it is
we ourselves who live, not vapours, not ghosts, but
in our present compound being, with our individual
personal lives, recognisable by others and recognising
them. We may dismiss the whole doctrine ; but to
do so we must first get rid of the Resurrection of
our Lord. If we accept that fact, we must accept
the doctrine of our own resurrection in this form, for
it is the only form in which it is taught in Scripture.

[1] John xiv. 19.

What was the case with our Lord must be the case with all His people. In the great day of account no vast array of shadowy figures will issue from the tombs, with nothing to distinguish them from one another. Separated by distinct individualities in this world, they will be not less separated in the next; and, as the Risen Lord was known and clung to by His disciples who had followed Him upon earth, so every member of His mystical body shall be known and clung to in the unity of love by those who, side by side with them, ran His race and fought His fight before they died.

It may be thought by some that it is too much to anticipate such results, and that this spiritualising of man,—this penetrating his whole frame with the power of the Divine Spirit,—this making him a " partaker of the Divine nature," is either inconceivable or that it is at once a humiliation of the Divine and an undue exaltation of the human. But philosophy, in the most aspiring of its modern developments, rejects such a conclusion, and seeks rather to show that humanity itself is God. Religion no less rejects it. The lesson of Scripture is that, if it is the property of our human nature to seek after the Divine, it is also a property of the Divine nature to communicate itself to the human ; that neither is satisfied in itself alone ; and that, to the full attainment of their mutual desires, each must find itself in the other. Thus it is that, on the one side, St. Paul teaches us that in every age and nation there is an impulse in man to " seek after

God, if haply he may find Him;"[1] and thus it is
that, on the other side, our Lord Himself used these
remarkable words to the woman of Samaria, "An
hour cometh and now is, when the true worshippers
shall worship the Father in spirit and truth : for the
Father also is seeking such, even them that worship
Him."[2] Man is seeking after God : God is seeking
after man ; and the union of the two is the highest
revelation both of the Divine and of the human.[3]

If this be so, it follows that that penetrating of
man by the Divine spirit which we have seen to be
the great lesson of the Resurrection of our Lord,
ought not to startle us ; and when it does not, what
a high and glorious hope does it present ! How lofty
is that conception of man's destiny which it unfolds !
how exalted the result at which it bids us aim ! We
are often told that the Gospel of Christ fails to do
honour to the capabilities of man's nature ; that it
is unable to stimulate his powers ; and that, by its
lessons on human corruption and human weakness, it
tends to sink him in degradation and hopelessness.
How utterly false and groundless is the charge ! No-
where else has so noble an ideal been presented for
man to aim at. To be united to the "only God;"
to be brought into harmony with the love which is
the foundation of all being ; to have every jarring
element in ourselves for ever done away; to become in

---

[1] Acts xvii. 27.

[2] John iv. 23.      [3] Note 64.

character as well as privilege the sons and daughters
of the Lord Almighty; and to look downward through
eternal ages, when, with bodies wholly adapted to our
spirits, we shall rejoice in the reign and in the service
of perfect righteousness,—that, and nothing less than
that, is what the Resurrection of our Lord both fore-
shadows and secures.

# LECTURE VI.

"And He is the head of the body, the church : who is the beginning, the firstborn from the dead ; that in all things He might have the pre-eminence."—COL. i. 18.

WE have considered the Resurrection of our Lord in its bearing upon Christian life and hope, but it is impossible to rest there. The Christian does not stand alone. He is not merely an individual, nourishing the hidden life in the secret of his own heart, and walking above the world even while he is in it. He is a member of that community which we name the Church. He stands in the closest relation to that system of things which, using the word in its widest sense, we name the World ; and the question therefore meets us, Does the Resurrection of our Lord affect these two great wholes ? and if so, How does it affect them ?

## I.

In the first place, as to the Church. The slightest glance at the New Testament is sufficient to show that, in founding what He called the "kingdom of God" or the "kingdom of heaven" in the world, our Lord contemplated more than dealing with men as

individuals.   He did not think that the object of His
Mission would be accomplished by simply implanting
in scattered members of the community that new and
higher life which should fill them with its influence
as members of the family, of society, and of the State.
He aimed also at constituting a community, a Church.
He described the relation of His disciples to one another by figures which implied that they constituted
a new organization.   He pointed out to them the
nature of the duties to which mutual fellowship introduced and bound them.   He encouraged them by
promises peculiarly applicable to their condition when
thus combined.   Let us suppose that at any particular period in the history of the past the number of
believers in the world had been exactly what it was;
that their faith and hope and love had corresponded
with the highest demands of Christianity; that their
general walk in life had been thoroughly leavened by
the heavenly leaven; that in every public and private
relation they had been made new creatures in Christ
Jesus;—even then the end which our Lord proposed
to accomplish would not have been fully reached.   In
the want of cohesion which would have marked His
followers, in their want of union, in their failing to
gather themselves together into one Body for common
work and mutual strength, there would have been
something wanting.   As private Christians they might
have been all that could be wished; but they would
not have been the Church.   Had our Lord not in-

tended to institute a Church which should represent
Him after He had gone away, much of His own teaching, as well as of that of His Apostles, would have
been meaningless; and " I believe in the Holy Catholic Church" would never have found a place in that
Creed which has been the chief symbol of the Christian
faith in every age and land.

We have not now, however, to defend the idea of
the Church as a Body which our Lord designed to
establish upon earth. However various the senses in
which they use the word, all Christians allow that
the Church does exist, that she ought to exist, and
that her existence will never end. What we have at
present to do with is the relation in which the Resurrection of our Lord stands to her, and more especially
to her Institution and her Mission in the world. The
subject is one which seems to have been hardly, if
at all, dealt with in the theology of our Presbyterian
Churches. Yet it occupies a most important place
in the teaching of the New Testament,—a place indeed not less remarkable than we have already found
to be that of the Resurrection of our Lord in relation
to Christian life and hope.

1. It was by the Risen Lord that the Church was
instituted. Except in so far as she was summed up
in Himself, she was called into existence, not during
His earthly ministry but after His Resurrection. Two
great epochs may here be distinguished from each
other; but both of them belong to the period after

o

Jesus rose from the dead. The first is that of which
the third and fourth Gospels give us the account,
when the Risen Lord appeared for the first time in
the midst of the disciples.[1] The second is that mentioned in the Acts of the Apostles in connexion with
the day of Pentecost.[2] We need not enter here upon
the distinction between the two.[3] It is enough to
notice that, be the distinction what it may, it was
only after He rose from the dead that our Lord sent
forth His disciples on their mission ; that, after that
event, we read for the first time of " the Church."[4]
The nature of the case indeed forbade that it should
be otherwise, for it was in the power of the Spirit
that the Church was constituted, and the power of
the Spirit " was not " before Jesus was glorified.[5]

2. Not only, however, was the Church thus constituted by the Risen Lord, it was from Him when
risen that the disciples received full instructions
for her work. They had, no doubt, been instructed
by their Lord and Master all along ; and in particular
the last discourses, recorded in John xiv. xv. xvi.
have a special bearing upon Christian work rather
than upon general Christian life ;[6] but there seems to
have been a teaching of a higher kind during the
forty days spent by our Lord upon the earth between
His Resurrection and Ascension. It is a mistake to
think that His object in then meeting with the dis-

[1] Luke xxiv. 36 ; John xx. 19-23.    [2] Acts ii.    [3] Note 65.
[4] Acts v. 11.   Note 66.    [5] John vii. 39.    [6] Note 67.

ciples so frequently as He did was to convince them
that it was indeed Himself: the events of the day
of the Resurrection had already convinced all of them,
except Thomas, upon that point.  It was rather to
instruct them in the nature of the work upon which
they were to enter.  " Speaking to them of the kingdom of God" is the description given us by St. Luke
of the manner in which He spent the time;[1] and
when we gather together His various topics of instruction during these days, as they are scattered
throughout the different Evangelists, we find that
they refer to the most important lessons and the
highest gifts by which the Church was to influence
the world.[2]  This consideration, indeed, in all probability explains the fact that the interval between the
Resurrection and the Ascension was exactly what it
was; and that the latter event took place ten days
before the day of Pentecost rather than upon the very
eve of that festival.  Our Lord's own temptation in
the wilderness had extended over forty days; and we
know, from the special nature of the temptations
recorded, that the purpose of that time was to prepare Him for the ministry on which He was immediately to enter.  A similar period of preparation,
though filled, in a way corresponding to the change
of circumstances, with wholly different events, was
now given to the disciples.  That was the preparation; and then came the work.[3]

[1] Acts i. 3.          [2] Note 68.          [3] Note 69.

3. In the Risen Lord the Church reads the true nature of her Mission. It will hardly be denied that, considered in its first and greatest aspect, that Mission is to *be* rather than to *do*. Life itself must precede the exercise of the powers of life ; and it lies in the very nature of the Church's work that every effort to perform it must, in order to be successful, breathe the Divine spirit by which she herself is animated. To win the world to faith Jesus set before it what He *was* rather than what He *did;* and in this, as in all else, He has left us the pattern which the Church must imitate. But if so, the chief element of the Church's being, as pointed out to us in the New Testament, is that which makes her a witness to men of the fulness of heavenly life in her Exalted Lord. The teaching of the fourth Gospel, in particular, upon this point is not less striking than clear. It can only be summarised at present in the briefest possible manner, but its general purport is as follows :—The Lord Jesus Christ is no more in the world. He is gone to the Father. The heavens have received Him until the restitution of all things. We cannot hear His voice, or see our children folded in His arms, or behold such a look of tender expostulation as that which sent a pang to the Apostle Peter's heart, and made him go out and weep bitterly. Is there nothing to supply the want ? or to let the world see that there is still in the midst of it a " witness " to the immediate presence of the Divine ? It is not enough to say,

There is the Bible, of which the Church is the guardian
and keeper.   The Bible is a book.    It is not in itself
a living thing : it is words, and all words are meaningless until the reader is able to put their meaning
into them.   And again it is not enough to say, There
is the work that the Church does.  She cannot do more
than " compass sea and land to make one proselyte,"
and we know of whom these words were spoken.[1]   The
Church might map out the whole world into parishes;
she might have a church and a minister in each ; she
might preach the truth, administer the sacraments,
institute a discipline of morals, and yet she might be
what she was in the days of degenerate Israel, what
what she has again and again been in Christian
history,— a selfish, worldly institution, seeking the
glory that cometh from man, and not from the only
God.[2]   The Church has committed to her a higher
task even than that of converting the world.   She
has to do that by which alone the world can be converted.   She has to declare Christ as He declared the
Father.   She is the " sent " of Christ as He was the
" sent " of the Father.[3]   And just as our Lord Himself said, "He that hath seen Me hath seen the
Father,"[4] so, when the Church at any time reviews
her manifestation of herself, she ought to be able to
say, He that hath seen me hath seen my Lord.

   The point, however, to be especially noticed now
is this, that the witness which the Church is to bear

[1] Matt. xxiii. 15.    [2] John v. 44.    [3] John xx. 21.    [4] John xiv. 9.

to her Lord is to be borne to Him as not only the crucified but the Risen Lord. It is not enough for her to witness to Him as He was on earth; she must witness to Him as He is in heaven. " Verily, verily, I say unto you," are Christ's own words, " He that believeth in Me, the works that I do shall he do also; and greater works than these shall he do; because I go unto the Father."[1] Greater works than those of Jesus upon earth! The words admit of no other interpretation, and they could not be more definite than they are. Greater works than the Lord Jesus did shall His people do! Why? Because He will Himself be greater; He will have gone unto the Father, who is greater than He.[2] He will be one with the greater Father, and in that oneness both the Father and the Son will come unto them, and make Their abode with them, and fill them with Their spirit, and endow them with Their power. In other words, the Church of Christ is the organ not simply of a humbled and an earthly, but of an exalted and a heavenly Lord. "As He is," says St. John in his first Epistle, in words full of meaning,— " As He *is*" (not as He was), " so are we in this world."[3]

Out of this idea flows all that is most character- istic of the Church, all that is peculiarly to distinguish her in the execution of her Divine commission. Let us advert to one or two of these characteristics for a moment; and, as it is impossible to notice all of them, it may be well simply to mention three which seem to be most frequently forgotten.

[1] John xiv. 12.          [2] John xiv. 28.          [3] 1 John iv. 17.

(1.) From the idea of the Church now before us, we gather the most powerful impression of that *visible unity* which ought to bind all her members into one great whole. The life of the Risen and Glorified Lord is not a life in spirit only, but in an exalted and glorified body; and, so lived, it is at the same time alike one and visible. It exhibits no discordant elements; its different sides or aspects present no hindrances to the accomplishing of the common end. The Divine does not obliterate the human; the human does not limit the Divine. The body of the Risen Lord is not lost in His spiritual existence; the manifold operations of His spirit find their appropriate expression through the different members of His body. In the perfect harmony of both body and spirit He is one. But He is not only one. He is also visible both to His angels and to His saints. To the former He "appeared" after His resurrection;[1] the latter "follow the Lamb whithersoever He goeth."[2]

If, therefore, it be the duty of the Church to represent her Lord among men, and if she faithfully performs that duty, it follows by an absolutely irresistible necessity that the unity exhibited in His person must appear in her. She must not only be one, but visibly one in some distinct and appreciable sense—in such a sense that men shall not need to be told of it, but shall themselves see and acknowledge that her unity is real. No doubt such unity may be,

[1] 1 Tim. iii. 16.  [2] Rev. xiv. 4.

and is, consistent with great variety—with variety in
the dogmatic expression of Christian truth, in regula-
tions for Christian government, in forms of Christian
worship, and in the exhibition of the Christian life.
It is unnecessary to speak of these things now.
Variety and the right to differ have many advocates.
We have rather at present to think of unity and the
obligation to agree.    As regards these, it can hardly
be denied that the Church of our time is flagrantly
and disastrously at fault.    The spectacle presented by
her to the world is in direct and palpable contradiction to the unity of the person of her Lord; and she
would at once discover its sinfulness were she not too
exclusively occupied with the thought of positive
action on the world, instead of remembering that her
primary and most important duty is to afford to the
world a visible representation of her Exalted Head.
In all her branches, indeed, the beauty of unity is
enthusiastically talked of by her members, and not a
few are never weary of describing the precious oint-
ment in which the Psalmist beheld a symbol of the
unity of Israel.[1]    Others, again, alive to the useless-
ness of talking where there is no corresponding reality, seek comfort in the thought that beneath all the
divisions of the Church there is a unity which she did
not make, and which she cannot unmake.    Yet, surely,
in the light of the truth now before us, we may well
ask whether either the talking or the suggested

[1] Psalm cxxxiii.

comfort brings us nearer a solution of our difficulties.
The one is so meaningless that the very lips which
utter it might be expected to refuse their office.  The
other is true, although, according as it is used, it may
either be a stimulus to amendment or a pious plati-
tude; and generally it is the latter.  But neither words
about the beauty of unity, nor the fact of an invisible
unity, avail to help us.  What the Church ought to
possess is a unity which the eye can see.  If she is
to be a witness to her Risen Lord, she must do more
than talk of unity, more than console herself with the
hope that the world will not forget the invisible bond
by which it is pled that all her members are bound
together into one.  Visible unity in one form or another is an essential mark of her faithfulness.  Let it
be allowed that differently organised branches of the
one Church of Christ may exist in different lands, or
even in the same land, they must occupy such a relation to each other that their unity shall be manifest
to the world.  There must be intercommunion, mutual
helpfulness—even to a certain extent confederation—
among them.  Unless it be so, the unity of the Church
of Christ is destroyed, and without it she cannot fulfil
her mission.  Nay, the very aim, in the thought of
which she finds consolation for the loss of unity, will
be itself defeated.  The world will never be converted
by a disunited Church.  Even Bible circulation and
missionary exertion upon the largest scale will be
powerless to convert it, unless they are accompanied

by the strength which unity alone can give. Let the Church of Christ once feel, in any measure corresponding to its importance, that she is the representative of the Risen Lord, and she will no longer be satisfied with mere outward action. She will see that her first and most imperative duty is to heal herself, that she may be able to heal others also.

(2.) From the idea of the Church now before us, we learn the nature of that aspect in which she must present herself to the world. Would she fulfil her mission, she must be recognised by the world as a Church suffering, yet triumphant over suffering. Such is the life of Him to whom she witnesses. He bears the marks alike of suffering and of triumph. Both are manifest, both are visible, in Him. Amidst all the glories of His heavenly abode He exhibits the tokens of His sufferings on earth, and the song of His redeemed is "Worthy is the Lamb that was slain." Throughout everlasting ages these tokens of suffering will continue to be visible, and that song will never change. It follows, therefore, that the Church, which is His representative on earth, must be seen both to suffer and to triumph over suffering. It is not merely that she must suffer. No one denies that in the case of every follower of Jesus the cross must precede the crown. The point to be at present particularly noticed is, that the Church must be known, that she must appear, to suffer; and that she can no more produce her legitimate effect upon the world without such a manifesta-

tion of herself than our Lord could have produced
His effect, had His sufferings not been as visible as
they were real. We are prone to forget this, and
to think that the impression produced by our Lord
when He was on earth depended chiefly upon His
miracles. It may well be doubted if we are correct in
thinking so. When the Jews beheld Him weeping at
the grave of Lazarus, and Mary weeping at His feet,
they said, "Behold, how He loved him." These are
the same Jews of whom we are told at a later point
in the narrative, that, having "come to Mary," and
having seen the "things" which He did, they believed
in Him.[1] Of all that had passed, what, we may ask, had
most to do in thus bringing them to faith? It may
have been the miracle, although they had before
resisted many miracles, although our Lord Himself
had said, "If they hear not Moses and the prophets,
neither will they will be persuaded although one rise
from the dead."[2] But the special mention of them
in connexion with Mary, and the use of the word
"things," instead of "thing," appear to say that it was
quite as much the tears, the tokens of the suffering
love of Jesus, that produced the effect, as the majestic
word instantly obeyed, "Lazarus, come forth." The
power of Christ's mission upon earth depended not
merely on suffering but on suffering seen. It is not
otherwise in heaven, where the garment that He
wears, as He is followed by the armies of the re-

[1] John xi. 45.　　　　[2] Luke xvi. 31.

deemed, is said to be a "garment sprinkled with blood." [1]

Again, therefore, it must be with the Church of the Lord Jesus Christ as it is with the Lord Himself; and if she is not seen both to accept suffering and, in accepting it, to triumph over it, she is deprived of one of the main elements of her strength. It would of course be utterly wrong in her to make suffering for herself; and it may be urged that there come times when the providence of God does not send suffering, and when, therefore, owing to no fault of her own, she cannot be seen to suffer. The reply is easy. It lies in the very nature of the case that the Church's testimony must always be offensive to the world. She speaks of things seen and temporal in a light the very opposite of that in which the world is accustomed to regard them. She calls to a separation from ends to which the world is devoted. She enjoins the exercise of virtues which the world does not appreciate. The very existence of the Church, when exhibiting her true spirit and leading her true life, is a protest against the spirit and life of the world. " Woe unto you," said our Lord, " when all men shall speak well of you;" [2] " I came not to send peace, but a sword." [3] On the other hand, there will always be sin and sorrow in the world. But sin can only be healed by our stooping to its misery; sorrow can only be healed by our pouring human words into its ear, and wiping

[1] Rev. xix. 13.          [2] Luke vi. 26.          [3] Matt. x. 34.

away its tears with human hands ; and works like these
can never be accomplished without pain.　The Son of
God Himself,

> " In doing good,
> Was fain to look to heaven, and sigh."

The Church, therefore, does not require to make
suffering for herself.　Simple faithfulness will do it.
Neither the rich nor the poor, when wicked or worldly,
will tolerate those who are true to the teaching and
life of their great Master.　But if so, the inquiry can
hardly fail to force itself upon us, whether the position
occupied by the Church in our own day, in respect to
suffering, is such as to entitle her to think that she is
a true witness to her Lord, and a true exhibiter of
His life.　Are her labours, pains, self-denials, sufferings, self-sacrifices, the marks by which the poor, the
worldly, and the criminal, chiefly know her ?　Are
they not more likely to think of ministers, elders, and
multitudes of Christian men and women living at ease,
not unfrequently in luxury, with little hardship and
little toil ?　When they thought of our Lord in the
days of His earthly ministry they thought of one
who had not where to lay His head.　They would
hardly think thus of His representative now.　The
Church of Christ rides too much, and not too little,
on the high places of the earth ; and the world's first
impression of her not unfrequently is, that it has only
to offer her more purple and fine linen and sumptu-
ous fare, in order to secure her co-operation for the

accomplishment of its own selfish purposes. She
would need more, not less, of her Master's cup put into
her hands, and more, not less, of His cross to bear,
before the world will acknowledge her spiritual power.

After all, however, it must always be remembered
that, just as suffering is not the only, or even the chief
mark of the Risen Lord, so it is not that which only
or even chiefly distinguishes the Church. Her most
characteristic feature is rather triumph over suffering,
light springing out of darkness, joy out of sorrow, and
life out of death. "We are pressed on every side,
but not straitened; perplexed, yet not unto despair;
pursued, yet not forsaken; smitten down, yet not
destroyed; always bearing about in the body the
dying of the Lord Jesus, that the life also of Jesus
may be manifested in our body." [1] Such is the true
spirit of the Church's life; not despondency, or
mourning, or sighs "even when thanking God;"
but the voice of praise, the shout of victory, the confidence and hope of men who are even now seated with
their Lord in the "heavenly places." It is not merely
a crucified but a Risen Lord that we proclaim.

(3.) Once more, from the idea of the Church now
before us, we learn that she is not only to develop her
inner life, but that she is to find for it an outward
and appropriate expression. This expression, when we
think of the Church's being rather than of her doing,
is her worship,—those rites, or forms, or ceremonies in

[1] 2 Cor. iv. 8-10.

which she utters to the eye and to the ear of others
the emotions of her heavenly life.  The Church can
no more live without a worship than thought can live
without words to fix it and to lend it permanence.
Spirituality is indeed the deepest and most fundamental element of her existence.  The Risen Lord is
spiritual.  Even the very body which He possesses in
heaven is so penetrated and pervaded by the Spirit
that it may be spoken of as a " spiritual body," and
that He himself may be described as " spirit." [1]
The Church, therefore, which represents Him must
first of all be spiritual.  By whatever marks, whether
of doctrine, or worship, or government, we endeavour
to distinguish her, there is one that she must possess, and to which all her other gifts must minister
even when they have been bestowed upon her in their
most perfect form,—she must present to the world
a manifestation of spiritual life.  Without this, she
would fail to manifest her Lord in the most essential
characteristic of His being.  No outward worship can
supply its place.  The Risen Lord, it cannot be too
frequently repeated, is essentially spiritual, and it is
in the spiritual life of humanity that He lays the
foundation of His Church.  To Him all is nothing
that is not spiritual; and outward rites, however well-
ordered, or beautiful, or magnificent,—however vener-
able with age, or rich with the pious associations of
the past,—have value only when they express spiritual

[1] Comp. Note 15.

realities, or promote the growth of spiritual feelings
and purposes and aims. Christ's kingdom is first in
the soul of man. All holy thoughts, all heavenly
aspirations, all sighs of contrition, all tears of peni-
tence, all faith and hope and love, all that is meek
and gentle, and lowly and self-sacrificing, and
patient and forgiving,—all these are the main elements of His kingdom ; and if they do not speak to
the world in the Church's life, the most imposing
ceremonial will be nothing but the cerements of death.

Considerations such as these, however, lend no
support to the conclusion that in the thought of the
Church's spirituality we may neglect her worship ;
for the Risen Lord is not simply spirit. He has a
body, and He included the perfecting of the body
in His perfecting of human nature as a whole. The
moment the Church grasps this truth, her outward
not less than her inward worship must assume that
importance in her eyes, the denial of which will
always be found fatal to healthy spiritual life. To
tell her that she has only to do with spirit is to lead
the way to the practical denial of her Lord's Resurrection in the body. It is to introduce a false antithesis between spirit and body, whereas the true
antithesis is between spirit and flesh. And it is to
undervalue one of the essential verities connected
with Him whose personality in its completeness is
the Church's life. We violate, therefore, the truth of
our Lord's human nature, as well as of our own, when

we allege that our worship may be independent of the outward,—of the day of rest, of the sanctuary, of an appointed ministry, of united praise and prayer, and of the Sacraments. By such reasoning we do more than sin against ourselves. We sin against Him whom we worship, not simply that we may derive benefit from doing so, but that in our worship we may show forth His praise. The worship that truly performs its part of witnessing must include bodily as well as spiritual service; and these, so far from being inconsistent, are necessary to each other. The doctrine of the Risen Lord, in whom spirit and body are bound together in perfect and endless unity, consecrates them both.

It follows, too, that the outward service of the Church, if thus essential to her work of witnessing, ought to be unfolded and beautified to the highest degree consistent with maintaining the supremacy of the spirit. Nothing is more foolish if not more selfish, than to plead that we may be indifferent to outward worship because God is spirit. At the very time when the Psalmist celebrates the king's daughter as "all glorious within" he immediately adds that "her clothing is of wrought gold."[1] In the Revelation of St. John, the most precious stones, the most costly metals, and the richest dyes, are employed to set forth the splendour of the bride, the Lamb's wife; and surely, if Mary expressed by a

---

[1] Ps. xlv. 13.

P

lavish gift her homage to her Lord when He was preparing for His burial, much more may we be lavish in
our gifts when we follow in the train of One who has
ascended up on high in all His royal dignity. The
thought of danger to which we are thus exposed is no
argument against a course of conduct rooted in the
very conception of the Church's being. Such danger
is simply that which must be met on every side so
long as the flesh lusteth against the spirit ; and the
only way to avoid it is to see that the worship of
the Church be a witness to her Risen Lord in the
completeness of His exalted state. Let her express
as far as possible in her worship what He is, and her
path is sure.

We have considered several leading characteristics
of the Church, dwelling especially upon such as in
this land are peculiarly apt to be forgotten, and we
have seen that they flow directly from that conception of the Church which teaches us to regard her as
the manifestation upon earth of the Risen Lord. The
characteristics which have been spoken of relate
especially to the Church's *being* in the world,—to
her unity, her triumph over suffering, and her worship. The thought of the Risen Lord is, however,
not less applicable to the Church's field of *action*
than it is to her sphere of being, and it throws as
bright a light on the former as on the latter. The
fact that the Lord is risen is that upon which Scripture rests the *universality* of the Gospel message, and

by which it most of all impresses on the Church her *responsibility* to plant everywhere the kingdom which that message brings with it.

(1.) The New Testament constantly reminds us how close the connexion is between the Resurrection of our Lord and the evangelization, not of any one portion of the human race, but of the whole. Upon this point the words of our Lord Himself are peculiarly instructive, "And I, if I be lifted on high out of the earth, will draw all men unto Me."[1] From the expression "lifted on high" it is impossible to separate the Resurrection of Jesus and the glory following it; and when the Evangelist, immediately after he has recorded these words of his Divine Master, adds, "This He said, signifying by what manner of death He should die,"[2] his object is to *include* the lifting up upon the cross in the "lifting on high," not to *exclude* the Resurrection and the Ascension from it.[3] Here, therefore, our Lord Himself distinctly teaches us that with His being "lifted on high out of the earth," with His being separated from the limitations of His earthly state, is associated the drawing of "all" men unto Him. Thus also, when we read in the Epistle to the Hebrews, "But we behold Him who hath been made a little lower than the angels, *even* Jesus, because of the suffering of death crowned with glory and honour, that by the grace of God He should taste death for every man,"[4] we

---

[1] John xii. 32.　　[2] Ver. 33.　　[3] Note 70.　　[4] Hebr. ii. 9.

cannot dissociate the last clause of the verse from the clause immediately preceding it. In other words, the lesson of the passage is, that it is through His being "crowned with glory and honour" that our Lord is in a position to apply the benefit of His death to "every" man.[1] Scripture, in short, always teaches that the universality of the application of the Gospel is to be traced to the action of the Risen Lord. Only when He burst the bonds of death did He pass from the limited to the unlimited, and from the local to the universal. But, because He has now done so and is seated at the right hand of God, "there cannot be Greek and Jew, circumcision and uncircumcision, Barbarian, Scythian, bondman, freeman; but Christ is all and in all."[2] The universality of the application of the Gospel depends upon our Lord's Resurrection, and not merely on His death.

(2.) Not only, however, is this the case, the teaching of Scripture leads also to the conclusion that the responsibility of the Church to spread the Gospel thus universally depends upon the fact that to her, and to her alone, as the representative of the Risen Lord, is the power entrusted by which the world is to be saved. We know that this great end can be accomplished by no other means than the agency of the Spirit; and it would seem that the gift of the Spirit is bestowed only through the Church as the organ upon earth of the Risen and Glorified Lord in heaven. We dare

---

[1] Note 71.        Col. iii. 1, 11.

not indeed restrain the power of the Almighty; but what we have to do with is His *plan*; and of that plan what has now been said appears to be one of the most striking characteristics. There is a want of all proof that the Spirit in His fulness is ever given *directly* to the world; or that, apart from the medium of those whom He has called to a knowledge of Himself, the Almighty sends down His influences, now here, now there, upon such as He would awaken to a sense of sin and lead to righteousness. On the contrary, it appears to be the teaching of the New Testament that, as it is the prerogative of Christ in His glorified humanity to bestow the Spirit, so it is only through the Church, as the representative of that glorified humanity, that the influences of the Spirit are communicated to the world. There is no separate witnessing on the Spirit's part. Through men he witnesses to men. Through the Church alone is He brought to bear upon those who are without her pale.[1]

The lesson is a solemn one; and it places the Church as the body of Christ, and every part of the Church as a part of the body, in a position of peculiar responsibility. It reminds us of what we constantly forget. We look abroad upon the world—upon what it is and upon what it ought to be. We dwell upon its evil, and upon the manner in which it resists all argument and entreaty to lead it to the knowledge of

[1] Note 72.

the truth. We feel our own weakness, as if nothing that we can do will be of the least avail. Then we cry in our despondency, God Himself will interpose; He will accomplish by the power of His Spirit what we are unable to effect; let Him break these hard hearts, and bend these stubborn wills; let Him take His own work in hand; and let it be ours to stand by, like Moses on the shores of the Red Sea, looking in awe and wonder upon Israel saved, and the enemies of God overwhelmed in the mighty waters.

There seems to be no foundation in Scripture for language such as this,—no ground to think that the Spirit of God is ever given except through the instrumentality of those who are the members of Christ's body. The Glorified Redeemer acts through them. They are the channel by which He sends His all-powerful Spirit down to make the wilderness a garden of the Lord.

Thus it is, then, that everything most distinctive of the Church of Christ, alike in her inward and outward life, in her relation to her various members and to the world, flows out of the fact that she is the representative not only of the humbled and suffering but of the Exalted and Glorified Lord. The Church has often been spoken of as a kind of continuation of the Incarnation; but there is a sense in which she may be spoken of as more. The great Head from whom she draws all that is most characteristic of her being and her duties is no longer upon earth; He is

in heaven,—His humiliation over, His cup of sorrow
drained, His eternal and glorious reign begun. To
that Head the Church is united in the bonds of closest
fellowship. She is one with Him who in all His
Divine majesty, in all His heavenly power, with all
the influences of His Spirit, is at the right hand of
the Father, that she may dwell in Him, and may
produce even here below the fruits of that tree of life
which grows by the river of the water of life, which
bears its fruits throughout the year, and the leaves
of which are for the healing of the nations. The
Church of Christ is not an institution of this world's
policy, nor does she exist for this world's ends. It is
presumption on the part of men clothed with mere
worldly power to think that they can lend her strength,
or that they can save her when she is in danger. She
can lend strength to them and save them; they can
do none of these things for her. Her spirit, her
strength, her life are from above. She is the child of
heaven upon earth, that she may witness to the
heaven which she now partially introduces, and for
the full manifestation of which she prepares and waits.

Did the Church of Christ only realise more fully
than she does what is thus her true position and character and power, how different would she be from
what she often is! How different would be her tone,
her life, her work! Instead of contention amidst her
various branches, she would exhibit unity; instead of
simple freedom from outward trouble, the joy that

rises superior to all trouble; and instead of a worship in which the form not unfrequently restrains the spirit, a spiritual worship shaping itself into forms of appropriate and natural expression. She would not only acknowledge that her mission-field was "the world," but would see the principle by which she is encouraged in every part of it to expect success; and she would advance to her work as alone in possession of the true remedy for the world's ills. Glorious things would again be spoken of her; and the time would not be distant when both Jew and Gentile shall be gathered into her fold.

## II.

If such is the bearing of the Resurrection of our Lord upon the Church, the bearing of the same great fact upon the world is not less worthy of our notice. The Church and the world indeed cannot stand wholly apart from one another, and Scripture often reminds us of those secret and mysterious links which bind man and nature together, and which make nature follow man, whether in his fall or in his rising. She followed him at the first, when the ground was cursed for man's sake, and when it brought forth thorns and briers instead of nothing but what was pleasant to the eye and good for food. She follows him now, when she has risen in his progress: and with the Resurrection of our Lord there is held out to her the hope of a more complete deliverance; "For the earnest

expectation of the creation waiteth for the revealing
of the sons of God.　For the creation was subjected
to vanity, not of its own will, but by reason of Him
who subjected it in hope, because the creation itself
also shall be delivered from the bondage of corruption
into the liberty of the glory of the children of God.
For we know that the whole creation groaneth and
travaileth in pain together until now."[1]

　Looked at in the light of the Resurrection of our
Lord, what a prospect even for nature opens on the
view!　It is true that in one aspect there is decay.
The mountains are gradually crumbling into the val-
leys; "the waters wear the stones;" and different
species both of animals and plants have passed and
are passing away.　Sin, too, with its dissolving power,
has still a terrible intensity of existence around us,
and forces are at work threatening to break up the
very foundations of society, and filling the heart with
dismay.　Neither the philosopher nor the poet can
give us hope.　The Resurrection of our Lord, which
derives its greatest value from this, that it is not a
mere miracle of the past, but is full of the promise of
the future, alone can do so.　In its light not decay
but advance, not pulling down but building up, not
falling back but reaching forward, become the main
characteristics both of nature and of human history.
Once the earth was without form and void; scientific
men tell us that in still remoter ages it existed only

[1] Rom. viii. 19-22.

in the shape of endlessly-multiplied particles of matter, which swept through space without having been as yet gathered together into a mass. Be it so. At all events the earth passed through that stage. Then came successive stages of its history, during which plants covered its surface, and animals in ever-rising forms of existence appeared to live upon the plants. Each stage gave way to another, not lower but higher than what went before it. Last of all, man came upon the scene, the highest and fairest of the Creator's works; but the progress did not stop. Even the Fall did not stop it, for through the Fall, however disastrous it was in some respects, men became as gods, knowing good and evil. Then came the remedial process,—first darkly hinted at, afterwards revealed in ever-brightening light until it was fulfilled in Christ. Still the progress did not stop. It has not stopped now. The purpose of the ages was an increasing purpose as the world hastened onward to the Resurrection of our Lord; and looking back upon that event now, we read in it not something peculiar to Him, but the token of a higher destiny towards which both the spiritual and the material creation are moving on. We cannot therefore join either philosopher or poet in their desponding moods. The culminating point of the world's progress has not yet been reached. But in due time it will be reached, and in sharing the " liberty of the glory of the children of God," whatever be the way in which we endeavour to conceive of it, its final purpose will at last be gained; "The mountains and the hills will break forth into singing, and all the trees of the forest will clap their hands." [1]

I must bring these Lectures to a close. We have been dealing with a question upon which it is no exaggeration to say that Christianity, in everything peculiarly distinctive of it among the religions of the world, depends. Such facts as the Incarnation and Resurrection of our Lord are either true or false; and the Christian faith is so intimately bound up with them that, if they are false, the only alternative left us is to abandon it, and to seek in some other way satisfaction for our religious needs and guidance in our religious life. It is impossible to enter into the language of those who urge that, altogether apart from the supernatural foundation upon which it rests, Christianity ought to be preserved for the sake of the moral system which it inculcates, or of the natural piety which it promotes. That moral system and that natural piety are not so exclusively dependent upon the revelation of the Bible as to justify our seeking them where they are associated with statements not only believed to be false, but proved alike by history and experience to be the source of a very large amount of mental anxiety and pain and terror. Could we indeed eliminate from the Christian system all that is directly

[1] Isa. lv. 12.

supernatural or Divine, and yet leave men those other parts in which alone, it is pled, there is eternal value, we might at least listen to the arguments employed in favour of the propriety of doing so. But to eliminate the one and to retain the other is impossible. A teacher who should feel himself constantly called upon to explain away the Divine facts of Scripture, and to show that, while a precious kernel was enclosed in them, they were themselves no more than the fruit of ignorant superstition or poetic fancy, would soon discover that he was weakening the respect of his hearers for it all. He would find that the only course open to him was to teach it as it is; and, although he might hope that advancing knowledge will gradually expose the fallacies of the pulpit, he would be constrained to leave the furthering of this advance to others. He dare not startle too suddenly the mass of common minds. He dare not insinuate to the many what he may whisper to the few. In his public position he must teach the whole word of God, or at least much of it belonging to another department than that of morals or natural piety; and his sole consolation, while he speaks, will be that he is yielding to a necessity which, in a happier future, will have vanished away.

In such circumstances, however, it is surely worth while to consider whether the good to be gained from this temporary honour to the Divine word is not purchased at an enormous price. There are two

sides to the picture of results to be anticipated from
such teaching, and both ought to be looked at.   Let
us suppose that the preaching of natural religion and
morals produces its beneficial effect.   What are we
to expect from those other truths which, far more
than moral precepts or lessons of natural piety, not
only permeate the Bible, but penetrate every confession of the Church, are breathed forth in every
prayer, are sounded aloud in every psalm or hymn
of praise?   Let those who, under the pressure of
necessity, teach these things while they would fain
eliminate them, trace back the history of eighteen
centuries, or even consider what is passing around
them now.   Do they not see results of a very different kind from those which they desire to produce,
and which may well make them doubtful as to the
course they are pursuing?   Have they no compas-
sion for the millions of human hearts that Christianity, on their supposition, has torn with anguish as
causeless as it was unutterable?   Have they no
sympathy with the countless multitudes whom it has
driven to despair through a revelation of God thought
to be Divine, when their teachers knew that it was
really human?—no pity for the alarms of conscience,
or the agonies of remorse, that have needlessly embit-
tered so many lives?—no feeling for the pangs of
unnumbered loving spirits who have lived in perpetual self-reproach because they thought that they
were not loving God enough?—no sense of shame

when they have seen how often a revolt against the
terrors of hell has made wicked men only more
wicked than they would otherwise have been? All
these things, they must allow, might have been
saved had they, or those who before them have
entertained the same views, not thought, or rather
pretended to think, that for the unenlightened the
morals of Christianity were necessary, and that as
they were inseparable from its doctrines, the preaching of the doctrines ought to be countenanced for the
sake of the morals. Or, if they are not ashamed,
do they never mourn over the loss to society and the
world occasioned by what they must consider the
diversion of so many minds from the real to the
delusive, from the substantial to the shadowy,—by
this standing face to face with fancies instead of
things? They tell us of a gain to morals; but, upon
their own showing, we may tell them of thoughts
turned aside from the useful to the useless, of strength
wasted, of souls harassed by problems that ought never
to have been raised, of tears poured forth without
measure in silent chambers, of minds in which reason
even threatens to desert her seat;—and, when we set
the one picture over against the other, can they honestly
say that such results ought to be endured for the
sake of benefits that may be gained by other means?

In the finer class of spirits it is a strange hallucination and one-sidedness that leads to such a conclusion. More common men are led to it by their

own selfish interests, by their love of position, or honour, or gain.

Mental anxieties like those now spoken of ought to be endured, although with increasing effort on the Church's part to mitigate them, if the supernatural facts of Christianity are true; for in that case we must give account to God, and eternity is in the balance. But certainly they ought not to be endured for any prudential reason which it is possible to assign. The man who tolerates them for the sake of the moral precepts of our Lord, or of natural piety, is not only false to what he thinks the cause of truth, but to the very humanity which he professes to reverence and love. Let it not be said that faith is cowardly when the cowardice of unbelief is so much more marked.

Once more, it may be said that it is possible to retain the *idea* of our Lord's Resurrection while we give up the *fact;* and that the story of it is one of those beneficent illusions by which the human race is educated, and which it is the part of wisdom to encourage for the sake of infant nations or of children. Supposing that it were so, it is nevertheless incontrovertible that it is the duty of every man to dispel these illusions at the earliest possible moment. To substitute for them the reality, though it may be the far sterner reality, of truth, is the education which a generous mind must desire both for itself and for all in whom it feels an interest. Truth is the best educator of man. In the Providence of God it was not all revealed at once, because men would have been unable to comprehend it. There was a growth of revelation as there was a growth of man; and the Redeemer of the world did not come until the times were full. But it is our duty to use for ourselves, and to impress on others, any measure of positive enlightenment we may enjoy. We may be taught by illusions, but we cannot acquiesce in them. They are "childish things;" and when we become men we put them away. Our nobility lies in being witnesses to truth.

On the other hand, if the Resurrection of our Lord be a fact, it is undeniable that it ought to occupy a far more important place than it generally does, alike in our theological systems and in our religious life. The Romish Church has practically expelled it by making the mass the centre of her worship. The Protestant Church has done the same by the almost exclusive attention which she has directed to the death of Christ, and by her utterly inadequate teaching, that the Resurrection of our Lord is the guarantee of the acceptance of His work, instead of the culminating part of the work itself. To the neglect of the great fact with which we have been dealing are to be largely traced those defects in the Christian life of the members of our Churches which it is impossible not to observe and to lament. Take all classes of society among us, from the highest to the lowest, and we cannot deny that, even where Christianity is professed and where the ordinances of the Church are faithfully used, there is yet, with many honourable exceptions, a worldly tone of life,—a life of worldly luxury in some, of worldly aims in others,—affording a melancholy contrast to the life of Christ, whether in earth or in heaven.  There is no want of evangelical preaching, as it is called, and no want of admiration for it.  Nay, the most thoroughly selfish members of our Churches, the most thoroughly immersed in all the frivolities of fashionable life, are often the greatest admirers of that preaching.  Preach the death of Christ, they cry to us.  We do preach it.  To preach it is to preach one of the fundamental doctrines of the New Testament. But to preach the death of Christ alone does not seem to disturb the selfish heart of man.  It often flatters him with the thought of what was endured for his sake.  It makes a free offer of forgiveness, which it pleases him to hear of,—always supposing that he needs it.  It tells him that he has nothing to "do" to be saved.  It even frowns upon self-sacrifice, as if it were the same thing as self-righteousness ; and the popular preacher is not unfrequently most successful when he discredits the self-chosen poverty and the severe self-discipline of members of the Romish Church, and shows to the gratified self-satisfaction of his hearers that those who choose such unpleasant paths are simply working out a salvation for themselves, which will fail them in the great day of account.  What is known as evangelical preaching may have saved many souls, but it has not succeeded

Q

in raising the tone of our Christian life in such a way
as to make the world "marvel." The Church must
teach the whole truth if she would effect this. She
must teach the Resurrection of her Lord as well as
His death; and she must teach it, not as a reward
for His work, but as a part of the work itself,—as
a part that, not less than His death, is to be "fulfilled"
in us. This will lead us beyond the thought of dying
to sin to the thought of living in righteousness; this,
and this alone, will bring the raising up of the new
man within us into inseparable connexion with the
death and burial of the old man.

Then too will the Church exert her due power
upon the world. We learn from the Acts of the
Apostles that the fact most of all proclaimed by the
first teachers of the Gospel was the Resurrection of
their Lord; and the proclamation appears to have
gone home with singular power to the hearts of those
who heard. Yet it may be inferred from different
passages, both of the same book and of the Epistles
of St. Paul, that the success of the Apostles in gather-
ing their numerous converts into the Church was in
no small degree owing, not to the mere preaching of
the fact, but to the life of the Christian community
as it was moulded by it. The early Christians lived
in the thought of their Risen Lord; and this so lifted
them above a present world as to bring near that
better world to which every labouring and heavy-
laden heart is drawn. A similar power ought always

to go forth from the Church of Christ; and it can go forth from her only when her life,—life in a Risen and Living Lord,—is a light of men.

I cannot close these Lectures without expressing the earnest hope that, notwithstanding their manifold deficiencies, they may, by the blessing of God, be the means of directing the thoughts of those who have heard them to the vast importance of the subject with which they have been occupied.  Christ has died; and we cannot too frequently, too earnestly, or too lovingly, visit the grave where He who gave His life for us was laid.  But when we go there to weep, let us see that we listen also to the voice which says to us, " He is not here, but is risen."  " Weeping may endure for a night, but joy,"—both for ourselves and the world,—" cometh in the morning."  And the morning has come; the dawn has broken; and we who believe in the Risen Lord have passed out of the valley of the shadow of death into unclouded light and life for ever.

---

I say to all men, far and near,
　　That He is risen again;
That He is with us now and here,
　　And ever shall remain.

And what I say, let each this morn,
　　Go tell it to his friend,
That soon in every place shall dawn
　　His kingdom without end.

Now first to souls who thus awake
   Seems earth a fatherland,
A new and endless life they take
   With rapture from His hand.

The fears of death and of the grave
   Are whelm'd beneath the sea,
And every heart, now light and brave,
   May face the things to be.

The way of darkness that He trod
   To Heaven at last shall come,
And he who hearkens to His word
   Shall reach His Father's home.

Now let the mourner grieve no more,
   Though his beloved sleep,
A happier meeting shall restore
   Their light to eyes that weep.

Now every heart each noble deed
   With new resolve may dare,
A glorious harvest shall the seed
   In happier regions bear.

He lives, His presence hath not ceased,
   Though foes and fears be rife ;
And thus we hail in Easter's feast
   A world renew'd to life !

Lyra Germanica.

# NOTES

# NOTES.

### NOTE 1, p. 11.

Even Dr. Hodge of Princeton ("System. Theol." iii. p. 775), from whom the words quoted in the text are taken, is hasty enough to declare that there "can be no doubt that it was so," and that "otherwise there would have been no Resurrection." In this Dr. Hodge expresses the general opinion of at least all the Presbyterian Churches. An elaborate discussion on the point, by Professor Robinson of New York, will be found in the "Bibliotheca Sacra" for May 1845, reprinted in "Kitto's Journal of Sacred Literature" for July 1852, p. 341. He takes the same view as Dr. Hodge.

### NOTE 2, p. 11.

Thus, when Mary Magdalene, standing weeping by the empty grave, turned suddenly round and saw Jesus beside her, but supposed Him to be the gardener (John xx. 15), her mistake in all probability arose as much from her eyes being blinded with her tears, and her mind preoccupied with her grief, as from any change in Him. When the two disciples on the way to Emmaus not only walked but conversed with Him for a considerable space of time, we are expressly told that "their eyes were holden that they should not know Him" (Luke xxiv. 16); and that language leads directly to the inference that, had their eyes not been holden, they would have known Him. Once more, if the seven disciples fishing on the Sea of Galilee did not at once recognise Jesus on the shore, the words of the Evangelist, "when morning was now coming" (John xxi. 4), almost force on us the conclusion that daylight had not yet broken, and that, in that Eastern land, there would be no small amount of darkness in the sky.

NOTE 3, p. 11.—See Note 6.

NOTE 4, p. 11.

The "honeycomb" mentioned in the Authorised Version has no place in the best-attested reading of the original. We may here take the opportunity of remarking that the difficulty occasioned by this text to the view of our Lord's resurrection-body advocated in these Lectures is at least a solitary one. Acts x. 41 may indeed seem, at first sight, to imply the contrary; but, whether or not we adopt the idea of Bengel, that all the words from οὐ παντὶ to αὐτῷ are parenthetical, it is most probable that the last clause of verse 41, "after He rose from the dead," is to be connected with the clause "gave Him to be made manifest" of verse 40. Certainly there is no instance recorded in the Gospel of our Lord's eating and drinking *with* His disciples after His Resurrection. At Emmaus (Luke xxiv. 30, 31) such an idea is rather expressly excluded by the language of the Evangelist. At John xxi. 13 we read only, "Jesus cometh and taketh the bread, *and giveth them* and the fish likewise : " it is not said that Jesus Himself ate. At Luke xxiv. 43 there is no common eating, "He took it and did eat *before them*." Comp. Krüger ("Die Auferst. d. H.," p. 30, note), who, however, attaches undue importance to our Lord's own words in Luke xxii. 18. The language there is too figurative to be relied on for the deter-mination of a fact; and it is possible that, according to our Lord's meaning, the Kingdom of God came with His Resurrec-tion. The view of Luke xxiv. 43 commonly taken by com-mentators, both ancient and modern, is that the eating was de-signed as a proof by our Lord that His form was no phantom of the imagination (see Plumptre, Wordsworth, Denton, Gloag, etc., on Acts x. 41). This, however, does not even touch the difficulty of the verse. It seems better to say that I neither know nor can offer any satisfactory solution of this act of our Lord's eating, than to profess acceptance of solutions which only evade the difficulty.

## Note 5, p. 13.

For a fuller description of the remarkable incidents recorded in John xx. 19, 26, I may be allowed to refer to the Commentary on St. John's Gospel by Milligan and Moulton, in the Commentary on the New Testament edited by Professor Schaff. In addition to what is there said, it may only be remarked that Calvin has rightly styled all the remarks that had been made in his day, and that have been repeated by so many down to the present hour, as to our Lord's entering the room through the pores of the wood of the closed doors, *pueriles argutiæ*. Such a thought, obviously, never entered the Evangelist's mind. At the same time, Calvin's own explanation, though adopted by Beyschlag, ("Die Auferstehung Christi," p. 24), that the doors opened of their own accord, is equally untenable. Not less to be at once rejected is the idea that Jesus knocked at the door of the room and was admitted in the usual way ; or that adopted by Michaelis ("On the Burial and Resurrection of Jesus Christ," p. 255, Translation), that Jesus Himself opened the doors miraculously without noise, and entered the room unperceived, the minds of the disciples being too much preoccupied to notice Him.

## Note 6, p. 13.

The words used by our Lord when He says, "A spirit hath not flesh and bones as ye see me have," are undoubtedly attended with great difficulty. It may be well to make a few observations upon them in a note. One thing is clear, that "flesh and bones" is not synonymous with "flesh and blood." The latter expression, either in the form "flesh and blood," or in the form "blood and flesh," occurs frequently in the New Testament (Matt. xvi. 17; 1 Cor. xv. 50; Gal. i. 16; Heb. ii. 14; Eph. vi. 12); the former is found only once, for in Eph. v. 30 the words "of his flesh and of his bones" ought to be omitted from the text. In these circumstances no careful interpreter will doubt for a moment that "flesh and bones" are here deliberately spoken of by our Lord, and that they express a different idea from that conveyed by "flesh and blood." The late Dr. Candlish, in his "Life in a Risen Saviour" (Discourse XV.), has argued, with no small measure of acuteness, that, while "flesh and blood" denotes community in the lower animal life, "flesh and bones" denotes community, kinship, close personal union, and relationship,—the analogy of a kinship like that of Gen. ii. 23, and illustrated by such passages as Genesis xxix. 14; Judges ix. 2; 2 Samuel v. 1, xix. 12, 13. If this explanation be accepted, it is obvious that our Lord, by the words which He here used, intended to express two things,—(1) That His state was *not* the same as that of His disciples, or as it had been before; (2) that He was yet one with them—their human companion and friend. It was necessary to express the latter point in some way, for the disciples had imagined that He was a mere formless spirit (verse 37), what we should call a ghost. But to have said that he was "flesh and blood" would have misled them into the idea that He was exactly what He had been. He therefore says that He has "flesh and bones," in proof that, while He had undergone a change, that change still left Him truly human. The conclusion often drawn from the words, when compared with 1 Cor. xv. 50, that the Lord's resurrection-body was bloodless, seems somewhat precarious, unless we are careful to explain that our only meaning is that the blood was not in the same condition as that in which it had previously been. There seems no reason for saying that the blood might not be glorified in the same way as the more solid portions of the earthly body.

## NOTE 7, p. 14.

John xx. 17.—The difficulty occasioned by the comparison of these words with those of John xx. 27 will at once disappear, if it be observed that the expression used in the original does not indicate a momentary touch, but is equivalent to "Handle me not," "Cling not to me." It is addressed to a state of mind wholly different from that of Thomas, and is intended to point out to Mary that the old relations between her Lord and her were changed. She may no longer cling to Him with the grasp of earthly friendship and love. The relation between them must henceforward be entirely spiritual. Had Thomas attempted thus to "touch" Jesus after he had uttered his confession "My Lord and my God," he too would have been addressed in the same way. In conformity with this, it ought to be particularly observed that the message committed to Mary has reference not merely to the fact of our Lord's Resurrection, but to *His resurrection-state*,—a state which was not the same as it had been, and which could not be known by the disciples until they received the truth that He was in the condition of One "ascending to the Father." Then they may all touch Him, cling to Him, but not till then.

### Note 8, p. 15.

It is probable that this idea is very commonly entertained. It was that of the late Dr. Wardlaw ("System. Theology," ii. p. 620); of the late Dr. Hodge of Princeton, who, allowing that there was some change at the Resurrection, and making no mention of development during the forty days, says distinctly that it was at the end of these days that the body of our Lord "passed into its glorified state" ("System. Theology," ii. p. 628). See also Dr. Robinson in "Journal of Sacred Lit.," July 1852, p. 352.

### Note 9, p. 15.

John xx. 6, 7.—It seems probable that the circumstances thus noted by the Evangelist are designed to do more than to give "proof of a thoroughly tranquil occurrence in contrast to a tumultuous ravishment" (Lange *in loc.*) They indicate also that the Risen Lord had left behind Him, when He rose, the last traces of His connexion with this mortal scene.

### Note 10, p. 16.

Among the number of eminent theologians who have held this view the following may be mentioned:—Julius Müller, "Die Lehre von der Sünde," ii. p. 396 ; Schmid, "Die Bibl. Theol.," i. p. 118 ; Martensen, "Dogmatik," p. 364 ; Beyschlag, "Die Auferstehung Christi," p. 26 ; Pressensé, "Jesus Christ," p. 545 ; Godet on Luke xxiv. 28 and elsewhere. Meyer, on Luke xxiv. 51, holds that the body of our Lord was not yet glorified, but in an intermediate condition between its earthly and its glorified state.

On the other hand, Hofmann ("Schriftbeweis," vol. ii. p. 523)

denies the gradual transfiguration of Jesus.  Compare also Krüger,
"Die Auf. d. H.," pp. 22-37 ; and Weiss's remarks on Luke xxiv.
in his edition of Meyer on Mark and Luke.


### NOTE 11, p. 17.

On the force of the word "manifested," in John xxi., compare
the Commentary above referred to on the Gospel of St. John, by
Milligan and Moulton, and especially the comment on John xxi.
1, 14.  It is peculiarly important to observe that the word means
much more than that Jesus made Himself known or displayed
Himself to His disciples.    Nor is it possible to avoid observing
that it is the purpose of the Evangelist to draw a marked contrast between the appearance to Mary Magdalene and the three
"manifestations" following it.    The contrast would seem even
to justify the conclusion that between the appearance to the
Magdalene and the next following manifestation, Jesus had
already ascended to His Father, and that out of the glory there
surrounding Him He subsequently manifested Himself.  If this
be the case, we shall also be better able to explain the $\dot{a}\nu a\beta a\dot{\iota}\nu\omega$
of chap. xx. 17, both in itself, and in its contrast with the
$\dot{a}\nu a\beta\dot{\epsilon}\beta\eta\kappa a$ of the earlier part of the same verse.  It ought to be
hardly necessary to say that the notion of a return of Jesus to
His Heavenly Father immediately after His Resurrection is by
no means inconsistent with the Church doctrine of His Ascension
at the end of the forty days.   This last is simply His final act of
departure, made visible because it was final.


### NOTE 12, p. 19.

1 Cor. xv. 44.—It will hardly be denied that the above
translation is the true translation of the text.  With the rendering of the English version, whether Authorised or Revised, there
is nothing for the "it" to refer to.  The only subject capable
of supplying a nominative to the verb is the $\dot{\eta}$ $\dot{a}\nu\dot{a}\sigma\tau a\sigma\iota s$ $\tau\hat{\omega}\nu$
$\nu\epsilon\kappa\rho\hat{\omega}\nu$ of ver. 42, which cannot be said to be sown in "corrup-
tion" or "weakness."  The importance of marking the correct
translation may be seen in the argument drawn from the passage,
among others, by Hodge ("Systematic Theology," iii. p. 775),
that "it is the same body that rises."   The real argument of the

Apostle is that, at the Resurrection, the body which rises if in one sense, because *our* body, the *same*, is, in another and most important sense, a *different* body. Were it not different, we should have to suppose that the same change will take place on it *after* its resurrection, as that described by the Apostle in 1 Cor. xv. 52, and there confined by him to those who have not "fallen asleep." A double change would await believers who have died,—a resurrection to their old condition, and then a change to a new condition. Scripture knows nothing of this double change.

### NOTE 13, p. 21.

Compare Carpenter's "Mental Physiology," especially chap. xix. Dr. Carpenter finds nothing improbable in the remarkable, and at first sight almost incredible, case of Louise Lateau. For an interesting account of this case see "Macmillan's Magazine" for April 1871.

### NOTE 14, p. 23.

It is not denied in the remarks made in the text, that there is a vast difference between the glory of Sonship as it belongs to Jesus before His death and after His Resurrection. In both cases, indeed, the Sonship is itself the same, and its glory is essentially the same; but in the one state it is hidden from the eye. None but the few who are one with their Lord can see it. The world scorns it. In the other case the world, even though not submissive, is compelled to own it. The *bringing out* of this glory of Sonship is the point of the word "glorify," and we cannot too completely dismiss from our minds the impression that outward light or brightness is necessarily implied.

### NOTE 15, p. 24.

In connexion with the important subject thus alluded to, it is the aim of this Note to submit to students of the New Testament a brief examination of several difficult texts, which seem to show that the condition of our Lord after His Resurrection was viewed by the sacred writers as essentially a state of πνεῦμα. Not indeed that our Lord had then no *body*, for it is the constant lesson of Scripture that a body was possessed by Him; but that

the deepest, the fundamental characteristic of His state, inter-
penetrating even the body, and moulding it into a complete
adaptation to and harmony with His spirit, was πνεῦμα. In
other words, it is proposed to inquire whether the word πνεῦμα
in the New Testament is not used as a short description of what
our Lord was after His Resurrection, *in contrast with* what He
was during the days of His humiliation upon earth. Such a
supposition, it appears to us, will be found to afford a satisfactory
explanation of statements to which it is otherwise difficult to
attach a clear meaning. One caution only it may be well to
interpose at the very outset. We do not for a moment mean to
deny that in our Lord, even during His sojourn upon earth, there
was the very same condition and state of highest life, of spirit,
which there was after He rose from the dead. Nay, further, we
should even be disposed to urge that this state of spirit-existence,
of spirit-life in Himself, continued even in the very article of
death, rendering it impossible that His body should see corruption. But previous to His resurrection-state this spirit-existence
was so fettered by the limitations of the σάρξ, that it could not
be spoken of as the absolutely *ruling* element in His being, as the
one and complete master of the field. At His Resurrection these
limitations were broken through ; and hence, in a sense peculiar
to itself, our Lord's state after that event may be described as
πνεῦμα. The question is, Is this description of it actually given
in the New Testament ? Or are there passages in which, by so
understanding the word πνεῦμα when applied to our Lord, we are
able to throw light on what is otherwise dark ? We must indicate what we mean by brief hints, having no space to attempt a
full discussion.

1 Cor. vi. 17.—" He that is joined to the Lord is one spirit."
There can be no doubt that by " the Lord " in this text we are to
understand the Risen Lord, for the Apostle himself distinctly tells
us that it is of the Risen Lord that he speaks, " And God both
raised the Lord, and will raise up us through His power (ver. 14).
The argument is, he that is joined to a harlot is one flesh with
her,—is lowering the members of his body to union with a person acknowledged even in Corinth to be sinful and degraded ;
but he that is joined to the Risen Lord is one spirit, *i.e.* is one
spirit with Him. The argument, therefore, proceeds on the

supposition that the Risen Lord is essentially and characteristically spirit—that "spirit" is a correct description of His present condition or state. It is the ruling element in His heavenly existence: His resurrection-state is πνεῦμα.

2 Cor. iii. 17, 18.—"Now the Lord is the Spirit: and where the Spirit of the Lord is, there is liberty. But we all, with unveiled face reflecting as a mirror the glory of the Lord, are transformed into the same image from glory to glory, even as from the Lord the Spirit." There is, however, no article before the last mentioned, although there is before the first mentioned, "Spirit;" and it may be questioned, therefore, whether the closing words of ver. 18 ought not to be translated "from the Lord, *who is* spirit." Apart from the general usage of the Apostle, it will hardly be denied that the whole context and argument of the chapter compel us to understand by the words "the Lord" the Risen Lord. It is "the glory of the Lord" in His heavenly condition that we behold, as Moses beheld the glory of God upon the mount; and, as we behold it, gazing upon it with ever increasing love and fervour, we are enabled to reflect it better, until we are transformed into the same image from glory to glory. Here then the Risen Lord is expressly described as πνεῦμα, not as the personal Holy Spirit, but as Himself in that condition of spirit by which He is enabled to shine upon us "all" with His glory, and to transform us into a likeness with Himself.

1 Tim. iii. 16.—"And, without controversy, great is the mystery of godliness: He who was manifested in flesh, justified in spirit." We forbear from any attempt to discuss the different modes in which commentators have proposed to arrange the six clauses of this verse expressive of the "mystery of godliness." It is enough to say that it seems best to take them in three groups of two each, the two members of each group being successive to each other both in time and thought; and each of the two last groups being equally successive both in time and thought to the statement or statements by which it is preceded. In the first group we shall thus find Christ, *as He is in Himself*, described in two particulars; in the second, Christ, now considered as being what He has been shown to be, *proclaimed to angels and men;* in the third, Christ, now thought of as thus proclaimed, *acknowledged and owned by the earthly and the heavenly worlds.* The contrast

between the two particulars of the first group will not then lie,
as is often supposed, between the lowliness of our Lord's human
life and that power of spiritual life which He exhibited in the
midst of it, but between His state of humiliation here when He
was manifested *in flesh*, and His state of exaltation now when He
has been "justified *in spirit*," when He has been gloriously vindicated before the universe by His Father in heaven through His
Resurrection from the grave (comp. John xvi. 10). The word
πνεῦμα, therefore, here again expresses the uncontrolled dominion
of that spirit which our Lord indeed possessed even on earth,
though then in a manner limited by other conditions of His earthly
existence, but which, after His Resurrection, was wholly free.
In other words, πνεῦμα is a short expression for our Lord's resurrection-state. This view is confirmed by one or two considerations
which it may be well to notice. 1. The use of the word ὤφθη
in the first particular of the second group. That word cannot
refer to those occasions on which angels ministered to our Lord
during His earthly life. It cannot be said that He then " appeared " to them : they came to Him. On the other hand, the
word is continually used in the New Testament of our Lord's
appearances after His Resurrection. 2. The connexion between
our Lord's resurrection-state and the *universality* of His mission.
This universality is the point of the second member of the second
group, "preached among Gentiles" (for, if among them, then
among *all*); and it is important to remember, what we shall have
further occasion to dwell upon in these Lectures, that, according to
the teaching of the sacred writers, it was the Resurrection of our
Lord which opened up to Him this new and unbounded field of
labour. 3. Who, we may ask, was thus preached to Gentiles ?
Surely Christ as risen, and not simply as He lived on earth. We
expect, therefore, in a short *summary* of doctrine such as this,
some allusion to the Resurrection, and we have it in the mention
of πνεῦμα.

It may be objected that the last clause of the third group is
opposed to the principle of interpretation upon which we have
proceeded. Did that clause simply refer to the *fact* of the Ascension, the objection might have force. But to give the words
such a reference alone is incompatible with any interpretation
whatever that can be applied to the verse as a whole. In no way

can the five points mentioned before the last be made to precede the *instant* of time at which the Ascension took place. We must regard the words as a kind of *constructio pregnans*. Christ "believed on in the world" evidently implies *continued* faith in Him, the world's being brought to *rest* on Him in faith. So Christ "received up in glory" implies the continued glory of His resurrection-state. He was "in glory" when He ascended; He ascended "in glory;" in the same "glory" He continues for ever. The words are an abbreviated form of Ephesians i. 20-23; and thus they constitute most appropriately the culminating point of that "mystery of godliness" of which Christ is both the beginning and the end. Looked at in this light, the last clause of the verse leaves ample scope for that succession both in time and thought of which we have spoken.

Rom. i. 3, 4.—"Concerning His Son, who was born of (out of) the seed of David, according to the flesh; who was established as the Son of God in power, according to the spirit of holiness, out of the resurrection of the dead,—*even* Jesus Christ our Lord." It will be at once admitted by every one that the Apostle deals here with the Risen Lord. His allusion to the "resurrection of the dead" proves it, to say nothing of the fact that the connexion between verses 4 and 5 renders such a view absolutely necessary. It is through the Risen Lord that the limitation of the Messianic kingdom to the Jewish people is brought to a close, and that the Mission of Christ, and of His Apostles in Him, assumes its universality.

Of the numerous attempts to discover the relation in which the different clauses of this passage stand to one another, or of the interpretations of these clauses which have been given by others, we say nothing. It seems clear that we have before us two contrasted aspects of one Person, God's Son; the first point of the first side of the contrast being His birth into this world; the last point of the second side of the contrast being that state of resurrection-glory from which (ver. 5) He commissions St. Paul to be the Apostle of the Gentiles. Between these two points the contrasts lie, and the particulars of them are so many as to make it reasonable to think that each will be carefully set over against another corresponding to it. These particulars are—

R

## " His Son "

| " Born, Son of God in weakness (implied in γενομένου), Out of the seed of David, According to the flesh." | " Established,[1] Son of God in Power, Out of the resurrection of the dead, According to the spirit of holiness." |
| --- | --- |

The fact that the " resurrection of the dead " holds the last place in St. Paul's enumeration of the terms of his second series, while, strictly speaking, it corresponds to the third term of the first series, is easily explained. It was of importance to bring the Resurrection of Jesus into the closest possible connexion with the Gentile mission. If, as will not be denied, " born " is in contrast with " established ; " " according to the flesh " in contrast with " according to the spirit of holiness " (as shown by the double κατά) ; and the thought of " the Son of God in weakness "[2] in contrast with that of " the Son of God in power," there remains nothing for " out of the seed of David " to be in contrast with, except " out of the resurrection of the dead." The use of the same preposition in the two last-quoted clauses confirms this view. The one clause marks the source, earthly and limited, out of which the Son of God sprang when He assumed humanity ; the other the source, heavenly and unlimited, out of which He

[1] The rendering of the original word here used by "declared" is extremely insufficient. In addition to the fact that the proper meaning of ὁρίζω is to constitute, to fix by decree (which is something very different from declaring), we urge only that "declared" supplies no proper contrast to "born." An act is referred to in the one case ; we look for an act in the other.

[2] The danger of misinterpreting the passage before us, if we do not supply the whole clause now spoken of, is illustrated in the case of Godet, who (Comm. in loc.) maintains that Jesus at His Incarnation renounced the position of Son of God, recovering it only at His Resurrection. " Jesus was restored," he says, " and restored wholly,—that is to say, with His human nature,—to the position of Son of God, which He had renounced on becoming incarnate." Godet has failed to observe that the words " His Son " belong to all the terms of both series of contrasts. The difference, as regarded Sonship, between the two states of Jesus was, that in the first, though still Son of God, He was so in weakness, that in the second He was so "in power." It ought not to be necessary to prove that the word γενομένου, the same as that used in John i. 14, in implying transition, change, implies change to weakness.

sprang when He entered on the glorious condition in which He
is "the Son of God in power." These things being so, it will
follow that the words "according to the flesh" describe our
Lord's earthly state, that the words "according to the spirit of
holiness" describe His state after He rose from the grave. All
through His earthly life Jesus was Son of God, but not "Son of
God in power,"—His power being checked by the restraints to
which He had voluntarily submitted; only after His Resurrection did He resume the fulness of that power of which He had
once "emptied" Himself. All through His earthly life His spirit
was limited because His state was one "according to the flesh;"
only after His Resurrection was His spirit unfettered because
His state was one "according to the spirit." The apprehension
of what has been said will be rendered easier if we observe that
no article is used with either "flesh" or "spirit," and if, therefore, for the moment we translate, in unidiomatic English,
"according to flesh" "according to spirit." The latter expression thus denotes neither the personal Holy Spirit, nor the
sacred human spirit of Christ, nor His Deity regarded as spirit.
It denotes His resurrection-state as contrasted with His state of
humiliation upon earth. Let us look at the passage in this
light, and it assumes in its well-balanced clauses a meaning that
is both clear and in harmony with the whole range of New
Testament teaching upon the truths expressed in it. There
is a difficulty, no doubt, connected with the use of the word
ἁγιωσύνης. Why is it added? and why does not the Apostle
content himself with simply saying "according to spirit"? The
answer may depend upon the real meaning of ἁγιωσύνη. That
word occurs three times in the LXX., in two of which (Ps. cxlv. 5,
and xcvii. 12, A. V.) it is applied to the glorious holiness of
God, in the third (Ps. xcvi. 6), to the holiness of His Sanctuary.
In the New Testament it is found only twice in addition to the
passage before us. In one of these (1 Thess. iii. 13) it is to be
connected closely with "at the coming of our Lord Jesus with
all His saints," and it points therefore to the holiness of the
*perfected* kingdom of God. In the other (2 Cor. vii. 11) it
is connected with a verb ("perfecting") which in the original
(ἐπιτελεῖν) does not so much describe the process of improvement
as the bringing improvement to its perfect end,— *ad finem*

*perduco* (Grimm). The word ἁγιωσύνη thus expresses not the progressive sanctification of earth, but the fully and gloriously accomplished holiness of heaven, the holiness of God and of His heavenly abode. It is, accordingly, quite in place here. The idea of the post-resurrection glory of Jesus might have been expressed without it by the simple phrase " according to spirit;" but the addition of the words " of holiness " magnifies the thought, and brings out more fully the Divine and glorious elements which characterised the condition of the Risen Lord.

1 Peter iii. 18.—" Being put to death in flesh, but quickened in spirit." These words will be found to confirm what has been said. The contrast drawn in them is not between our Lord in His earthly state and in some state of disembodied spirit between His death and His Resurrection. Whether it is possible to understand ἐν ᾧ, in verse 19, of the latter we shall not enquire. The enquiry would involve a discussion of the whole question of the *Descensus ad inferos;* and a discussion upon that point, because unnecessary, would be out of place. We urge only that, in ver. 18, the word πνεύματι cannot be understood of such a state. " Flesh" and " spirit," in that verse, cannot mean " body " and " soul," as if the Apostle's object were to tell us in the first clause that Christ was put to death in the body, in the second that, notwithstanding this, He lived on in the soul. It is our Lord's mortal life *as a whole* that is thought of under " flesh," the life in which he endured those sufferings on our behalf which at length culminated on the cross of Calvary. The proper contrast to this is not any disembodied life (even supposing that there were one) between His death and His Resurrection, but is the post-resurrection life itself. Nor was the surviving of His soul in death the reward bestowed upon our Lord by the Father, but the glory of the new state upon which He entered when He rose from the grave. In like manner it is not the surviving of our souls in death to which Christ leads us, if we imbibe His spirit and imitate His example of patience amidst undeserved suffering; it is to the presence of God (note the word προσαγάγῃ), when, possessed of our full human nature, we shall forget in the bliss of the future the trials of the past. The only true contrast to our Lord's or to our own life in " flesh" is His life or our own life in heaven; and to this latter the word πνεύματι must refer.

What has been said will be made still clearer if we observe that the word " quickened " associated with " spirit " in ver. 18 must express more than mere survival, and must point to the beginning of a new life. It is also confirmed by the words of ver. 21, " through the Resurrection of Jesus Christ," which must be brought into the closest possible connexion with ver. 18, all that comes between them and the beginning of ver. 19 being really parenthetical. No other conclusion, therefore, seems open to us than that πνεύματι in ver. 18 denotes our Lord's post-resurrection state, as distinguished from his state of weakness and limitation during his earthly life. It may be added that those who find no *Descensus ad inferos* in this passage ought to feel even more than others the force of what has been said. They will see that the contrast drawn in verses 19-21 lies between what Christ accomplished ἐν πνευμάτι at the time of the Flood and what He now accomplishes ἐν πνευμάτι after his Resurrection. The waters of the flood bearing up the ark of Noah meet us in the one case ; the waters of Baptism meet us in the other ; and it ought to be remembered that there was no Christian Baptism until after the Resurrection. They will see that the main thought of the passage is that Christ, who in Noah's days executed a mission of mercy, executes the same mission now, but far more powerfully, there being no longer only " few " that are saved (see some admirable though only too brief remarks of Prof. John Forbes in an appendix to the second edition of his treatise on " Predestination and Free Will "). They will see that, according to the Apostle, Christ is the same Saviour now as He was of old, but greater ; and they will hardly fail to acknowledge that as, in ver. 18, " flesh " denotes the earthly state, the humiliation, the weakness of Jesus, so in the same verse " spirit " denotes the exalted state, the strength and glory of Jesus in that condition which began with His Resurrection.

Heb. ix. 14.—"How much more shall the blood of Christ, who, through eternal spirit, offered Himself without spot to God, purge your conscience from dead works to serve the living God ?" This verse must be taken in connexion with verse 12, of which, as appears by the " for " of verse 13, it is explicative, " nor yet through the blood of goats and calves, but through His own blood, Christ (verse 11) entered in once for all into the holy place, having obtained eternal redemption." The words are not so directly to our purpose as those of the texts already considered, but they have a certain bearing on it. In the first place, it is necessary to observe that the aorist participle of verse 12 " having obtained" is contemporaneous with, not precedent in time to, " entered " of the same verse (see Delitzsch *in loc.* and on Heb. ii. 10), so that the " offered " of verse 14 must be referred to the same period of Christ's work. If so, it will follow, in the second place, that the offering thus spoken of is not so much Christ's oblation of Himself upon the cross, as His offering of Himself in heaven. This, though denied by many eminent commentators, is allowed by Bleek (*in loc.*), and seems to be admitted, at least in part, by Dr. Moulton, who says, "He who was typified in every high priest and in every victim, ' through an eternal spirit,' of Himself laid down His life (John x. 18), offering Himself to God in the moment and article of death,—offered Himself in His constant presence in the holiest place" (verse 24). (See Moulton *in loc.* in the " Commentary on the New Testament," edited by Bishop Ellicott). If then it be so, we can now mark the course of thought in the writer's mind. It appears to be as follows,— Christ has obtained eternal redemption, so that, purged from dead works, we can serve the living God. But He can obtain nothing for us which He has not Himself, for all our blessings are summed up in Him. He, therefore, must not only be in that state of " spirit," in which alone it is possible to serve God fully, but in that state of spirit which is " eternal," at once without limitation and without end. It is through His being so that He is able to complete our redemption. Therefore may it be said that, " through eternal spirit," He offered Himself to God when He entered into the holiest place. " Eternal spirit " is not therefore the Divine inward being of Christ, so called here because " absolute, divine, and purely self-determined " (Delitzsch), and in which Christ offered Himself to death ; it is rather the state of unlimited, absolute, Divine spirit in which He presented Himself to His Father when He entered within the veil.[1] Even Delitzsch,

[1] It seems not improbable that the preposition διά in Heb. ix. 14 is employed in the sense explained and illustrated by Winer when he says, "More loosely used, this preposition denotes that with which some one is furnished, the circumstances and relations amid which he does something" (*Moulton's Winer*, p. 474).

who contends strongly for the view commonly received, is compelled, apparently without noticing the effect upon his general argument, to interpose a clause in his explanation of the words, "eternal spirit," which coincides with all that we need contend for. "By διὰ πν. αἰων.," he says, "I understand the whole Divine human, but more particularly the Divine inward being of Christ, that Divine personality which, at the Resurrection, interpenetrated, and, as it were, absorbed, the σάρξ, so that He is now altogether πνεῦμα."

The passages now considered appear thus to find their best explanation if we understand the πνεῦμα spoken of in them to be a short description of that mode of existence upon which our Lord entered after His Resurrection. On earth His state could not be so described—"The Word became flesh" (John i. 14). He was then subject to all the limitations and weaknesses of the flesh. The πνεῦμα was, no doubt, the foundation of His Being even then, but in His great act of self-denial and self-sacrifice, He had taken into union with it our "flesh." That flesh He had to interpenetrate and to transfigure by its power, completing the work of doing so at His Resurrection. He then entered on the full condition of πνεῦμα in which He had existed before all time, but with this change, that transfigured human nature was now a part of His Being or mode of existence. And thus it is that He effects our redemption from the power of the σάρξ. By that faith which is communion with Him we are made partakers of His πνεῦμα, and are thus gradually raised more and more above the limitations and sufferings of our natural condition. The work in us, however, is not completed here. The "Spirit" of Christ has first to take full possession of our spirits, and then, at the resurrection, to effect that work upon our bodies which was effected on Christ's body at His Resurrection. "But if the spirit of Him that raised up Jesus from the dead dwelleth in you, He that raised up Christ Jesus from the dead shall quicken also your mortal bodies, because of His spirit that dwelleth in you" (Rom. viii. 12).

An element of confusion is introduced into all our thoughts upon this subject by the ambiguity of such words as "spirit" and "spiritual." We are apt to think of them as antithetical to "body" and "bodily." How far this is from the view of the New Testament the single passage, 1 Cor. xv. 44, is sufficient to prove. The antithesis of Scripture is not that of the spiritual and the bodily, but that of the spiritual and the carnal.

### Note 16, p. 25.

May the suggestion be offered, that the Evangelist John seems to have looked at what we would call miraculous acts on the part of our Lord in the light in which they are presented in the text? Students of his Gospel must be struck with the fact that the miracle of the walking on the sea, in chap. vi. 15-21, appears to occupy a position wholly peculiar to itself among the miracles of the fourth Gospel. It is not called a " sign ;" it has no discourse connected with it ; there is nothing in the narrative to suggest that it was intended symbolically to teach some deeper truth. Besides which, it gives us one more miracle than the sacred number seven, which the peculiar structure of that Gospel would lead us to expect. How is all this to be explained? The answer seems to be that St. John would not have spoken of it as a miracle. In his eyes it was only a part of the *natural* working of Him who was quite as much above as within those laws which regulate the lives and acts of ordinary men.

### Note 17, p. 28.

The use of the word "man" in John xvi. 21, possesses in this point of view a peculiar interest. Our Lord is alluding to the joy which His disciples should experience when they should " see Him again." It would be like the joy of a mother when she is told that she is safely delivered of a son. But our Lord does not use either the word son or child. He uses the word " man,"—" for joy that a *man* is born into the world." It can hardly be doubted that the reference is to the Resurrection of Jesus, when, not after a slow growth, but instantaneously, in the full glory of that Resurrection in which He lives His new life, and upon which His Church for ever rests, He should be born into the world.

### Note 18, p. 29.

Two small books in the " Nature Series," entitled " Transformations of Insects," and " What is a Frog ?" may be referred to for highly interesting illustrations of what has been said. They are easily accessible to all.

## NOTE 19, p. 31.

" The Roman world might live in the fear that the terrible
Nero was yet to return to vex and disturb it. Mediæval
Germany might believe that Barbarossa was asleep in his
mountain cave, and would yet awake and come forth to restore
the glories of the Empire, and the House of Hohenstaufen.
Our own legends might tell how Arthur had sailed away to his
island home of Avilion, whence, when happier days dawned, he
would come to erect his table round, and open his chaste and
chivalrous court. But all these rest on similar ideas, speak of
the mythical imagination, as they speak to it. Death is in each
case denied ; the men can return because they have escaped
death, and are only absent or asleep."—Principal Fairbairn's
" Studies in the Life of Christ," p. 345.

## NOTE 20, p. 40.

Such is without doubt the true order of these clauses in the
original. The clause " Am I not free ? " then stands first, and the
two here quoted are brought into immediate contiguity and
forcible connexion with each other.

## NOTE 21, p. 43.

Principal Barry (General Introd. to the Epistles of St. Paul's
First Captivity, in the Commentary on the New Testament,
edited by Bishop Ellicott) has some interesting remarks on the
order of St. Paul's preaching, which may be quoted to illustrate
what has been said. Among other things he says, " It may be
noted that as, when we dig through the strata of the earth, we
uncover first what is latest, and come only at last to what is
earliest in deposition, so in the realisation of Gospel truth the
order of preaching is the reverse of the order of actual occurrence
of the great facts of the Divine manifestation."

## NOTE 22, p. 43.

Not that the term κύριος may not be applied to our Lord in
circumstances where the thought of His life on earth may seem
to be prominent, as at John iv. 1, 1 Cor. ix. 5, etc., yet even then
His higher, His Divine nature is in the writer's mind. While

He tabernacled here Jesus was Divine as well as human, and a term expressive of this is therefore with all propriety applied to Him during the time of His humiliation. But a careful consideration of the very numerous passages in which our Lord is spoken of as κύριος, will show that in the minds of the sacred writers it is especially as the Risen Lord, returned to the presence of His Father, and clothed with all authority and power, that He is so thought of. Comp. among many others that might be mentioned, Acts iv. 33 ; Rom. i. 4 ; iv. 24 ; viii. 34-39 ; 1 Cor. iv. 5 ; vi. 14, 17 ; ix. 1 ; xi. 23 ; xv. 47. By keeping this constantly in mind, instead of thinking of " the Lord " as applying mainly to what Jesus was on earth, it will be found that the spirituality and heavenliness of view which mark the New Testament are immeasurably heightened.

### Note 23, p. 48.

The most probable enumeration of the different appearances of Christ, after His Resurrection, seems to be as follows :—

(1.) To certain women, " the other Mary," Salome, Joanna, and others, as they returned from the sepulchre, after having seen the angel who told them that the crucified Saviour was risen. Of this appearance St. Matthew alone gives us the account, chapter xxviii. 1-10 ; but some details of the company and of the visit, not given by St. Matthew, are to be found in St. Mark xvi. 1-8, and St. Luke xxiv. 1-11.

(2.) To Mary Magdalene at the sepulchre, in all probability upon her second visit to it that morning, and after she had run to tell Peter and John, " They have taken away the Lord out of the sepulchre, and we know not where they have laid him." This appearance is recorded at length by St. John alone, chapter xx. 11-18, although it is also alluded to in St. Mark xvi. 9-11.

(3.) To the Apostle Peter, under circumstances of which we have no particular account. It must, however, have taken place on the day of the Resurrection, and before evening. It is alluded to by St. Luke, xxiv. 34, and by St. Paul, 1 Cor. xv. 5.

(4.) To the two disciples on the way to Emmaus. This appearance is spoken of in St. Mark, chapter xvi. 12-13 ; but a full account of it is given by St. Luke alone, chapter xxiv. 13-35.

It took place, like the preceding, on the day of the Resurrection, but later in the day.

(5.) To the ten Apostles (Thomas being absent) and others " with them " (Luke xxiv. 33), whose names are not given, when they were assembled together on the evening of the day of the Resurrection, and at their evening meal. Of this appearance we have an account in each of the Evangelists, except St. Matthew, whose place, however, is here taken by St. Paul (Mark xvi. 14-18; Luke xxiv. 36-40 ; John xx. 19-23; 1 Cor. xv. 5).

(6.) To the eleven Apostles, Thomas being now one of the company, when Jesus permits the latter to put his hand into the prints of the nails and of the spear, and draws from him the confession " My Lord and my God." Of this appearance St. John alone gives us the account, chapter xx. 26-28. It took place also at Jerusalem, and most probably in the same apartment as the last.

(7.) To several of the disciples, of whom four at least were certainly, the rest probably, Apostles, at the Sea of Galilee when they were fishing. Again St. John is the sole recorder of this appearance, chap. xxi. 1-23.

(8.) To the Apostles and about five hundred brethren at once, upon an appointed mountain in Galilee. Of this appearance we seem to have an account by St. Matthew, xxviii. 16-20. It is also mentioned by St. Paul, 1 Cor. xv. 6.

(9.) To James, under circumstances of which we have no information. The fact is mentioned by St. Paul alone, 1 Cor. xv. 7.

(10.) To the Apostles at Jerusalem, immediately before the Ascension, when they accompanied their Lord from the city to Mount Olivet, and there beheld Him ascend to heaven, till a cloud received Him out of their sight. Of this appearance several particulars are furnished us by St. Mark, xvi. 19; and others by St. Luke, xxiv. 50-52; Acts i. 3-8.

(11.) To the Apostle Paul on his way to Damascus. St. Paul claims this as a special manifestation to him of the Risen Saviour, Acts ix. 3-9, 17; 1 Cor. xv. 8, ix. 1.

## NOTE 24, p. 53.

Comp. Acts iv. 2, where the Authorised Version unfortunately conveys an entirely false idea of the situation. They " came

upon them," we are told, " being sore troubled because they
taught the people, and proclaimed (not "through Jesus," but)
in Jesus (that is, in the person of Jesus) the resurrection from
the dead."

### NOTE 25, p. 54.

I should certainly hesitate to refer seriously to such an
objection, were it not that so much has been and is still made
of it by the opponents of the Resurrection of our Lord.   Comp.
Strauss, " Das Leben Jesu, f. d. D. Volk," p. 287 ; " Supernatural
Religion," iii. 449, 524.

### NOTE 26, p. 56.

"I know not a more rash or unphilosophical conduct of the
understanding than to reject the substance of a story, by reason
of some diversity in the circumstances with which it is related.
The usual character of human testimony is substantial truth
under circumstantial variety.   This is what the daily experience
of courts of justice teaches.   When accounts of a transaction
come from the mouths of different witnesses, it is seldom that it
is not possible to pick out apparent or real inconsistencies
between them.   These inconsistencies are studiously displayed
by an adverse pleader, but oftentimes with little impression upon
the minds of the judges.   On the contrary, a close and minute
agreement induces the suspicion of confederacy and fraud."—
Paley, "Evidences of Christianity," Part iii. chap. 1.

### NOTE 27, p. 58.

" The men who were enabled to penetrate most deeply into
the mysteries of the new revelation, and to apprehend with the
most vigorous energy the change which it was destined to make
in the world, seem to have placed little value upon the written
witness to words and acts, which still, as it were, lived among
them. . . . But while everything shows that the Apostles
made no conscious provision for the requirements of after times,
in which the life of the Lord would be the subject of remote
tradition, they were enabled to satisfy a want which they did not
anticipate. . . . That which was in origin most casual became
in effect most permanent by the presence of a Divine energy ;

and the most striking marvel in the scattered writings of the
New Testament is the perfect fitness which they exhibit for fulfilling an office of which their authors appear themselves to
have had no conception."—Westcott, "Introd. to the Gospels,"
First Edit., p. 150.

## NOTE 28, p. 60.

The precise object which our Lord had in view in thus asking
for something to eat has been mistaken by the commentators.
It was not to give proof of the reality of His human body.
This proof had been already given at verses 39, 40. A second
demonstration upon the same point was unnecessary. The unbelief still resting in the minds of the disciples (verse 41), was
not unbelief in the strict sense of the word; it was the unbelief
of Mark ix. 24, which Jesus recognised as faith. The object
of the eating here was to illustrate His fellowship and sympathy
with His disciples. The expression used in the original seems to
indicate this,—not "food" or "meat," but anything "that may
be eaten," the emphasis lying not on the idea of nourishment,
but on the act of eating.

## NOTE 29, p. 61.

A comparison of the accounts of the Ascension in Luke
xxiv. and Acts i. will confirm what has been said in the above
note on the object of the third Evangelist in this part of his
narrative. It is in the Gospel account only that he mentions
that Jesus lifted up His hands and blessed the disciples, and
that He parted from them while engaged in doing so.

## NOTE 30, p. 62.

The following are the words of Baur, "The Christianity of
the First Three Centuries," p. 42:—"The question as to the
nature and the reality of the Resurrection lies outside the sphere
of historical inquiry. History must be content with the simple
fact that, in the faith of the disciples, the Resurrection of Jesus
came to be regarded as a solid and unquestionable fact. It was
in this faith that Christianity acquired a firm basis for its historical development. What history requires as the necessary ante-

cedent of all that is to follow, is not so much the fact of the
Resurrection of Jesus as the belief that it was a fact." The
view of Baur is fully adopted by Strauss ("Das Leben Jesu,
f. d. D. Volk," pp. 288, 289), although he feels that he cannot
dispense with inquiry into the origin of the belief.

### Note 31, p. 64.

See Strauss, "Leben Jesu, f. d. D. V." p. 288.

### Note 32, p. 65.

An interesting example of this will be found in Acts xx. 7,
where the sense is obscured by the translation of the A. V.,
"Paul preached unto them." The true rendering is rather "discoursed with them," and the compound verb in the original
implies distinctly that the discoursing or the conversation was
not all on one side. Comp. Grimm in his "Clavis N. T." under
the words διαλαλέω and διά. He explains the preposition as
denoting in compound words *id quod alternatim vel utrinque fit.*

### Note 33, p. 75.

The theory was adopted by Paulus, and became the
favourite explanation of all the Continental writers belonging
to the school known as that of the *Rationalismus Vulgaris.*
It is more remarkable that it should have been countenanced
in later times by Hase ("Geschichte Jesu," § 112). The latter
writer is disposed to ascribe the Resurrection to the wonderfully
healing or restorative powers which resided in Jesus, and which,
as they had often been exerted on others, so now were exerted
on Himself.

### Note 34, p. 76.

No more is necessary upon this point than to quote the
words of Strauss ("Leben Jesu," *u.s.,* p. 298),—"It is impossible that one who had just come forth from the grave
half dead, who crept about weak and ill, who stood in need
of medical treatment, of bandaging, strengthening, and tender
care, and who at last succumbed to suffering, could ever

have given to the disciples that impression that he was a conqueror
over death and the grave,—that he was the Prince of life,—
which lay at the bottom of their future ministry.   Such a
resuscitation could only have weakened the impression which he
had made upon them in life and in death,—or at the most could
have given it an elegiac voice,—but could, by no possibility, have
changed their sorrow into enthusiasm, or elevated their reverence into worship."

NOTE 35, p. 83.

Attention does not seem to have been sufficiently drawn
to the fact that the words of Gal. i. 16, " that I might preach
Him among the Gentiles," really express the *contents* of the
inner revelation to which St. Paul had just referred.   The
statement, too, that the giving of this inner revelation was *subsequent* to the outward manifestation of the Risen Lord, is in
strict accordance with the narratives of St. Paul's conversion in
the Acts of the Apostles (chaps. ix. 15 ; xxii. 15 ; in this last,
mark the " all men").   We shall also afterwards see how close is
the connexion between the truth that the gospel is designed for
" all men," and the fact that Christ is the *Risen* Lord.   This is
precisely the order of thought in the passage before us, and it
shows clearly that the inner revelation is not the manifestation
itself, but something that followed it.

NOTE 36, p. 87.

It is at once to be admitted that the verb, ὤφθη, in 1 Cor.
xv. 6-8, is to be understood always in the same sense.
What the manifestation spoken of in verse 8 was to St. Paul,
it was to all the others mentioned in the 6th and 7th verses,
and *vice versâ*.   It can hardly admit of dispute, however, that in
their case a personal manifestation of the Risen Lord Himself,
and not a mere appearance in a vision, is expressed.   The constant use of the verb in the New Testament connects it with
persons or things either seen or supposed to be seen in their
reality, and not thought of as visionary appearances.   In Acts
xvi. 9, indeed, it is employed with reference to a vision, but
there the word " vision " is introduced by the writer along with

it, so as to prevent what would have otherwise been the conclusion of the reader. The use of the word in 1 Tim. iii. 16 is
peculiarly instructive,—"appeared to angels." Have angels
visions? It may be well to notice that the appearance to St.
Paul, mentioned in 1 Cor. xv. 8, cannot be assigned to any period
*after* his call to the apostleship. The article before ἐκτρώματι
forbids any such supposition; compare Hofmann *in loc.* in his work
"Die Heilige Schrift Neuen Testaments." The present may be
a fitting opportunity for observing that the value of the evidence
contained in 1 Cor. xv. 6-8 is not in the least degree affected, although we may not be able to discover the principle upon which St.
Paul makes his selection of witnesses there mentioned. We know
that a Jew did not write history upon exactly the same principles
as a modern historian, and that he was often guided in his selection of particulars by some idea dominating his mind at the
moment. The genealogy of our Lord, as given in Matt. i.,
affords a striking example of this. Thus, in the present instance,
it is perfectly evident that the list of witnesses is given neither
upon chronological grounds, nor because of any superior importance due to these appearances, as appearances, above those with
which others were favoured. The mention of "all the apostles"
in verse 7, after that of "the twelve" in verse 5, is conclusive
upon this point. Perhaps, following out a hint of Luthardt, in
his note on John xxi. 14, we may suggest that the whole number
is divided into two groups of three each. If it be so, the first
group will then have special relation to Christ's disciples in their
own home life, and that in three rising gradations—Peter, the
twelve, the five hundred; the second, to Christ's disciples looked
at in their action on the world, again in three rising gradations—James, all the Apostles (viewed as sent out with their
commission), the Apostle of the Gentiles. The death of James,
recorded in Acts xii. 2, might easily lead to his receiving the
place thus assigned to him. It may only further be noted that
should the correctness of the hint thrown out in Note 11 be
admitted, the similarity of the successive manifestations here
recorded will be still more marked. All of them will then be
manifestations of One who had already ascended to His Father,
and who revealed Himself from His heavenly abode.

## NOTE 37, p. 89.

The unwillingness of St. Paul to give an account of the vision related by him in 2 Cor. xii. is particularly worthy of notice, as it appears alike in verse 1 and afterwards in his speaking of himself in the third person. How strikingly do his words here contrast in this respect with the manner in which he is wont to refer to the manifestation near Damascus.

## NOTE 38, p. 93.

The author of "Supernatural Religion" (iii. p. 479, etc.) has indeed endeavoured to show that the words of Herod with regard to John the Baptist in Matt. xiv. 2, illustrate the "familiarity of the age with the idea of the resurrection of the dead," and show "how common was the belief in a bodily resurrection." Yet it is obvious that this case is far too isolated, and that the words of Herod were spoken in circumstances far too peculiar, to afford a good foundation for so wide an inference. It is much more probable, especially when we take into account the statement of Luke ix. 7 (Herod was "much perplexed"), that we are to see, with almost all commentators, in the language of the crafty and cruel king, simply the terrors of a guilty conscience. A still more entire failure is the same author's disingenuous attempt to show, from the accounts of the raisings of the widow's son at Nain and of the daughter of Jairus, that "such a miracle as the resurrection was commonplace enough in the view of these (the Gospel) writers" (p. 478). A single glance at the narratives is sufficient to show in what a solemn and imposing light these raisings were regarded by their reporters; while the popular feeling is strikingly expressed in the narrative of St. Mark, who tells us that when the daughter of Jairus was raised "they were amazed straightway with a great amazement" (Mark v. 42).

## NOTE 39, p. 97.

Dr. Westcott has justly called attention to the fact, that, instead of there being any popular expectation of the rising of Jesus in the form in which it actually occurred, "as a

S

matter of experience, the popular conceptions of a carnal resurrection very speedily overpowered the teaching of the New Testament in the early Church."—" Gospel of the Resurrection," 4th Edition, Appendix, p. 287.


## NOTE 40, p. 97.

It is extremely doubtful, indeed, whether there were not many in the early Christian Church who maintained that the day of the Lord was actually come. The verb $\dot{\epsilon}\nu\acute{\epsilon}\sigma\tau\eta\kappa\epsilon\nu$ in 2 Thess. ii. 2, can hardly be translated by "is at hand." In the New Testament it is uniformly employed to denote what has already happened, or what is now in existence around us. The Revised version, accordingly, properly renders the Greek here, "as that the day of the Lord is now present." Yet, even if thought of as present, the day of the Lord was not accompanied with visions of Him who, it was believed, would then take unto Him His great power and reign.


## NOTE 41, p. 112.

"Les Apôtres," Ch. I. Dr. Fairbairn, in the work formerly spoken of, has distinguished between the theory of Renan and the ordinary visional theory, calling the former the Phantasmal, p. 341. That there is such a distinction may be allowed, in so far as the immediate origin of the belief is concerned. But, whatever may have been the state of Mary's own mind, it was still upon supposed visions, seen by themselves, that the belief of the other disciples rested. It is not necessary, therefore, for my purpose to draw the above distinction, and to treat the phantasmal and visional theories as distinct.


## NOTE 42, p. 113.

The words of Keim (Jesus von Nazara, iii. p. 600), at the close of his valuable discussion on the Resurrection of Christ, ought to be quoted :—" After all that has been said it must be allowed that the theory (that, viz., of visions) which has of late become so popular, is only a hypothesis ; that, while it explains some things, it fails to explain the main substance of the narrations to be dealt with ; nay, that it leads us to look at facts historically attested from a distorted and untenable point of view."

## Note 43, p. 116.

Mr. Prudot, in his work "La Résurrection de Jésus Christ," p. 299, gives a Declaration signed at a General Conference of Pastors and Elders of the French Protestant Church held in Paris, A.D. 1865, which contains the following statement :—

"The undersigned Pastors and Laymen, considering that the modern religious conscience instructed in the school of Jesus Christ Himself, and slowly developed by eighteen centuries of Christian education, has learned, on the one side, not to make the Divinity of the Master's teaching depend upon His bodily reappearances ; on the other, to consider as independent of this fact the certainty of eternal life, in such a manner that faith rests henceforth not upon the perilous arguments of critical erudition unapproachable to simple believers, but upon the evidence of truth itself :

"Declare that, divided as they are among themselves upon the historical question, they frankly acknowledge the right of distinguishing between this question and Christianity itself, and of founding the simple and living demonstration of faith upon the agreement of the Holy Word of Jesus Christ with the principles and the needs of the human soul."

## Note 44, p. 117.

It is hardly necessary to name particular persons for views expressed by almost all writers on the subject. The following may, however, be mentioned:—Horsley, " Nine Sermons," p. 124 ; Dr. A. A. Hodge, "Commentary on the Confession of Faith," p. 147 ; Bishop Ellicott, " Lectures on the Life of Christ," p. 367 ; Hodge, " Syst. Theol.," ii. p. 627.

## Note 45, p. 119.

The preposition ἐκ used in this passage by our Lord ought to be allowed its proper force, and ought not to be translated as

if it were simply equivalent to ἀπό.   It is said by Delitzsch (on
Heb. v. 7) that ἐκ may mean either to rescue out of death one
who has died, or to preserve from death.   For the latter meaning he refers to Ps. xxxiii. 19, and Jas. v. 20.   Neither text
proves the point.   On the contrary, in both death, viewed meta-
phorically, is supposed to have taken place, and the persons
" delivered " or " saved " are rescued out of it.   Buttmann
("Grammatik d. N. T.," p. 281) holds that the prepositions are frequently interchangeable, and refers to John i. 44 ; 2 Cor. iii. 5 ;
Apoc. ix. 18 ; and Winer ("Moulton's Ed.," p. 456), while
urging that there is a distinction between them, allows that they
are used synonymously in John xi. 1 and in Apoc. ix. 18.
Winer compares also for synonymous use Luke xxi. 18 with
Acts xxvii. 34.   This last comparison proves nothing ; the use
of the preposition depends on the manner in which at the moment
the hairs of the head are supposed to be connected with the head.
Apoc. ix. 18 may also be set aside, the style of the book being
peculiar.   A careful consideration of the other passages referred
to will show that the prepositions are used with a strictly independent force.   In John i. 44 and xi. 1, the two towns mentioned
have a double aspect in the eyes of the Evangelist.   Philip is
" from " the one, Lazarus " from " the other ; but in both cases
there is a still more intimate relation between the persons
spoken of and the town to which they respectively belong.
Philip belongs to the town of Andrew and Peter, who had just
been spoken of as drawn to Jesus ; he has breathed the same
atmosphere, and is prepared to be a partaker of the same faith,
with them.   Lazarus belongs, in like manner, to the town of
Martha and Mary ; he has the same spirit as they have, and is,
like them, one in whom the " glory of God " may be fitly shown
forth.   The form of expression in 2 Cor. iii. 5 is itself sufficient
to show that the prepositions are not synonymous, the ἀπό denoting the outward act of judging, the ἐκ the internal source out
of which the outward act must come (comp. Hofmann *in loc.*)
The distinction is further illustrated by Luke ii. 4 (comp. Winer,
p. 456).   It may be added that Westcott adopts the view of
John xii. 27 taken in the text, " so that the sense appears to be,
' Bring me safely out of the conflict ' (Heb. v. 7), and not simply
' Keep me from entering into it ' " (*in loc.*)

## NOTE 46, p. 120.

The correctness of the view thus taken of the meaning of the word ἔξοδος in Luke ix. 31 may be at once illustrated and confirmed by the use of the contrasted word εἴσοδος in Acts xiii. 24. The Apostle is there speaking of the coming of our Lord into the world, and the word employed by him is εἴσοδος, which our translators have indeed rendered "coming." But this translation is manifestly inadequate for the remarkable expression of the original, "When John had first preached, πρὸ προσώπου τῆς εἰσόδου αὐτοῦ, the baptism of repentance to all the people of Israel." We ought to render, "before the face of his entering in." The allusion is to the entering in of Joshua into Canaan,—an allusion made clear by the fact that we read immediately before of God's having "brought unto Israel a Saviour, Jesus." Jesus is Himself the true Joshua, entering first, and bringing His people with Him, into the promised inheritance.

## NOTE 47, p. 122.

In contrast with the passages of St. Paul quoted in the text, it is possible to refer to the Apostle's words in writing to the Corinthians, "For I determined not to know anything among you, save Jesus Christ, and Him crucified" (1 Cor. ii. 2). But these words cannot be understood in the sense in which they are generally interpreted,—that the doctrine of a crucified Redeemer constituted the only or even the main substance of the Apostle's teaching in Corinth. The simple fact that in none of his Epistles does St. Paul enlarge so much upon the doctrine of the Risen Lord as he does in 1 Cor. xv., is sufficient to show this. In addition, however, it may be observed—(1.) That the Apostle is not so much describing the *contents* of his preaching as that particular aspect of the truth which affected his *method* of preaching. "He had come to them not with excellency of speech or of wisdom" (ver. 1), "*for*" (ver. 2) that which rendered his simple, unostentatious manner of speaking necessary was, that he had to deal with a topic alike familiar and offensive to them, viz. the *crucified* Christ. By this he could make no carnal show; from this he could gain no worldly honour. Such ends, therefore, he could

not have in view. (2.) The verb "to know" is not equivalent
to the verb "to preach;" it has reference to his attitude towards
himself, and not towards them. St. Paul, in short, is not describing the *whole* truth which he proclaimed, but that part of it
which determined himself to his unpretending style of utterance.
How could one who had the "offence of the cross" to preach seek
glory in the manner of preaching it? The translation of the
verse, indeed, as given above, is hardly correct. It ought rather
to be, "For I did not determine to know anything among you,"
etc.

### Note 48, p. 123.

The point adverted to in the text finds a striking illustration
in the manner in which the inquirer into the structure of St.
John's Gospel finds it necessary, even on totally independent
grounds, to consider chaps. xviii.-xx. as one Section. Chap. xx.,
although containing the narrative of the Resurrection, cannot be
separated from chaps. xviii. and xix., containing the narrative of
the trial and crucifixion. The main thought of these last chapters
is not that of Jesus in humiliation, but of Jesus "lifted on high,"
rising triumphant above the humiliation to which He is subjected.
That is exactly the thought of chap. xx. The Section must take
the three chapters together,—having for its theme not defeat
followed by victory, but real victory in the midst of apparent
defeat. See also the next Note.

### Note 49, p. 123.

The scenes in chap. xii. of St. John's Gospel are a striking
illustration of what has been said in the text. We do not appreciate them aright unless we bear in mind that the Redeemer
who here pursues His path of glory has at this moment the
sentence of death upon Him (see chap. xi. 53, 57); and that
although He is on His way to Jerusalem to die, He has before
Him, in Lazarus "whom He had raised from the dead" (ver. 1,
comp. ver. 17), the great token which He had just given of His
power over death.

### Note 50, p. 123.

This remarkable expression is, in the fulness of its meaning,
as applied to Jesus, peculiar to the fourth Gospel, and it is by no

means adequately represented by the English words "lifted up."
It refers first of all to the Glorification of our Lord, and in that
sense we find it used in Acts ii. 33, v. 31. But St. John, when
he quotes it in chap. xii. 32, includes under it, as he himself
distinctly intimates in the following verse, not only the Glorification but the crucifixion. It ought to be noticed that the object
of chap. xii. 33 is not to *limit* the term to the crucifixion, but
to show that, contrary to all that we should naturally expect, the
crucifixion is included under it. The *one* thought is, glory through
crucifixion. Crucifixion breaks the bond to earth, takes the
Redeemer "out of" it, and is thus the transition or introduction
to heaven and glory. For the force of "out of" in chap. xii. 32
compare what has been said in Note 45.

### Note 51, p. 123.

It is worth while to mark the emphatic position of these
words "for ever" at the end of the verse in Heb. vi. 20, when
the writer has brought his digression to an end, and is about to
resume the great topic which he had left for a few moments.
The Authorised Version has failed to do them justice.

### Note 52, p. 126.

1 Cor. xv. 47.—In this verse the words "the Lord," which
are found in the common reading before "from heaven," are
omitted by the best critical authorities. The change of reading brings out with force that the Apostle is dealing with the
thought of the first *man* and the second *man*, the two great heads
of lines of human beings descended from them. Commentators
have differed much as to the point of time referred to in the
words "from heaven," but the whole argument of St. Paul requires us to understand it of our Lord's Resurrection.

### Note 53, p. 135.

The procedure with the blood referred to in the text, and the
import of the ritual connected with it, appear to demand further
consideration.

It is admitted by all inquirers that the sprinkling of the
blood of the victim upon the Horns of the altar in an ordinary

Sin-offering, and upon the Mercy Seat in the Sin-offering of the great Day of Atonement, constituted the culminating point of the Sacrifice. This circumstance alone ought to guard us against two mistakes into which, in considering the subject, we are prone to fall. The first is that of supposing that the Sprinkling of the blood had essentially the same meaning as the Slaughtering; or that the one was simply a continuation of the other, though expressing the common idea in a different and higher form. The second is that of looking upon the two acts as wholly distinct in meaning, and as related to one another merely by succession of time. If the sacrifice *culminated* in the Sprinkling, we may start with the fact that the entire procedure with the blood of the Sin-offering had one object in view; and that, in attaining that object, each of the two parts with which we are now dealing occupied a necessary place, and expressed an idea to a certain extent independent of, although at the same time closely related to, that of the other. It was necessary that the victim should be slaughtered. To have obtained the blood in any other way, as, for example, by the opening of a vein, would have been invalid. It was not less necessary that the blood thus obtained should be sprinkled upon the appointed place. We may expect, therefore, that each of these two actions will have a meaning of its own, and that both will combine together into some conception higher and more general than either separately would have been able to express.

It will help our inquiry if, in the first place, we endeavour to determine the object of the Sin-offering as a whole, after which we shall be better able to fix the interpretation of its different parts. In doing so, it will not be disputed for a moment that the Sin-offering must share in the general meaning and purport of all sacrifice, although in its case that meaning may receive a particular modification, owing to the particular light in which the offerer is viewed. This general meaning, again, may be best ascertained by starting from the thought of that relation in which Israel was to stand to God. On this point no doubt can exist. Israel was God's covenant people, designed to walk with Him in the closest possible fellowship, the seed of Abraham His "friend." But Israel perpetually violated the Covenant, provoked the anger of the Almighty, and separated itself from Him by sin. Sacrifice, then, was a merciful institution by which such breaches of the Covenant might be repaired, and the people restored to their old and true relation with their covenant God, and to a walk with Him in the enjoyment of His love and favour. Pardon of sin was not the chief aim of Sacrifice. The undue prominence given in the Theology of the Reformation to this aspect of the truth, though easily accounted for, and perhaps unavoidable in the earlier history of the Churches of that era, has been attended with no small injury to the very truths which these Churches were most anxious to conserve.

Passing from a too one-sided conception of the doctrine of salvation through Christ alone to its treatment of the Old Testament, the Theology of the Reformation was, in its turn, acted upon by the views of the Old Testament doctrine of Sacrifice to which it had itself given birth; and the grand end aimed at in the work of our Lord is, in consequence, to this day obscured. Hengstenberg is unquestionably right when he says, "The false assertion that atonement is the fundamental idea of Sacrifice in general has created very much confusion" ("The Sacrifices of Holy Scripture" appended to Commentary on Ecclesiastes in Clark's Translation, p. 371). The leading or central idea of Sacrifice was not mere pardon of sin, or atonement, or the procuring of the Divine favour, by which the relation of only one of the two parties to the other—that of God to His creature—was affected; while the love of God, contemplated by faith, was simply left to work as a motive of gratitude upon the heart. The relation of both parties to one another was involved in the Sacrifice itself. That act expressed all that was implied, alike for God and Israel, in the restoration of the covenant. It brought both back into a state of mutual reconciliation and fellowship. Out of this idea flowed the two parts of the ritual of Sacrifice which we have at present to consider.

I. *The Slaughtering.* This part of the ritual ought certainly to be treated separately; and it is a misfortune that the late Principal Fairbairn, in his valuable remarks upon "The subject of Sacrifice by Blood" ("Typology," vol. ii., Appendix C, p. 531), has taken it along with the Sprinkling, "as going in a manner together with it." Had he not done so he might perhaps have been led to unfold more at length certain expressions which he has used (see especially p. 533), and might have come to what seems to us the right conclusion. Looking then at the Slaughtering by itself, it is impossible with many modern inquirers either to consider it simply as a means of getting at the blood of the victim, or to be satisfied with regarding it as expressive of nothing more than a surrender on the part of the offerer of his old and selfish, in order that he might enter on a new and unselfish, life. The place constantly occupied by the thought of death in the Old Testament, and the manner in which the death of Christ, the undoubted Antitype of the Sin-offering, is spoken of in the New Testament, alike demand a deeper meaning for the Slaughtering than is afforded by the first of these suppositions; while the fact that the victim had been already presented to God before the Slaughtering took place forbids the adoption of the second. It is impossible indeed to rest short of the idea that in the *particular mode* of procuring the blood there was something penal. The Israelite had sinned, and he deserved to die. Before he could be brought again into fellowship with God, it was necessary for him to acknowledge this ; he made the acknowledgment in the putting to death the spotless victim from his own fold which he presented as a sin-offering in his stead. In its death he consented to die.

If this be so, it ought next to be observed that, when the blood flowed from the slaughtered victim, it was not merely blood, but blood bearing with it and in it the acknowledgment of which we have spoken, an acknowledgment by the offerer of his free acceptance of death as a penalty due to him on account of sin. This gave its value to the slaughtering as a part of the sacrifice. No reflecting person can imagine for a moment that blood, simply as blood, could be acceptable to God. What made the blood acceptable was that, as it flowed, it "cried," confessing sin and desert of punishment. It thus could not be dead. It was alive. Not indeed that it was physically alive. It was rather ideally alive,—alive with a life which had now assumed its true attitude towards God, with a life which confessed, as it flowed forth in it, that it was surrendered freely, and in harmony with the demands of God's righteous law. We know that the idea of blood thus speaking was familiar to the Jew (Gen. iv. 10 ; Job xvi. 18 ; Ezek. xxiv. 7, 8 ; Heb. xii. 24) ; but what speaks must either be, or must be thought of as being, alive. The living nature of the blood is indeed expressly declared to us in the law itself. In Lev. xvii. 11, it is said, "For the life of the flesh is in the blood: and I have given it to you upon the altar to make an atonement for your lives: for the blood atones through the life." The meaning of this passage—the *locus classicus* upon the point under discussion—seems obvious. The blood is a conventional hieroglyphic labelled as the life. It is the bearer of the life of the animal offered ; and because it is looked at in this light, because it is the vehicle of a life substituted for the life of an offerer who is setting himself in a right relation towards God, it possesses expiatory virtue.

The Slaughtering was thus more than a mere means of getting at the blood ; it was a means of getting at the blood in a *particular way*—in a way without which the offerer would not have acknowledged his own desert of punishment. It was also more than the expression of the offerer's surrender of himself to God ; it was such an expression in a *particular way*—in a way without which the offerer would not have accommodated himself to the great law everywhere pervading a sinful world—that only through death freely accepted is the first step taken in the path of life. The blood, after it has been shed in the slaughtering, has thus a compound aspect. It is not simple life : it is life of a peculiar kind. Life it always was ; but a new and peculiar element has just been added to it. It is *life which has willingly passed through death* as through a doom both deserved and necessary ; and it is this compound thought that constitutes the action, up to the point that we have reached, a sacrificial action by which, when complete, sin will be covered or atoned for. The main idea, then, which has as yet met us is neither that of blood alone, nor of death alone. It is blood obtained by "Slaughter:" it is life in death. In other words, the free acceptance by the will of deserved death,—a process during which the will lives,—constitutes the kernel and heart of the Slaughtering ; " Lo, I come to do thy will, O God."

II. *The Sprinkling of the blood*. This is the second and most important of the two actions with which we are at present concerned. The question is, What are its object and meaning? These cannot be the same as in the first action of which we have spoken, for the second action is wholly different from the first, and is regulated by strict prescriptions, as well as fenced about by solemn sanctions of its own. The Sprinkling, therefore, cannot represent the surrender of the sinner by himself to the just doom of sin, for we should thus have the same thing represented by two entirely different actions. It has indeed been urged that the Horns of the altar upon which the blood of the ordinary sin-offering was sprinkled, or the Mercy Seat upon which the blood was sprinkled on the great Day of Atonement, are to be regarded as expressive simply of greater nearness to God than was obtained upon the altar itself (Hofmann, "Schriftbeweis," ii. 1, p. 157). Were this view correct, it might be pled that the same idea which utters itself in the Slaughtering utters itself in the same way also in the Sprinkling, with only the additional thought of greater nearness to God. The second action might then have substantially no other meaning than the first, though the meaning might be expressed in a more intensive form. But there is a want of all sound warrant for such an interpretation either of the Horns of the altar or of the Mercy Seat. The Horns (and the same remark applies in principle to the Mercy Seat) did not represent nearness to God. They represented a higher potency of the Divine idea than that expressed in the Altar itself. They were the symbols of the Altar in the greatest fulness of its signification. The Sprinkling of the blood upon them, therefore, cannot be only the bringing nearer God a sinful life yielded up to merited punishment. It must have expressed something else ; and what we contend for is, that it expressed the bringing of the offerer's life, after it had been so yielded up, into loving communion and fellowship with God. The Sprinkling was, in short, the culminating point of the restoration of the Covenant. In the Slaughtering the first step towards a full reconciliation between God and His creature had been taken. The blood of the victim bore along with it the life of the offerer, and it was poured out even unto death. Now the blood of the same faultless animal, still bearing along with it the life of the offerer, was sprinkled. In other words, the life which had passed through death was brought near to God, and was dedicated to Him for the future. Two different considerations may help to establish this.

(1.) The blood in the second action must be looked at in the same light as in the first. All, it may be presumed, will agree thus far. But we have already seen that in the first action the blood is not dead but living; and, as nothing has occurred between the two actions to alter its constituent elements or typical character, it must, in the second action, be not less living than in the first. It is not death, therefore, but life, that is sprinkled upon the Horns of the altar or upon the Mercy Seat, and that is thus brought by the priest, the representative of God, into the closest embrace of God's loving mercy. This point may be said to be distinctly implied in the words of the law already quoted from Lev. xvii. 11, "I have given it to you *upon the altar* to make an atonement for your lives." The reference here is to the Sprinkling; that is, at the very moment when the blood is declared to be the life, the declaration is made in immediate connexion with the Sprinkling. The blood, then, was here a living thing, brought into the most intimate relation with the grace of God in its greatest potency. Once more, if any doubt could remain upon our minds that the blood, when sprinkled, was living not dead blood, it would be dispelled by the fact that death could not have been placed in such close contiguity with the Living God. No thought was more deeply impressed upon the whole ritual of Israel than that of the impassable gulf between God and death. Nothing defiled like contact with death, and so alien was it to the nature of God, that, from the simple circumstance that the Almighty had called Himself the God of Abraham, of Isaac, and of Jacob, long after these patriarchs were in their graves, our Lord deduced what His opponents felt to be an unanswerable argument that the dead are raised (Luke xx. 37, 38). Surely, then, the blood sprinkled upon the Mercy Seat, the most holy spot of the Sanctuary, that over which God Himself was throned in glorious majesty, could not be blood of death. It was blood of life. The life, not the death, of the sinner was so given over to, and embraced by, the Divine mercy that sin was covered.

(2.) While the blood must thus be looked at in the same light throughout the whole offering, it is further to be observed that it was by the sprinkling of the blood that the atonement was completed and sin covered. But sin can be thus covered only when union with God has been effected.    This union is not sanctification, which is the fruit of union not union itself.    Only in union with God, then, is sin covered.    Death cannot extinguish sin : it simply puts an end to the power of sinning. Reconciliation of the life with God, union of the life with Him, must take place before the full meaning of the word atonement is exhausted, or sin can be spoken of as ready for dismissal into the land of darkness.

Principal Fairbairn has so nearly expressed what seems to be the truth upon the point before us, that his words may with propriety be quoted.    " It was otherwise, however," he says, ".with the sprinkling of the blood, which completed the work of atonement ; for this respected the acceptance of the substituted life for that of the offerer, and could only be done by God's accredited representatives—the consecrated priesthood.    The mere bringing of the victim to the altar, laying on it the guilt which burdened the sinner's conscience, with other collateral acknowledgments, and taking from it its life-blood in token of what the offerer felt himself bound to render, however necessary and important, were still not sufficient to restore peace to his conscience.    There must be the formal approval of Heaven, or the palpable acceptance of the one soul as a covering for the guilt of the other.    And this was done by the pouring out or sprinkling of the sacrificial blood on the altar—not as that which, according to Hofmann, had *once had* the life of the animal (for apart from this it was only so many particles of blood, meaningless and worthless), but which, as flowing fresh and warm, still in a sense had it—the very life of the animal—in its immediate seat and proper representation.    This blood so presented gave assurance to the offerer both of a satisfaction rendered for him by death, and of a pure life granted to him in the presence of God " (" Typology," ii. p. 533).

It is strange that immediately after this passage Dr. Fairbairn speaks of " Christ's work on the cross " as that in which the Old Testament doctrine of sacrifice *rose to its proper consummation.* But it is unnecessary to dwell on this.    The longer passage which we have quoted is important as coming from a theologian so careful and justly esteemed, and the view to which it points, although not thoroughly worked out by its writer, cannot be

mistaken. The following also are the words of Mr. Jukes in his
" Law of the Offerings : "—" As to the sprinkling of blood, I need
scarcely say it refers to atonement by sacrifice ; it signifies that
the thing or person sprinkled is thereby brought from a state of
distance from God to a state of nearness. The sprinkling, then,
of blood upon the incense-altar implied that until this act was
performed the altar was unapproachable ; and consequently, that
all priestly service, and therefore all service of all kinds, was
stopped between God and Israel. In like manner, the sprinkling
of blood upon the brazen altar implied that till this was done,
that altar too was regarded as unapproachable. In each case
sin is apprehended to have interrupted communion ; in the one,
the communion of priests ; in the other, the communion of Israel ;
while the sprinkling of blood declares that communion restored
through the sin-offering on the incense-altar to the priests, on the
brazen altar to the people " (p. 155). What we urge, therefore, is
that restored communion of the life with God, perfect dedication
of the life to Him in His own Covenant of love, is the meaning
of the sprinkling of the blood in the sin-offering of Israel.

Let us now look at the Sin-offering as a whole, and we can
hardly fail to see that, so far from terminating with the death of
the victim, or being occupied solely with the idea of death, it had
special regard to the life of the victim and to the presentation of
that life to God. Throughout all the parts of the offering the
blood was the life. It was never dead blood ; and the actions
with the blood—with the life—were not brought to an end until
the life was restored, by sprinkling upon the Horns of the altar
or upon the Mercy Seat, to communion and fellowship with God.
The blood was no doubt blood that had been poured out ; the
life was life that had been surrendered to death ; but it had
passed through death to a higher life in which the Almighty
was to be served through all time to come. Not death, then,
but life through death, was the meaning of the sacrifice. The
thought which it expressed was one.

Such is the type, and the Antitype strictly corresponds to it.
It is a fact worth noting that the almost uniform practice of the
Sacred Writers (exceptions can be easily explained) is to ascribe
our salvation to the " blood," not to the " death " of Christ ;
and the two terms, blood and death, are not synonymous.[1] In

---

[1] See Appendix to this Note.

our thoughts they are apt to be so, but not so in the thoughts
of a Jew. When a Jew thought of the blood, he thought of
more than death. He thought not only of the blood as poured
out when the victim died, but of the blood as carried into the
Most Holy Place. He thought of all that was done with it, of
the whole of that ceremonial in which it bore so important a
part. Nay, he must have thought even more especially (as we
see strikingly exemplified in the Epistle to the Hebrews) of that
Sprinkling for the sake of which, and as a means to which, the
blood-shedding took place. When, then, the Sacred Writers so
constantly ascribe our salvation to the blood rather than the death
of our Lord, we must connect with the words the whole range
of thought which would present itself to the Jew who heard
them. We must take in not only the death upon the cross, but
our Lord's presentation of Himself in heaven, in the true Holy
of Holies, when, not " through the blood of goats and calves, but
through His own blood, He entered in once for all into the Holy
Place, having obtained eternal redemption for us " (Heb. ix. 12).
We must think not *of death*, but *of life through death*, as the
essence of Christ's offering. We must think of Christ's blood
as living blood, and of the pardon of sin as only the initiatory
result of His sacrifice of Himself. In short, through all Christ's
offering we deal with life. Christ is " a living sacrifice ; " we
in Him, and sharing the blessings of His salvation, are also " a
living sacrifice " (Rom. xii. 1). The end and purpose of everything that is done is that we may be brought into loving fellowship with God, and into the holy life which such fellowship
involves ; " for if the blood of goats and bulls, and the ashes of a
heifer sprinkling them that have been defiled, sanctify unto the
cleanness of the flesh ; how much more shall the blood of Christ,
who through eternal spirit offered Himself without blemish
unto God, cleanse your conscience from dead works to serve the
living God ? " (Heb. ix. 13, 14).

Keeping these things in view, we may now be prepared to
estimate the force of a class of passages in which we read of the
blood of Christ as being taken into heaven and being continued
there. These passages occur chiefly in the Epistle to the Hebrews ; and the leading one may be said to be that in which,
along with other things belonging to the heavenly Jerusalem,—

such as innumerable hosts of angels, the general assembly and
church of the first born who are enrolled in heaven, and the
spirits of just men made perfect,—there is mentioned the "blood
of sprinkling, that speaketh better than *that of* Abel" (Heb. xii.
24). It is upon this passage that Bengel has the long and
elaborate note in which he endeavours to establish the proposition
that the blood of Christ, having been wholly poured out, partly
on the cross, partly in His other sufferings, has not been again
sent into His veins, but has been taken into heaven, where it
remains for ever as "incorruptible blood," separate from His
body, before the eyes of God.    This view has also been adopted
by Alford, who, in his note on Hebrews xii. 24, expresses himself
to the following effect :—" Our Lord's blood was shed from Him
on the cross. And as His body did not see corruption, it is obvious
to suppose that His blood did not corrupt as that of ordinary
men, being as it is so important a portion of His body.    Hence,
and because His resurrection-body seems to have been bloodless,
(see Luke xxiv. 39 ; John xx. 37, and notes), some have supposed that the blood of the Lord remains as it was poured out,
incorruptible, in the presence of God.    On such a matter I would
neither affirm nor deny, but mention with all reverence that
which seems to suit the requirements of the words before us.
By that blood we live, wherever it is ; but as here it is mentioned
separately from the Lord Himself, as an item in the glories of
the heavenly city, and as 'yet speaking,' it seems to require
some such view to account for the words used."

    Delitzsch again, who is unable to adopt this view, however
readily he allows that much may be said for it, after considerable
discussion sums up his view as follows :—" As far as concerns the
presentation of the blood, the Risen One has brought before
God, His Father, in the vessel of His body transfigured yet
identical with what it had been when crucified, His blood transfigured yet identical with what it had been when shed, and this
high-priestly self-presentation of the Redeemer is become the
eternally effective settlement of our eternal redemption."—
" Hebr. Brief.," p. 393.

    Both of these views appear to be untenable.    The first is so
realistic, that, if we are to accept, in the manner proposed, the
literal interpretation of the blood, there will be much else which

we shall be compelled to interpret with equal literalness. We shall have to admit the existence of a real and physical Tabernacle in heaven, of a Holy Place, and of a Mercy Seat,—to admit much that is altogether incompatible with the notions which Scripture itself teaches us to form of the heavenly abode. The second leaves altogether unexplained the prominence given to the blood in the language of the New Testament, and supplies no proper antitype to the type presented in the law. Neither supposition, we may reasonably believe, would have been resorted to had the point upon which we have been insisting been recognised— that the blood is the life ; that the offering of the law was not complete until the life, in the form of the blood, was reunited to God, and anew dedicated to Him in loving fellowship ; and that, in like manner, the offering of Christ was not complete until He presented His blood, that is His life, to the Father, that it might thenceforward be the Father's in the uninterrupted and perfect service of the eternal world.

The central idea, therefore, of our Lord's presentation of Himself, or of His blood, in heaven, is not that of a continued remembrance of His death alone, as if the blood were still no more than the blood poured out in the sufferings of earth ; nor is it a presentation only of His life—even His Divine and holy life— considered in itself alone. It is a continued presentation of His life, as a life which has accepted death, which has passed through death, and is now and for ever "an offering and sacrifice to God for an odour of a sweet smell" (Eph. v. 2). We dare not separate the thought of our Lord's sufferings and death from the thought of His glorified condition. It is true that the death is over. As an act, it belongs to the past ; but it is not to be forgotten. It must be as distinctly before us now, when we behold the Saviour in glory, as it was before the eyes of those who nailed Him to the tree. Scripture always reminds us of it, "I am the First and the Last, and the Living One ; and I was dead, and behold I am alive for evermore ;" "A Lamb standing as though it had been slain ; " "Ye proclaim the Lord's death till He come" (Rev. i. 18, vi. 6 ; 1 Cor. xi. 26). It is the more necessary for us to keep all this distinctly in view, for we are not in so favourable a position as the Jew was for seeing that the blood with which we deal has passed through death. Although in the sacrificial ritual the blood was conventionally alive, the Jew could not think of it except as gained by the death of the victim. We do not see this, and may forget it; as so much of the Theology of our day has done. The fact, therefore, that the *living* Lord has passed through *death* cannot be too earnestly insisted on. But what we have mainly to urge at present is, that in His state before the Father, He expresses an idea beyond or in advance of that of death. His offering has gone beyond its primary stage, having culminated in the complete restoration of the broken covenant ; and that restoration is life.

It is probably unnecessary to dwell upon the important consequences that must flow from such a view of the presentation of our Lord's blood or life in heaven, as we have now endeavoured to unfold. Yet we may briefly notice two points upon which its bearing is very close.

In the first place, it ought to go some way at least towards conciliating widely divergent views with regard to the true purport of the holy Sacrament of Communion. We start with at once accepting the proposition that the worship of the Church on earth ought to be moulded on her worship in heaven ; and that, inasmuch as our Great High Priest there presents Himself continually before the Father, as the offering in which His people are accepted and complete, the Sacrament of the Supper must here be the central rite of that worship. But in what sense? This must evidently be determined by the light in which we regard the heavenly worship of Him in whom His whole Church is gathered up. The Romish Church has rightly felt that the idea of Intercession cannot exhaust this worship, and has fixed upon the continued presentation of an offering which had been completed upon earth as its central thought. The development of the doctrine of the Mass immediately and naturally follows. Christ, it is held, is certainly present in the Eucharist. If present at all, He must be present in the same attitude and with the same functions as those which He has assumed in heaven. He must thus be present simply as an offering in the same aspect as that in which He offered Himself upon the cross. The Eucharist becomes the Mass,—a repetition, or, as Möhler ("Symbolik," Section 34) prefers to call it, a "continuation" of the one offering made on Calvary for the sins of men ;

and the distinction, utterly without foundation on the point before us, between a bloody and an unbloody sacrifice, is introduced. On the other hand, different branches of the Protestant Church, recoiling from the Mass and all the corruptions which it brought along with it, have too often practically eliminated the presence of the Lord from the Eucharist altogether, and have reduced that Sacrament to a mere commemoration of an offering made by the Lord in His death eighteen centuries ago. Both extremes are wrong; though the latter is even more clearly baseless than the former. The former too, however, must be set aside, for it proceeds upon the erroneous idea that the exalted Lord is now presenting Himself to God in His death instead of in His *life won through death*. The heavenly act of the Glorified High Priest of the Church becomes merely a perpetuated crucifixion, and the Church is practically robbed of the heavenly life of Him in whom alone her own heavenly life can be maintained. The view here advocated seems to point us to the true middle way, for the sacrifice of our Lord presented in heaven is not simply a continuation of that once presented on the cross; nor is the former a mere commemoration of the latter. The heavenly act is rather the completing part of the one sacrifice which embraces both what was done on earth and what is done in heaven. A true repetition, therefore, or imitation of the heavenly worship, does not lead to the Mass; it leads to the thought of the Eucharist as a service in which the redeemed, and already at least in principle triumphant, Church presents herself to the Father in her new and higher life, and in which she is nourished by the gracious provision made for her in that festival. The Eucharist is not mainly a remembrance of death; the thought of death lies indeed at the bottom of it; but death is surmounted, and the end for which it was endured has been reached. The Eucharist is life. It is the nourishment, the feast, of life. Hence, accordingly, the cruelty, to say nothing of the unscripturalness, of withholding the cup from the laity, for the cup is the culminating point of the service. It is " the new covenant in Christ's blood " (1 Cor. xi. 25 ; Comp. Luke xxii. 20); the " fruit of the vine " which it contained was His " blood of the covenant " (Matt. xxvi. 28, 29 ; Mark xiv. 24, 25) ; and it was so because the blood was the " life." To withhold the cup is thus to withhold that which especially sets forth the life of our Lord—that life which it is the main object of His work to communicate to man, as to procure it was the main purpose of the covenant.

In the second place, the view which we have endeavoured to unfold ought to conciliate divergent views as to our Lord's whole work on behalf of man. On the one hand, there is the merely legal or juridical view of that work, which has a paralysing effect upon the life of the Church. Taken by itself, it leaves the impression upon the mind of something outward and unreal. The truly awakened conscience cannot be satisfied with a mere verdict of acquittal at the bar of Divine justice. What it needs, and never can be at peace without having, is deliverance from sin itself, is a moral and spiritual change, through which there shall be produced a walk with God instead of a walk in sin. And this change must be involved in the very process of redemption. It is not enough for one who has felt the power and evil of sin in itself to be told that he is freely forgiven,—and that, if he will only open his heart to receive in faith the declaration of forgiveness, he shall also be strengthened from above to prove his gratitude for the Divine mercy. He must see that in the very plan of redemption holiness is secured ; that holiness is not a consequence of salvation, but an integral part of it ; that God has " called us in holiness " (1 Thess. iv. 7) ; and that, if we are interested in the sacrifice of Christ at all, we must be interested in it not simply for justification, but for a new life,— for the former indeed first in order, but only as inseparably connected with, and directly leading to, the latter. Thus we ought to find ourselves drawn to a Theology, less one-sided and more pervaded by Catholic elements than that of the Reformation, because dealing more with life than with death.

On the other hand, we ought to be equally saved from that opposite tendency of many earnest minds, to resolve the whole of Christ's work, when applied to us, into the exercise of a self-denial and self-sacrifice like His, to put out of view the sterner attributes of the Almighty, and to represent His whole manifest-ation of Himself in the Son as a manifestation of Fatherhood in the popular sense of that word. *Such* Fatherhood will never explain the ritual of the ancient sin-offering, and still less will it explain the far more awful sacrifice of the cross. Nor will it ever exercise the mighty power which the thought of God as just and righteous has exercised in past ages of the Church. It may do for quiet times; but in times of trouble, when men's hearts fail them, they need something sterner, something associated with the thought of judgment against sin, to afford a resting-place for the soul. What would have been left of ancient prophecy had this element of power been extinguished in it? Or what would the Scottish Covenanters have made of the doctrine of the Fatherhood as taught in our day? For them stronger meat was necessary; and it was in words like those of the 124th Psalm that they found courage. This strength, however, may easily become too harsh. What we require is a Theology that will mediate between the two extremes; and it seems as if this might be best obtained by a remoulding of the doctrine of Sacrifice upon the lines that we have indicated. The old one-sidedness was undoubtedly more Scriptural than the one-sidedness so widely accepted now; and a stern Theology is better than no Theology at all. But the Church is waiting to have more clearly expressed for her than was needed in the sixteenth century that moral and spiritual side of God's dealings with man which was forced into a too exclusively juridical direction by the peculiar struggles of the Reformation age.

---

## APPENDIX TO NOTE 53.

In the course of the above Note we had occasion to remark that the New Testament writers do not seem to speak of the "death" and of the "blood" of Christ, as if the terms were perfectly synonymous, but that under the latter they include a wider range of thought than under the former. The point is of sufficient importance to demand a few additional remarks. Before, however, turning directly to the texts which we propose to examine, it may be well to observe that a general distinction between the two words may really exist, even although it should be possible to cite a few cases in which they appear to be exchanged for one another. This may easily happen with any two words, the meanings of which, while not the same, are yet closely related. It may happen much more easily in the present instance where, the *sacrificial* nature of death and blood being in view, we can neither think of the former without also thinking of the latter which is procured by its means ; nor of the latter without thinking also of the former by which alone it is procured. When benefits are traced to that Sacrifice of the Lord Jesus Christ which involves the thought of both His death and His blood, it can hardly surprise us if the distinction generally traceable between the two words be not always observed with perfect strictness.

The passages in which blessings are spoken of as conferred on man by the "death" of our Lord are indeed less numerous than might be at first supposed, while those in which blessings are connected with His "blood" are of much more frequent occurrence. This circumstance alone may prepare us for the fact that the two words do not cover exactly the same ground ; but only an examination of the passages themselves can satisfy us that such is the case.

One of the most interesting of these passages is one in which both words meet us. In Romans v. 8-10, we read not only of the death, but also of the blood, of Christ. The translation is as follows (verses 8, 9) :—"But God commendeth His own love toward us in that, while we were yet sinners, Christ died for us. Much more then, having been now justified in His blood, we shall be saved through Him from the wrath *of God.* (verse 10.) For if, while we were enemies, we were reconciled to God through the death of His Son, much more, having been reconciled, we shall be saved in His life."

Before passing on it may be proper to notice that the " reconciliation " here spoken of is that of God to man, rather than that of man to God ; in other words, it is an objective rather than a subjective reconciliation. This interpretation is rendered necessary by the context, and by the general usage of the word καταλλάσσειν. It is also adopted by the best commentators, and it need not be further discussed at present. It will be seen that the passage, as a whole, consists of two very similar and parallel parts, which may be designated by the letters A and B. The two parts are not, indeed, expressive of precisely the same aspect of the common thought ; for the first, consisting of the

8th and 9th verses, presents that thought from the side
of what God does; the second, consisting of the 10th verse,
from the side of what man receives. The place occupied by the
words "much more" in both, and the general principles of
parallelism, justify this division.

The thoughts of the passage may be thus arranged :—

A (verses 8, 9).

God commendeth His own love towards us
In that, while we were yet sinners,
Christ died for us :
Much more then,
Having been now justified in His blood,
We shall be saved from the wrath *of God*
Through Him (as alive).

B (verse 10).

For if, while we were enemies,
We were reconciled to God
Through the death of His Son ;
Much more,
Having been reconciled,
We shall be saved
In His life.

This analysis demonstrates—(1) That in the last line of A,
corresponding to the last line of B, the word "Him" must be
referred to the living Saviour. (2) That the words in the fifth
line of A, "Having been now justified in His blood," corresponding to those in the fifth line of B, "Having been reconciled,"
express a state of effected reconciliation, that is, a *state* in which
we are placed when the *act* of reconciliation is viewed as past.
(3) That God has appointed the living Christ to give us complete
salvation after we have been presented to Him in the blood of
Christ, as men justified or reconciled. There are thus two
leading thoughts in the passage as a whole. First, we have
part in Christ's death; this reconciles God to us, and makes us
ready for further manifestations of His grace. Secondly, we
have part in Christ's life; this brings complete salvation. It is

true that at first sight the "blood" of Christ appears to be spoken of in connexion with our justification, and had the Apostle said that we were justified *by* His blood, we might have thought of nothing more; but he says *in* His blood, and that circumstance, taken along with the parallelism of the lines, shows us that he has a larger thought before him,—not merely that Christ's blood shed in death justifies us, but that, having had that blood applied to us, we are *in* it, as justified men, when the blessing of *salvation* is bestowed. Salvation is not here equivalent to justification; it is more. The "wrath" spoken of is not wrath from which we have been delivered; it is "*the*" wrath of God, the wrath to come, from which we shall be delivered, from which the justified man shall be *saved*. The blood, therefore, is not thought of only as blood shed in Christ's death *for* us, but as blood *in* which we enter into life. The death of Christ makes provision for God's love being extended to us as sinners; the blood of Christ "in" which we are presented to God after reconciliation, makes provision for the bestowal of life upon us as persons in a state of reconciliation. Thus the death and the blood do not cover the same sphere of thought; they are related to one another, as the death of the sin-offering was related to the blood of the sin-offering when it was taken into the Holy of Holies.

The "death" of Christ, along with the effect accomplished by it, is spoken of in two passages of the Epistle to the Hebrews.

The first of these is Chap. ix. 15,—"And for this cause He is the Mediator of a new covenant, that, a death having taken place for the redemption of the transgressions that were under the first covenant, they that have been called may receive the promise of the eternal inheritance." It is unnecessary to say anything of the question raised in connexion with these words, —Whether the beneficial effects of the death of Christ were limited to "the transgressions that were under the first covenant,"—the general teaching of the Epistle forbidding any such limitation. But it is important to observe that Christ's death is viewed simply as a ransom for transgressions. The sacred writer does not say that it gives life. What it procures is the remission of sins, so that they who in faith present it as their offering may be accepted by God, and placed in a position in which the promise of "the eternal inheritance" may be received by them. This conclusion is rendered still clearer if we look at the words of the 14th verse, immediately preceding,— "How much more shall the blood of Christ, who through eternal spirit offered Himself without blemish unto God, cleanse your conscience from dead works to serve the living God?" In this verse the "blood" of Christ is spoken of, and why? There can be no hesitation as to the answer, which is rendered clear by verse 12, where the "entering once for all into the holy place" is mentioned, as well as by the words "eternal spirit" of the verse itself. It is because we are not dealing in verse 14 with Christ's death upon the cross, but with His presentation of Himself, as One who has died, to His Heavenly Father. And the instant we have this thought set before us, we pass beyond remission of sin to the new and spiritual condition of fellowship with God and eternal life; we pass beyond the thought of death to that of blood. "Blood" and "death" are here distinguished from one another.

The second passage in this Epistle of which we have to speak is Chap. ii. 14, 15,—"Since then the children are sharers in flesh and blood, He also Himself in like manner partook of the same, that through death He might bring to nought him that had the power of death, that is, the devil; and might deliver all those who through fear of death, were all their lifetime subject to bondage." It is not difficult to see what our Lord is here said to do "through death." There is not a word of positive union and fellowship with God. What is spoken of is the deliverance of believers from fear of death and the bondage induced by it. These spring from sin,—"the sting of death is sin,"—the consciousness of sin gives the "power of death" to the devil; and what is needed to extinguish that power is an assurance that sin is forgiven. This we have by the "death" of Christ, which is thus again connected with the initial rather than the advanced stage of Christian experience.

A third passage in this Epistle, Chap. ii. 9,—"That by the grace of God He should taste death for every man,"—seems to throw no light upon the present inquiry.[1]

---

[1] It might be otherwise did we read χωρὶς θεοῦ. But we shall not now attempt to defend a reading so universally rejected.

From the passages in which the death of Christ is spoken of, let us now turn to at least the chief of those which make mention of His "blood."

Acts xx. 28.—"Take heed unto yourselves and to all the flock . . . . to feed the church of God which He purchased with His own blood." The word thus translated "purchased" is more properly rendered "acquired as a possession." The thought of "blood" is associated not merely with the thought of our having been purchased, but with that of our having become the possession of God, so that we are His in reality and truth, as well as by legal right.

Eph. ii. 13.—"But now in Christ Jesus, ye that once were far off, are made nigh in the blood of Christ;" *i.e.* the Ephesian Christians are not merely pardoned, they are actually "nigh;" they are part of the "one new man" (ver. 15); they have "access in one Spirit unto the Father" (ver. 18); they are thus in communion and fellowship with God, and all is "in the blood of Christ." They are, in short, "in" the blood as sprinkled upon the Mercy Seat, and not merely as poured out in the Slaughtering, and with their being so are connected all the advanced privileges of their Christian condition.

Heb. x. 19-22.—"Having therefore, brethren, boldness to enter into the holy place, in the blood of Jesus, by the way which He dedicated for us, a new and living way through the veil, that is to say, His flesh; and having a great Priest over the house of God; let us draw near with a true heart," etc. Here the "blood" is so obviously and closely connected with more than the forgiveness of sin, viz. with entering into the immediate presence of God in His inmost Sanctuary, and with the positive dedication of ourselves to Him, that it is not necessary to dwell upon the words. Again, also, it may be noticed that it is not "by," or "through," but "in" the blood of Jesus that we thus enter. His life is in the place of our life, His blood in that of our blood; we are surrounded, as it were, with His blood, we are included in it, at the moment when we enter into the Holiest of all.

Heb. xiii. 11, 12.—"For the bodies of those beasts whose blood is brought into the holy place through the high priest for sin are burned without the camp. Wherefore, Jesus also, that

He might sanctify the people with His own blood, suffered without the gate." The sanctification, the consecration, not only outwardly but inwardly, of the people is here before the writer's eye, and he associates this great result with the "blood" of Christ as it is presented in the Most Holy Place.

Similar teaching to that which we have now met is found in the writings of St. Peter and St. John.

Thus, when St. Peter tells his readers that they have been redeemed from their "vain manner of life handed down from their fathers," he declares that this redemption has been effected with "precious blood, as of a lamb without blemish and without spot, even the blood of Christ" (1 Pet. i. 19); and when St. John says that we are "cleansed" from all sin, in a sense which certainly includes the bestowal of the new life as well as pardon, he brings distinctly forward the mention of the "blood,"—"and the blood of Jesus His Son cleanseth us from all sin" (1 John i. 7). Upon this last passage the following words of Haupt deserve quotation:—" It is undoubtedly biblical doctrine that Christ in His death has borne the penalty of our sin, and therefore released us from its punishment. *But the power of the blood of Christ is not limited to this.* The fundamental passage as to the question is the sixth of St. John. There the drinking of the blood of Christ is presented as the means of procuring eternal life. As the shedding of that blood brought about the death of redemption, so also it rendered it possible that the blood should be an open fountain which might overflow upon others: the death of the corn of wheat illustrates its effect—*that of life passing over as a power to others. Blood and life are, in the Scriptures, equivalent terms.* Where that is, there is this, for the life is in the blood according to Old Testament language. Thus, then, the καθαρισμὸς ἀπὸ πάσης ἁμαρτίας is possible only in consequence of the blood of Christ entering into our life as a new principle of life. There is absolutely no Christian sanctification imaginable which does not take place through the blood—that is, through the Redeemer's power of life working its effects and ruling within us."—(Haupt on 1 John i. 7, Clark's Translation.)

In the Revelation of St. John the connexion between deliverance from the power of sin, together with participation in the fulness of blessing prepared for the redeemed Church, and the "blood" of Christ, is especially marked. Thus in Chap. i. 5 we read, "Unto Him that loveth us and loosed" (not as in *Text. Rec.* "washed") "us from our sins in His blood." In Chap. v. 9, 10, where the four living creatures and the four and twenty elders sing the new song of the triumphant and glorified Church, it is of "blood," not of death only, that they sing,—"And they sing a new song saying, Worthy . . . for Thou wast slain, and didst purchase unto God in Thy blood *men* of every tribe, and tongue, and people, and nation, and madest them *to be* unto our God a kingdom and priests, and they reign upon the earth." In Chap. vii. 14 the great company before the throne of God and of the Lamb is described by the angel in the words, "they washed their robes, and made them white in the blood of the Lamb." And once more, in Chap. xii. 11, one of the means by which the redeemed in heaven have secured their victory is thus celebrated—"they overcame because of the blood of the Lamb."

Upon the great passage relative to the "blood" of Christ in the sixth chapter of the Gospel of St. John, we shall not dwell. It cannot be denied for a moment that the "blood" of Christ there spoken of is the "life" of Christ; and we remark only that it is impossible to exclude from the words the thought of the ever-living and glorified Redeemer, "He that eateth My flesh and drinketh My blood hath eternal life; and I will raise him up at the last day;" "What then if ye should behold the Son of man ascending up where He was before?" (John vi. 54, 60).

It is difficult to say whether there are any real exceptions to what has now been urged. Some of the exceptions that may be alleged are more apparent than real. They are passages in which, in speaking of the *death* of Christ, the sacred writer seems to connect it with the complete possession of Christ's heavenly life rather than with the initial act of forgiveness; or in which, speaking of the *blood* of Christ, he seems to connect it with the latter rather than with the former of these blessings. Of the first class of such passages we have examples in 2 Cor. v. 14, 15 and 1 Thess. v. 9, 10; of the second in Col. i. 20 and Eph. i. 7.

2 Cor. v. 14, 15.—"For the love of Christ constraineth us, because we thus judge, that one died for all, therefore all died; and He died for all, that they which live should no longer live unto themselves." These words, however, are immediately fol-

lowed before the conclusion of the sentence by others, "but unto
Him who for their sakes died and rose again." It is obvious
that the new life, as carried on in the soul, is thought of in connexion not merely with our Lord's dying but with His rising
again, in connexion with an aspect of His work which is wider
than death. In other words, the Apostle shows us that he has
here something more than Christ's death in view. Again, we
have 1 Thess. v. 9, 10,—" For God appointed us not unto death,
but unto the obtaining of salvation through our Lord Jesus Christ,
who died for us, that, whether we wake or sleep, we should live
together with Him." The last words, "together with Him,"
are, however, a sufficient proof that the Apostle, when he thus
speaks of "salvation," has in view not only the death of Christ,
but His life after death.

On the other hand, we have Col. i. 20.—" And through Him
to reconcile all things unto Himself, having made peace through
the blood of His cross." Yet it is unnecessary here to understand by "the blood of His cross," simply the blood as shed upon
the cross, and in the moment of its being shed. It is not less the
blood of His cross, though we think of it as taken within the veil,
because it was upon the cross that it was gained for our great
High Priest's further dealing with it. The expression, therefore,
may apply to the blood sprinkled as well as to the blood shed,
so that the reconciliation and making peace connected with it
will then have their customary, and not any exceptional, association. Remarks of a similar character will explain Eph. i. 7,
—" In whom we have our redemption, through His blood, even
the forgiveness of our trespasses ; " for, if we bear in mind not
only that the blood of the sacrifice is shed in its death, but that
the death is inflicted for the sake of shedding the blood, it is
obvious that the one may very easily be spoken of as accomplishing that which, *when the contrast of the two is distinctly before us,*
more properly belongs to the other.

Finally, there is yet one deeply important passage, which,
with its parallels in the Gospels, demands separate and special
consideration, 1 Cor. xi. 26,—" For as often as ye eat this bread,
and drink the cup, ye proclaim the Lord's death till He come."
Looked at in connexion with the words of institution, these
words of the Apostle seem at first sight to say that, even in the

highest act of the sacramental feast, that of *eating* the bread and *drinking* the wine, that is to say, in the moment when we have the most intimate communion and fellowship with our Lord, we are proclaiming His death alone. A closer attention to what is actually said will dispel this impression. For what is it of which St. Paul speaks? It is of the *Lord's* death,—the death, that is, not of Jesus of Nazareth only the humbled and suffering Son of man, but the death of Him who is now the Risen Lord, that same Lord spoken of in verse 23, and of whom the Apostle says, " For I received of the Lord that which also I delivered unto you." In the " Lord's death," therefore, which we proclaim in the sacrament of communion, we proclaim not only Jesus on the cross but the Lord exalted in heaven, and thus in the holy ordinance we have to deal with the loftiest not less than with the initial stage of Christian experience. In other words, the analogy of Scripture is still preserved when we speak of eating and drinking as associated not simply with the death of the suffering Redeemer, but with the death of Him who is our exalted and glorified Lord.

Nay, not only so. May we be allowed to submit for consideration that the two actions spoken of by the Apostle in the solemn passage before us hardly seem to be looked at by the Church in the light in which they presented themselves to St. Paul? In the way in which he is commonly interpreted, St. Paul is thought to speak of the death of Christ as represented in the ordinance of the Supper by the twofold act of breaking bread and pouring out wine. It will be observed, however, that the Apostle makes no mention of *pouring out*. He gives our Lord's words in the form, " In like manner also, the cup after supper, saying, This cup is the new covenant in My blood ; this do, as oft as ye drink it, in remembrance of Me " (1 Cor. xi. 25) ;[1] while immediately after-

[1] Even in the two earlier Gospels (Matt. xxvi. 28 ; Mark xiv. 24 ; comp. Luke xxii. 20), where the word " shed " can hardly be understood in any other light than as pointing to the death of Jesus, it does not appear to be necessary to confine the thought of the " blood " spoken of to the moment of bloodshedding. The clause, " for this is My blood," is immediately connected with the preceding " drink," and gives the ground ("for") why we are to drink. Then follows an explanation of the manner in which the blood is to be thought of as obtained,—a description given, because the *particular way* in which it has been obtained is that which makes it the foundation of our spiritual nourishment. It has been obtained by being " shed unto remission of sins." This description, however, is as truly applicable to Christ's

wards he dwells upon " eating" and " drinking " (ver. 26) as if the act of feasting were the point of view in which the ordinance is mainly to be considered by us; and feasting takes us beyond the thought of death or dying. Further, our Lord Himself speaks of His *body*, not of His flesh, as broken; and it seems difficult to answer the plea of Rome (however inadequate to justify her practice) in withholding the cup from the laity, that the blood is really given with the bread. Blood was a constituent part of the " body " of our Lord ; and it may be plausibly urged that the body cannot be given without it. In these circumstances we venture to ask, Whether the view is correct which looks upon the two actions referred to as designed, in their united character, to afford a representation of only one great fact—the death of Christ.[1] Is not the death expressed by the breaking of the bread alone? Is not the cup of wine representative of something more, of the blood of Christ as His continued *life*, of His exalted and glorified *life?* Do not the two actions, in short, divide themselves according to the words, " Ye proclaim the Lord's death until He come "?—the one symbolising " the Lord's death," the other, the life implied in the words " until He come." If there be any truth in what has now been said, it is obvious

blood in heaven as to His blood at the moment when it was shed. Throughout eternity it is blood "shed unto remission of sins." We are not, therefore, forbidden by the language of the first two Evangelists from thinking of Christ's blood in the words of institution as His blood, as His life, within the veil. The particular tense of the verb "shed" will even apply more easily to the thought of continued efficacy than to the thought of the one act upon the cross.

[1] It is thus, for example, that in the latest exposition of the doctrine of the Scottish Churches upon this point, Professor Candlish expresses himself— "It is plainly taught in Scripture that the Lord's Supper is a symbolical ordinance, and that the main thing that it represents is the death of Christ. This death is here symbolised, not as in the sacrifices of earlier ages, by the actual slaying of a living animal, but by the breaking of a piece of bread representing the body of Christ, and the presentation of wine in a cup representing the shed blood of Christ." And again, " We are not chiefly to think, in the Lord's Supper, of the body of Christ as now raised and glorified in Heaven, but rather of that body as it hung upon the cross, when His blood flowed forth, and He gave up His life a sacrifice to God ; we are to think of His body and blood with reference to this sacrifice offered on the cross" ("The Sacraments," pp. 93, 116. Comp. Hodge, "Syst. Theol." iii. p. 621. King, "On the Lord's Supper," p. 57 ; Bannerman, "The Church of Christ," ii. p. 132, etc.)

that the passage before us, so far from being at variance with the general view which we have been urging, is a powerful confirmation of its correctness.

What has been said with regard to the meaning of 1 Cor. xi. 25, 26, seems to be confirmed by the language of the same epistle in Chap. x. 15, 16,—"The cup of blessing which we bless, is it not a communion of the blood of Christ? The bread which we break, is it not a communion of the body of Christ? Because there is one loaf of bread, we the many are one body, for the whole of us partake from the one loaf." That St. Paul is here referring to the ordinance of the Supper no one doubts. But, if so, we are immediately led to ask why the natural order of the different parts of the service, the order of our Lord, the order of the Apostle himself in the following chapter, is changed. Hofmann answers the question by saying that St. Paul is occupied less with the thought of the nourishment afforded by the idol feast than with the thought of that joyful association of the participators which came to view with peculiar prominence in their common sharing of the wine. But Hofmann thus loses sight of the leading aim of the passage, which is to show that participation in idol feasts is, on the part of those who share in them, a communion not so much with one another as with demons (Comp. ver. 20). Their *mutual* communion is subordinate to this, and is mentioned mainly for the purpose of proving that no one who broke the bread of the Lord's Supper could possibly separate himself from the communion of the body of Christ implied in doing so. The true reason why the order of the service is changed in the Apostle's words appears to be, that the first part mentioned is more in accordance with his argument than the second. His readers would see that communion with demons supposed to be living was the meaning of the idol feast, if they bore in mind that communion with the Living Lord was the meaning of their drinking of the cup of blessing. In other words, the "blood" of Christ is here again the life of Christ, of Christ exalted and glorified. Christians at an idol feast sinned not merely against one truth, but against two truths expressed by them in their own sacred meal,—first, that they had their life in the Living Lord; secondly, that having their life in Him, they also shared a communion of His body which so united them to His body that they could not at the same time share a communion with a body of demon-worshippers. The first of these truths being at once the deeper and more important of the two, and that out of which the other flowed, is placed first in order. Had the thought of drinking of the cup not been a profounder thought than that of breaking the bread,—had the drinking only been one of two parts of a service which, in their union, expressed the same idea of participation in the death of Christ,—the Apostle would not have changed the order of the parts as he has done.

This steadfast adherence of the New Testament writers to the mention of the "blood" rather than the "death" of Christ, whenever they speak not of the pardon of sin only, but of full admission to all that is secured for us in the New Covenant, and especially of admission to the life of union with God, both here and hereafter, is surely very worthy of notice. That the connexion between the blood and the death is of the closest kind we most readily admit ; and had there been only one action with the blood in the Old Testament sin-offering, we should at once allow that, as the blood was obtained by the death of the victim, its "death" and its "blood" might be viewed as interchangeable terms. We know, however, that there were not only two actions with the blood, but that the latter of the two—the Sprinkling—was the culminating part of the ritual. We know, also, that every part of the ritual had a definite meaning. It is thus impossible to avoid the conclusion that the blood and the death were not entirely co-extensive with one another, and that the interpretation of the former is not to be limited by that of the latter. This conclusion is confirmed when we find that the New Testament writers, in making their application of the type, for the most part at least apply it in such a way that each part of the fulfilment corresponds, not merely to a separate part of the type, but to that part which was precisely fitted to express it. As the Slaughtering is the type of the penalty of sin, and the Sprinkling the type of the union of the life with God after the penalty has been paid, so the "death" of Christ is mainly connected with pardon, the "blood" of Christ with fellowship with the Father in all its blessed consequences, both for time and for eternity.

One remark only, already more than once indicated, either in the present Lectures or in these Notes, it is necessary emphatically to repeat. The death of Christ never loses its significance. That significance is eternal. To the latest moment of his life on earth the Christian traces all the privileges which he enjoys to the death of Christ, and beholds in it the first great act by which his Lord opened up to him the way to the Father. It is not otherwise when he enters the heavenly glory, where his song shall be to the Lamb that was slain. But it is not the less true that, if the views of which we have spoken, and which seem to be unfolded in the New Testament, are well founded, they must exercise a powerful influence over the whole Christian life. The blood of Christ is not simply His death ; it is more than blood shed on Calvary for remission of sin. It is Christ's life, the life by which we live ; and our Christian life is not led only in the grateful recollection of death endured for us, but is continually nourished by our living in the life of Him whose offering of Himself to the Father, with His people in Him, is only completed in the heavenly Sanctuary. Participation in this heavenly life is alone participation in the blood of Christ, for the blood of Christ is not His death, but His life, won through death, in heaven.

## Note 54, p. 141.

It seems to be now generally agreed, however much it may once have been disputed, that a distinction is to be drawn between the original word for spirit, when it has and has not the article prefixed to it. In the one case the expression denotes the Holy Spirit in His Personality, in the other the power or operation or gift of the Spirit. In the words quoted in the text the article is not found, so that they denote here not the Personal Spirit, but the Spirit as bestowed upon or received by man. "The necessary limitations," says Westcott (*in loc.*) "of Christ's historical presence with the disciples excluded that realisation of His abiding presence which followed on the Resurrection." It is much to be regretted that translators of the New Testament have not observed this distinction as they ought to have done. The idiom of the English language may not always easily permit it, but there are many passages—the present being one of them—where it is perfectly possible to indicate the true meaning. Even in most others the ear would soon have become accustomed to the sound, and it may well be doubted whether translators are entitled to sacrifice the sense of Scripture to the supposed requirements of English idiom.

## NOTE 55, p. 141.

John iii. 34.—It is of importance to observe that the words of the Authorised Version, "*unto him,*" as is indeed indicated by their being printed in italics, have no right to a place in the text. The giving of the Spirit here referred to is not to be confined to our Lord Himself. To Him indeed, as the "Sent of God," the Spirit is given first and in all His fulness; but He will be given equally without stint, according to their capacity for receiving Him, to all who are "sent" to do, in the name of Christ, God's work in the world.

## NOTE 56, p. 152.

The view taken in the text of the meaning of Rom. iv. 25, appears to be demanded by the principles of fair and legitimate interpretation. It is indeed difficult to account for the fact that any other view should ever have been adopted, and that the text should have occasioned such an amount of difficulty alike to Lutheran and Reformed divines. Perhaps no text in the New Testament has had to bear the burden of so many subtle distinctions, or of such far-fetched and roundabout explanations. This, too, is the more remarkable when we consider that the distinctions and explanations so ingeniously devised are more difficult to reconcile with the different systems of Protestant Theology than the simple and natural interpretation of the words. Two points must be kept distinctly in view; first, that in both clauses of the verse we have the preposition διά with the accusative case; and secondly, that in two clauses so obviously parallel, and so directly contrasted with one another, the meaning of the preposition must not be changed. Surely, had St. Paul designed to express in the second clause a relation between "our justification" and Christ's Resurrection different from that expressed in the first between "our trespasses" and Christ's death, he would have used a different preposition. The Greek language was abundantly able to supply him with what he needed, and it is unnecessary to say that the resources of that language were fully at his command. We must regard, therefore, the argument whether of Grammarians or Commentators, that the prepositions are here used loosely, as not less objectionable than the opinion that we have to deal with "rhetorical exaggeration of expression." Starting with these two points as accepted, it follows at once that in both clauses of the text before us διά denotes the *ground* upon which the thing spoken of rests, in neither clause the *end* for which it is done. Even Steinmeyer, who sees so clearly the errors of his predecessors, has contended that a distinction of this kind must be made. " Our offences," he says, "were the *ground* on account of which Jesus was offered ; our justification was the *end* for which God raised him from the dead " ("The Passion and Resurrection History," Clark's Translation, p. 253). Such a distinction, like every other proposed before, is inadmissible. The same preposition governing the same case in both clauses must be understood in both to express precisely similar relations between the things in connexion with which it is used by the Apostle. Christ's death rested upon the fact of our trespasses, His Resurrection upon the fact of our justification. We had sinned, therefore He died to procure for us the pardon of sin, and to restore us to the favour of God,—in other words, to justify us. He did thus justify us ; therefore He was raised again. Had we not sinned, His death would not have taken place ; had His death not accomplished its purpose, His Resurrection would not have taken place. The trespasses in the one clause, the justification in the other, are the *ground* upon which God delivered Him up to death, and afterwards raised Him from the grave. We urge that no other interpretation of these clauses is grammatically or exegetically possible.

If so, it may be added in one or two brief sentences that the gain of thus looking at the words is great. (1.) All danger of confounding justification with sanctification is avoided. How imminent that danger is may be seen in the laboured and anxious attempts of Lutheran expositors to escape the charge of failing, by their interpretation " for," to keep these two things sufficiently distinct ; by the utterly mistaken rendering of Olshausen, who is driven to the position that δικαίωσις is " the act which makes righteous and creates the new man " (*in loc.*) ; and by the fact that even Steinmeyer, who rejects this last view, hardly escapes it, if indeed he escapes it at all, when he urges that the only ground on which it becomes possible for God to impute to us the righteousness of Christ is, that He beholds in the Risen Christ "the pledge for believers *actually becoming righteous*" (*u.s.*, p. 256). (2.) The doctrine of the New Testament, that our justification is secured by the one complete sacrifice of Himself by our Lord upon the cross to expiate the guilt of sin, and that in no sense whatever is His Resurrection essential to the completion of that particular part of His work, is left untouched. (3.) We have a powerful confirmation of the truth, so often lost sight of, that "justification" is not "salvation." (4.) The mind is kept fixed on the point to which the whole context calls attention, viz. on *the fact that Christ was raised*, not on the purpose for which His Resurrection took place (comp. verses 17 and the first half of verse 24).

It is satisfactory to find Godet in his recent Commentary on the Romans defending the view here taken. But Godet is wrong in the idea which he seems to entertain, that his interpretation is new. It is found in the "Annotations" to the Bible prepared by order of the Westminster Assembly, A.D. 1651, in which (*in loc.*) it is said, " God having declared by raising him from the dead that he hath accepted of the death of his Sonne as of a sufficient ransom for our sinnes." Dr. Jukes, too, in his "Law of the Offerings," p. 146, speaks as follows :—" It is no future work, no promised work, no work to be yet accomplished, but a finished work, which is our sure foundation. 'He bore our sins;' this is God's testimony ; and having borne them he was raised *because we were justified* (Rom. iv. 25). Had we not been justified Christ could not have been raised. His Resurrection, and ours in Him, is the proof that we are justified." Comp. also Horsley, "Nine Sermons," p. 251.

## Note 57, p. 158.

John xvii. 21-23.—The reading which omits the word "one" in the clause "that they themselves also may be in us" of ver 21, ought not to pass unnoticed, or its effect in bringing out our union to the Son, and in Him to the Father, before we are united to our brethren in Christ.

## NOTE 58, p. 160.

It is impossible to discuss in such a note as can be given here the important reading adopted in the text. For an elaborate and able defence of it, reference may be made to a Dissertation by Dr. Hort of Cambridge, published by Macmillan and Co. A fuller explanation of the reading, as adopted, will be found in the Commentary on the fourth Gospel already mentioned in these Notes.

## NOTE 59, p. 163.

1 Cor. xv. 47.—The correct reading which here omits " the Lord" of the A. V. must first be noted (comp. Note 52). The immediate context, to say nothing of the whole strain of the chapter, is then sufficient to prove that the reference to Jesus as the Second Adam is a reference to Him, not as He came into this world at His Incarnation, and not as He manifested Himself on earth in *His whole personality as the God-man* (Alford *in loc.*), but in what He became at His Resurrection. Comp. especially verses 45 and 49. (See also Meyer, Hofmann, Kling, Stanley, *in loc.*)

## NOTE 60, p. 169.

2 Cor. iii. 18.—The argument of the Apostle seems distinctly to imply that by "the glory of the Lord" here spoken of we are to understand His glory in His Risen and Glorified condition, and that by the "mirror" referred to, the mirror of the Gospel "word" cannot be meant. The thought appears rather to be,—The glory of God's presence shone upon Moses when he was taken up into the mount; and, as it shone upon him, it changed his countenance into a likeness with itself, so that the face of Moses also shone. We Christians are now in the position of the great leader of Israel. We ascend spiritually into the mount where the Glorified Redeemer is. He shines upon us; and, as a mirror reflects the object placed before it, so we reflect the glory of the Lord in His exalted state. This, too, we "reflect from glory to glory;" *from* glory in Him, as the efficient cause of the change in us, *to* glory in us as the result produced; and all as "from the Lord *who is* spirit," because as spirit He acts upon our spirits, and conforms us to Himself.

### NOTE 61, p. 173.

The two places referred to are Heb. vii. 28 and x. 20, in the first of which for the word "consecrated" of the A. V. we ought to read "perfected;" and in the second "dedicated." On the other hand, there are not a few passages in which the substitution of "consecrate" for "sanctify" would bring out the meaning intended with new clearness and power. Comp. John x. 36; xvii. 17, 19; Heb. ii. 11; ix. 13; x. 10, 14, 29; xiii. 12. Dr. Moulton, on Heb. ii. 11, remarks most appropriately, "The special meaning of 'sanctify' in this Epistle seems to be *bringing into fellowship with God*, the Holy One."

### NOTE 62, p. 177.

An attentive consideration of the texts here referred to will at once bear out what has been said. It is only indeed in the case of John iv. 38, that any doubt upon the point for the sake of which they are quoted could be entertained. Yet the context in that case shows that, throughout the whole passage in which the text occurs, our Lord speaks of Himself (together, perhaps, with those who had gone before Him) as the only sower, and that He regards His disciples, not as men sent out to sow in a cold and ungenial Spring, but as men sent out to reap amidst the fruitfulness and joy of harvest. There can be no doubt as to the self-denial and suffering which are necessary in the living of the Christian life; but the pain of these, as they are rendered necessary by the prevalence of sin both without us and within us, is transformed in the service of Christ into an easy yoke and light burden. It is the world which presents a conflict: what Christ gives is victory; "This is the victory that overcometh the world, even our faith" (1 John v. 4).

### NOTE 63, p. 182.

An expression occurs occasionally in the Gospel of St. John to which less attention than it deserves seems to have been paid. It is the expression ἐν ἑαυτοῖς, in circumstances where we should rather expect to meet ἐν ὑμῖν—Chaps. v. 42, vi. 53. Comp. 1 John iii. 15, v. 10, though the reading in these two passages is somewhat doubtful. The emphasis belonging to this expres-

sion, which is very inadequately rendered "in you," may be best
seen by comparing other passages of the same Gospel, where our
Lord is spoken of in a precisely similar way—Chaps. v. 26,
vi. 61. The words seem designed to bring out in a forcible
manner that lesson of the personal individuality and moral
freedom of the believer which is so strikingly characteristic of
a Gospel often thought to teach the very contrary. It ought
hardly to be necessary to say that "*in* himself" conveys a very
different meaning from "*of* himself."

### Note 64, p. 189.

The rendering of John iv. 23 adopted in this Lecture has
not, so far as the writer knows, been before proposed by any
commentator. He may, therefore, be allowed to refer to the
Commentary on the Gospel of St. John already spoken of, where
it is defended at some length. The defence need not be repeated
here.

### Note 65, p. 194.

The relation in which the gift of the Holy Spirit spoken
of in John xx. 22 stands to that of Pentecost is not easily
determined.

In the first place, it may be observed that it is hardly possible
to draw any broad line of demarcation between them, as if the
latter alone were, strictly speaking, the bestowal of the Spirit,
the former that of the breath of our Lord's glorified humanity.
It is true that at John xiv. 16 our Lord says, "I will pray the
*Father*, and He shall give you another Advocate, that He may
abide with you for ever;" that at Chap. xiv. 26 He speaks of
"the Advocate, which is the Holy Spirit, whom the *Father* will
send" in His name; and that at Chap. xv. 26 the Advocate
is described as "the Spirit of truth which proceedeth from the
*Father*." These passages may appear to connect the gift of the
Spirit with the time when Jesus should have already ascended
to "His Father and our Father, to His God and our God." But,
on the other hand, we have seen in these Lectures that the
Session at the right hand of God is only a part of our Lord's
general Glorification, not a new stage of being, to be distinguished
from that upon which He entered when He came forth from the

grave; and in ver. 17 of this chapter Jesus had said to Mary Magdalene, not "I will ascend unto My Father," but "I ascend;" "I am even now in the act of ascending—My Ascension is begun" (Comp. Ellicott, "Life of Christ," p. 387). The circumstances of our Lord in John xx. and on the day of Pentecost are not so different as to lead to the idea that the gift bestowed on the two occasions was different. On both occasions our Lord's position was substantially the same.

In the second place, it hardly seems as if we were to seek the relation of the two gifts to one another in this,—that in the first we are to find only an initial fulfilment of what was afterwards perfectly accomplished, a first-fruits of the coming harvest; in the second the harvest itself. There is nothing in the words of Scripture to indicate that in the one case the gift was partial, in the other complete. It would rather appear as if the gift bestowed in John xx. were the more perfect, the more comprehensive, of the two. It is more immediately connected with the Person of the glorified Redeemer:—"He breathed on them, and said, Receive ye holy spirit." At Acts ii. 2, again, we are simply told that "suddenly there came a sound from heaven as of a rushing mighty wind. . . . . And they were all filled with holy spirit, and began to speak with new tongues, as the Spirit gave them utterance." While thus more immediately connected with Jesus as its source, the gift in John xx. is also associated with functions of a deeper and more intimate kind than belong to any miraculous agency whatever. In the one case it is breathed into, in the other it is poured upon, the disciples; and life itself is a greater gift than any of the powers of life.

In the third place, therefore, it would seem as if we were to seek the difference between the two gifts not so much in the *kind* or *degree* of either as in its *purpose* and *application*. The first had relation to the inner training of the disciples, the second to their more outward equipment for their work; the first to the enlightening and quickening of their own souls, the second to the furnishing them with what was needed to enable them to produce an effect on others; the first to the Church in her private chamber, the second to the Church as she is introduced to her mission in the world. At the baptism of our Lord the Spirit descended and abode upon Him; but He waited for a time before He entered "in the power of the Spirit" upon His public ministry. In like manner the disciples were made ready for their work at the time when their Risen Lord breathed on them; but they had to wait, before entering on their work, for the appointed hour when, at the great feast which had long foreshadowed the event, they were to offer up, not merely ripening ears of corn, but loaves baked and ready, the first-fruits of the new age.

## NOTE 66, p. 194.

It may seem as if Matt. xvi. 18 and xviii. 17 were at variance with the statements here made. But further consideration of these passages will show that in both our Lord has His future Church in view—certainly neither the Jewish Synagogue nor the Christian Hierarchy in any form. The words of Matt. xviii. 20 are sufficient to decide the question, where our Lord, in close connexion with what He had been saying, adds, "For where two or three are gathered together in My name, there am I in the midst of them." (Comp. the remarks of Stier upon this passsage in his "Reden Jesu," Part ii. p. 283.)

## NOTE 67, p. 194.

We believe that it will be found, upon careful examination of John xiv. xv. xvi., that these chapters do not refer to living, personal union with Christ considered in itself, so much as to the active Christian work which proceeds from such union, and is maintained in vigour by its means alone. This appears especially in the general contrast of Chap. xiv. with Chaps. xv. and xvi. The former exhibits the *preparation* of the disciples for their work; they "are" in Christ, and He in them. The two latter exhibit the disciples *in their work itself*, as they struggle, suffer, bear fruit, and triumph in it. They now "abide" in Christ; and *abiding* presupposes difficulty and trial.

## NOTE 68, p. 195.

Reference may be made to the valuable work of Bishop Moberly, "The Sayings of the Forty Days;" and also to Dr. Hanna's interesting volume, "The Forty Days after our Lord's Resurrection."

NOTE 69, p. 195.

Comp. Steinmeyer, " The Passion and Resurrection History,"
Clark's Translation, pp. 313, 337.

NOTE 70, p. 211.

Comp. the Comment. of Dr. Westcott on John xii. 32,—" The
phrase by which the Lord indicates His death (*be lifted up*,
iii. 14, viii. 28 ; comp. Acts ii. 32, v. 11) is characteristic of
the view under which St. John represents the Passion. He does
not ever, like St. Paul (*e.g.* Phil. ii. 8, 9) separate it as a crisis
of humiliation from the glory which followed. The " lifting up"
includes death and the victory over death. In this aspect the
crisis of the Passion itself is regarded as a glorification (xiii. 31) ;
and St. John sees the Lord's triumph in this rather than in the
return (Comp. 1 John v. 4-6). See also Note 50, p. 262.

NOTE 71, p. 212.

On Hebrews ii. 9 comp. the valuable note of Dr. Moulton
(*in loc.*) Speaking of the last clause, Dr. Moulton says, " We
cannot doubt that these words depend on those which immediately precede." Comp. also the following remarks of Godet on
Rom. i. 3, 4, which, always excepting his erroneous view that
Jesus, while on earth, was only Son of David, not Son of God,
deserve consideration :—" He (Jesus) has left in the tomb His
particular relation to the Jewish nation and the family of David,
and has appeared, through His Resurrection, freed from those
wrappings which He had humbly worn during His earthly life ;
comp. the remarkable expression, *Minister of the circumcision*,
xv. 8. Thus it is that in virtue of His Resurrection, and as the
Son of God, He was able henceforth to enter into connexion with
all mankind, which He could not do so long as He was acting
only as the Son of David ; comp. Matt. xv. 24 ; ' I am not sent
but unto the lost sheep of the house of Israel.' "

## NOTE 72, p. 213.

The statement made in the text is mainly grounded upon the general teaching of our Lord in the Gospel of St. John. There is one passage in that Gospel (Chap. xv. 26, 27) which at first sight may seem to lead to an opposite conclusion, but which, on further consideration, appears rather to confirm it. The words of this passage are,—" When the Advocate is come, whom I will send unto you from the Father, the Spirit of the truth, which goeth forth from the Father, He will bear witness concerning Me; and ye also bear witness, because from the beginning ye are with Me."

These words are so important, that I venture to quote the following remarks on them from the Commentary on the fourth Gospel already more than once referred to in these Notes:— " The Advocate shall be with them, and with them in a manner adapted to that stage of progress which they are thought of as having reached. In the promise of the Advocate here given there is an advance upon that of Chap. xiv. 16, 26. In the latter passage the promise had been connected with the *training* of the disciples for their work; in the present it is connected with the *execution* of the work. First of all, the Advocate ' will bear witness' concerning Jesus, will perform that work of witnessing which belongs to heralds of the Cross. *But He will do this in them.* We are not to imagine that His is an independent work, carried on directly in the world, and apart from the instrumentality of the disciples. It is true that there is a general influence of the Holy Spirit by which He prepares the ear to hear and the eye to see—such an influence as that with which He wrought in Judaism, and even in heathenism; but that is not the influence of which Jesus speaks in the words before us. It is a specific influence, the *power* of the Spirit, to which He refers,—that influence which, exerted through Himself when He was upon the earth, is now exerted through the members of His Body. In the two last verses of this chapter, therefore, we have not two works of witnessing, the first that of the Advocate, the second that of the disciples. We have only one,— outwardly that of the disciples, inwardly that of the Advocate.

Hence the change of tense from the future to the present, when Jesus speaks of ' ye,'—the Advocate ' will bear witness,' ye ' bear witness.' The two witnessings are not on parallel lines, but on the same line, the former coming to view only in and by the latter, into which the power of the former is introduced. Hence, also, the force of the emphatic ' Ye.' The personality and freedom of the disciples does not disappear under this operation of the Advocate ; they do not become mechanical agents, they retain their individual standing ; they are still men, only higher than they could otherwise have been."

# TEXTS MORE OR LESS DISCUSSED IN THE
## LECTURES AND NOTES.

THE END.

*Printed by* R. & R. Clark, *Edinburgh.*

*May,* 1879.

# A CATALOGUE of THEOLOGICAL BOOKS, with a Short Account of their Character and Aim,

### Published by

# MACMILLAN AND CO.

### Bedford Street, Strand, London, W.C.

---

**Abbott (Rev. E. A.)**—Works by the Rev. E. A. ABBOTT, D.D., Head Master of the City of London School :

BIBLE LESSONS. Second Edition. Crown 8vo. 4s. 6d.

"*Wise, suggestive, and really profound initiation into religious thought.*" —Guardian. *The Bishop of St. David's, in his speech at the Education Conference at Abergwilly, says he thinks "nobody could read them without being the better for them himself, and being also able to see how this difficult duty of imparting a sound religious education may be effected.*"

THE GOOD VOICES : A Child's Guide to the Bible. With upwards of 50 Illustrations. Crown 8vo. cloth gilt. 5s.

"*It would not be easy to combine simplicity with fulness and depth of meaning more successfully than Mr. Abbott has done.*"—Spectator. *The* Times *says*—"*Mr. Abbott writes with clearness, simplicity, and the deepest religious feeling.*"

CAMBRIDGE SERMONS PREACHED BEFORE THE UNIVERSITY. Second Edition. 8vo. 6s.

3,000 : 5 : 79.

**ABBOTT** (Rev. E. A.)—*continued.*

THROUGH NATURE TO CHRIST; or, The Ascent of
Worship through Illusion to the Truth.   8vo.   12*s*. 6*d*.

"*The beauty of its style, its tender feeling, and its perfect sympathy, the
originality and suggestiveness of many of its thoughts, would of themselves go far to recommend it.   But far besides these, it has a certain
value in its bold, comprehensive, trenchant method of apology, and in the
adroitness with which it turns the flank of the many modern fallacies that
caricature in order to condemn Christianity.*"—Church Quarterly Review.

**Ainger** (Rev. Alfred).—SERMONS PREACHED IN
THE TEMPLE CHURCH.   By the Rev. ALFRED AINGER,
M.A. of Trinity Hall, Cambridge, Reader at the Temple Church.
Extra fcap. 8vo.   6*s*.

"*It is,*" *the* British Quarterly *says,* "*the fresh unconventional talk of a
clear independent thinker, addressed to a congregation of thinkers* . . . .
*Thoughtful men will be greatly charmed by this little volume.*"

**Alexander.**—THE LEADING IDEAS of the GOSPELS.
Five Sermons preached before the University of Oxford in 1870—
71.   By WILLIAM ALEXANDER, D.D., Brasenose College; Lord
Bishop of Derry and Raphoe; Select Preacher.   Cr. 8vo.   4*s*. 6*d*.

"*Eloquence and force of language, clearness of statement, and a hearty
appreciation of the grandeur and importance of the topics upon which he
writes, characterize his sermons.*"—Record.

**Arnold.**—Works by MATTHEW ARNOLD :

A BIBLE READING FOR SCHOOLS.   THE GREAT
PROPHECY OF ISRAEL'S RESTORATION (Isaiah, Chapters 40—66).
Arranged and Edited for Young Learners.   By MATTHEW ARNOLD,
D.C.L., formerly Professor of Poetry in the University of Oxford,
and Fellow of Oriel.   Third Edition.   18mo. cloth.   1*s*.

*The* Times *says*—"*Whatever may be the fate of this little book in
Government Schools, there can be no doubt that it will be found excellently
calculated to further instruction in Biblical literature in any school into
which it may be introduced.* . . . *We can safely say that whatever school uses
this book, it will enable its pupils to understand Isaiah, a great advantage
compared with other establishments which do not avail themselves of it.*"

ISAIAH XL.—LXVI., with the Shorter Prophecies allied
to it.   Arranged and Edited with Notes.   Crown 8vo.   5*s*.

**Bather.**—ON SOME MINISTERIAL DUTIES, CATE-
CHISING, PREACHING, &c.   Charges by the late Archdeacon
BATHER.   Edited, with Preface, by Dr. C. J. VAUGHAN.   Extra
fcap. 8vo.   4*s*. 6*d*.

**Benham.**—A COMPANION TO THE LECTIONARY, being a Commentary on the Proper Lessons for Sundays and Holydays. By the Rev. W. BENHAM, B.D., Vicar of Margate. Cheaper Edition. Crown 8vo. 6s.

"*A very useful book. Mr. Benham has produced a good and welcome companion to our revised Lectionary. Its contents will, if not very original or profound, prove to be sensible and practical, and often suggestive to the preacher and the Sunday School teacher. They will also furnish some excellent Sunday reading for private hours.*"—Guardian.

**Bernard.**—THE PROGRESS OF DOCTRINE IN THE NEW TESTAMENT. By THOMAS D. BERNARD, M.A., Rector of Walcot and Canon of Wells. Third and Cheaper Edition. Crown 8vo. 5s. (Bampton Lectures for 1864.)

"*We lay down these lectures with a sense not only of being edified by sound teaching and careful thought, but also of being gratified by conciseness and clearness of expression and elegance of style.*"—Churchman.

**Binney.**—SERMONS PREACHED IN THE KING'S WEIGH HOUSE CHAPEL, 1829—69. By THOMAS BINNEY, D.D. New and Cheaper Edition. Extra fcap. 8vo. 4s. 6d.

"*Full of robust intelligence, of reverent but independent thinking on the most profound and holy themes, and of earnest practical purpose.*"—London Quarterly Review.

A SECOND SERIES OF SERMONS. Edited, with Biographical and Critical Sketch, by the Rev. HENRY ALLON, D.D. With Portrait of Dr. Binney engraved by JEENS. 8vo. 12s.

**Birks.**—Works by T. R. BIRKS, M.A., Professor of Moral Philosophy, Cambridge :

THE DIFFICULTIES OF BELIEF in connection with the Creation and the Fall, Redemption and Judgment. Second Edition, enlarged. Crown 8vo. 5s.

AN ESSAY ON THE RIGHT ESTIMATION OF MSS. EVIDENCE IN THE TEXT OF THE NEW TESTAMENT. Crown 8vo. 3s. 6d.

COMMENTARY ON THE BOOK OF ISAIAH, Critical, Historical and Prophetical; including a Revised English Translation. With Introduction and Appendices on the Nature of Scripture Prophecy, the Life and Times of Isaiah, the Genuineness of the Later Prophecies, the Structure and History of the whole Book, the Assyrian History in Isaiah's Days, and various Difficult Passages. Second Edition, revised. 8vo. 12s. 6d.

SUPERNATURAL REVELATION, or First Principles of Moral Theology. 8vo. 8s.

**Bradby.**—SERMONS PREACHED AT HAILEYBURY. By E. H. BRADBY, M.A., Master. 8vo. 10s. 6d.

*"He who claims a public hearing now, speaks to an audience accustomed to Cotton, Temple, Vaughan, Bradley, Butler, Farrar, and others......Each has given us good work, several, work of rare beauty, force, or originality; but we doubt whether any one of them has touched deeper chords, or brought more freshness and strength into his sermons, than the last of their number, the present Head Master of Haileybury."*—Spectator.

**Butcher.**—THE ECCLESIASTICAL CALENDAR; its Theory and Construction. By SAMUEL BUTCHER, D.D., late Bishop of Meath. 4to. 14s.

**Butler (G.)**—Works by the Rev. GEORGE BUTLER, M.A., Principal of Liverpool College:

FAMILY PRAYERS. Crown 8vo. 5s.

*The prayers in this volume are all based on passages of Scripture—the morning prayers on Select Psalms, those for the evening on portions of the New Testament.*

SERMONS PREACHED in CHELTENHAM COLLEGE CHAPEL. Crown 8vo. 7s. 6d.

**Butler (Rev. H. M.)**—SERMONS PREACHED in the CHAPEL OF HARROW SCHOOL. By H. MONTAGU BUTLER, Head Master. Crown 8vo. 7s. 6d.

*"These sermons are adapted for every household. There is nothing more striking than the excellent good sense with which they are imbued."*—Spectator.

A SECOND SERIES. Crown 8vo. 7s. 6d.

*"Excellent specimens of what sermons should be—plain, direct, practical, pervaded by the true spirit of the Gospel, and holding up lofty aims before the minds of the young."*—Athenæum.

**Butler (Rev. W. Archer).**—Works by the Rev. WILLIAM ARCHER BUTLER, M.A., late Professor of Moral Philosophy in the University of Dublin:

SERMONS, DOCTRINAL AND PRACTICAL. Edited, with a Memoir of the Author's Life, by THOMAS WOODWARD, Dean of Down. With Portrait. Ninth Edition. 8vo. 8s.

*The Introductory Memoir narrates in considerable detail and with much interest, the events of Butler's brief life; and contains a few specimens of his poetry, and a few extracts from his addresses and essays, including a long and eloquent passage on the Province and Duty of the Preacher.*

**BUTLER (Rev. W. Archer)**—*continued.*

A SECOND SERIES OF SERMONS. Edited by J. A. JEREMIE, D.D., Dean of Lincoln. Seventh Edition. 8vo. 7*s.*

*The* North British Review *says, " Few sermons in our language exhibit the same rare combination of excellencies; imagery almost as rich as Taylor's; oratory as vigorous often as South's; judgment as sound as Barrow's; a style as attractive but more copious, original, and forcible than Atterbury's; piety as elevated as Howe's, and a fervour as intense at times as Baxter's. Mr. Butler's are the sermons of a true poet."*

LETTERS ON ROMANISM, in reply to Dr. Newman's Essay on Development. Edited by the Dean of Down. Second Edition, revised by Archdeacon HARDWICK. 8vo. 10*s.* 6*d.*

*These Letters contain an exhaustive criticism of Dr. Newman's famous " Essay on the Development of Christian Doctrine." " A work which ought to be in the Library of every student of Divinity."*—BP. ST. DAVID'S.

**Campbell.**—Works by JOHN M'LEOD CAMPBELL :

THE NATURE OF THE ATONEMENT AND ITS RELATION TO REMISSION OF SINS AND ETERNAL LIFE. Fourth and Cheaper Edition, crown 8vo. 6*s.*

*"Among the first theological treatises of this generation."*—Guardian.
*" One of the most remarkable theological books ever written."*—Times.

CHRIST THE BREAD OF LIFE. An Attempt to give a profitable direction to the present occupation of Thought with Romanism. Second Edition, greatly enlarged. Crown 8vo. 4*s.* 6*d.*

*" Deserves the most attentive study by all who interest themselves in the predominant religious controversy of the day."*—Spectator.

REMINISCENCES AND REFLECTIONS, referring to his Early Ministry in the Parish of Row, 1825—31. Edited with an Introductory Narrative by his Son, DONALD CAMPBELL, M.A., Chaplain of King's College, London. Crown 8vo. 7*s.* 6*d.*

*These ' Reminiscences and Reflections,' written during the last year of his life, were mainly intended to place on record thoughts which might prove helpful to others. " We recommend this book cordially to all who are interested in the great cause of religious reformation."*—Times. *" There is a thoroughness and depth, as well as a practical earnestness, in his grasp of each truth on which he dilates, which make his reflections very valuable."*—Literary Churchman.

THOUGHTS ON REVELATION, with Special Reference to the Present Time. Second Edition. Crown 8vo. 5*s.*

**CAMPBELL (J. M'Leod)**—*continued*.

RESPONSIBILITY FOR THE GIFT OF ETERNAL LIFE. Compiled by permission of the late J. M'Leod Campbell, D.D., from Sermons preached chiefly at Row in 1829—31. Crown 8vo. 5s.
"*There is a healthy tone as well as a deep pathos not often seen in sermons. His words are weighty and the ideas they express tend to perfection of life.*"—Westminster Review.

**Campbell (Lewis).**—SOME ASPECTS OF THE CHRISTIAN IDEAL. Sermons by the Rev. L. Campbell, M.A., LL.D., Professor of Greek in the University of Glasgow. Crown 8vo. 6s.

**Canterbury.**—Works by Archibald Campbell, Archbishop of Canterbury :

THE PRESENT POSITION OF THE CHURCH OF ENGLAND. Seven Addresses delivered to the Clergy and Church-wardens of his Diocese, as his Charge, at his Primary Visitation, 1872. Third Edition. 8vo. cloth. 3s. 6d.

SOME THOUGHTS ON THE DUTIES OF THE ESTABLISHED CHURCH OF ENGLAND as a National Church. Seven Addresses delivered at his Second Visitation. 8vo. 4s. 6d.

**Cheyne.**—Works by T. K. Cheyne, M.A., Fellow of Balliol College, Oxford :

THE BOOK OF ISAIAH CHRONOLOGICALLY ARRANGED. An Amended Version, with Historical and Critical Introductions and Explanatory Notes. Crown 8vo. 7s. 6d.
*The* Westminster Review *speaks of it as "a piece of scholarly work, very carefully and considerately done." The* Academy *calls it "a successful attempt to extend a right understanding of this important Old Testament writing."*

NOTES AND CRITICISMS on the HEBREW TEXT OF ISAIAH. Crown 8vo. 2s. 6d.

**Choice Notes on the Four Gospels,** drawn from Old and New Sources. Crown 8vo. 4s. 6d. each Vol. (St. Matthew and St. Mark in one Vol. price 9s.)

**Church.**—Works by the Very Rev. R. W. Church, M.A., D.C.L., Dean of St. Paul's :

ON SOME INFLUENCES OF CHRISTIANITY UPON NATIONAL CHARACTER. Three Lectures delivered in St. Paul's Cathedral, Feb. 1873. Crown 8vo. 4s. 6d.

**CHURCH (Very Rev. R. W.)**—*continued.*

"*Few books that we have met with have given us keener pleasure than this....... It would be a real pleasure to quote extensively, so wise and so true, so tender and so discriminating are Dean Church's judgments, but the limits of our space are inexorable. We hope the book will be bought.*" —Literary Churchman.

THE SACRED POETRY OF EARLY RELIGIONS. Two Lectures in St. Paul's Cathedral. 18mo. 1s. I. The Vedas. II. The Psalms.

ST. ANSELM. Second Edition. Crown 8vo. 6s.

"*It is a sketch by the hand of a master, with every line marked by taste, learning, and real apprehension of the subject.*"—Pall Mall Gazette.

HUMAN LIFE AND ITS CONDITIONS. Sermons preached before the University of Oxford, 1876—78, with Three Ordination Sermons. Crown 8vo. 6s.

**Clergyman's Self-Examination concerning the** APOSTLES' CREED. Extra fcap. 8vo. 1s. 6d.

**Colenso.**—THE COMMUNION SERVICE FROM THE BOOK OF COMMON PRAYER; with Select Readings from the Writings of the Rev. F. D. MAURICE, M.A. Edited by the Right Rev. J. W. COLENSO, D.D., Lord Bishop of Natal. New Edition. 16mo. 2s. 6d.

**Collects of the Church of England.** With a beautifully Coloured Floral Design to each Collect, and Illuminated Cover. Crown 8vo. 12s. Also kept in various styles of morocco.

*The distinctive characteristic of this edition is the coloured floral design which accompanies each Collect, and which is generally emblematical of the character of the day or saint to which it is assigned; the flowers which have been selected are such as are likely to be in bloom on the day to which the Collect belongs. The* Guardian *thinks it "a successful attempt to associate in a natural and unforced manner the flowers of our fields and gardens with the course of the Christian year."*

**Congreve.**—HIGH HOPES, AND PLEADINGS FOR A REASONABLE FAITH, NOBLER THOUGHTS, LARGER CHARITY. Sermons preached in the Parish Church of Tooting Graveney, Surrey. By J. CONGREVE, M.A., Rector. Cheaper Issue. Crown 8vo. 5s.

**Cotton.**—Works by the late GEORGE EDWARD LYNCH COTTON, D.D., Bishop of Calcutta :

**COTTON** (Bishop)—*continued.*

SERMONS PREACHED TO ENGLISH CONGREGA-
TIONS IN INDIA. Crown 8vo. 7*s.* 6*d.*

EXPOSITORY SERMONS ON THE EPISTLES FOR
THE SUNDAYS OF THE CHRISTIAN YEAR. Two
Vols. Crown 8vo. 15*s.*

**Curteis.**—DISSENT in its RELATION to the CHURCH
OF ENGLAND. Eight Lectures preached before the University
of Oxford, in the year 1871, on the foundation of the late Rev.
John Bampton, M.A., Canon of Salisbury. By GEORGE HERBERT
CURTEIS, M.A., late Fellow and Sub-Rector of Exeter College;
Principal of the Lichfield Theological College, and Prebendary of
Lichfield Cathedral; Rector of Turweston, Bucks. New Edition.
Crown 8vo. 7*s.* 6*d.*

"*Mr. Curteis has done good service by maintaining in an eloquent,
temperate, and practical manner, that discussion among Christians is
really an evil, and that an intelligent basis can be found for at least a
proximate union.*"—Saturday Review. "*A well timed, learned, and
thoughtful book.*"

**Davies.**—Works by the Rev. J. LLEWELYN DAVIES, M.A.,
Rector of Christ Church, St. Marylebone, etc. :

THE GOSPEL AND MODERN LIFE; with a Preface
on a Recent Phase of Deism. Second Edition. To which is
added Morality according to the Sacrament of the Lord's Supper,
or Three Discourses on the Names, Eucharist, Sacrifice, and Communion. Extra fcap. 8vo. 6*s.*

WARNINGS AGAINST SUPERSTITION, IN FOUR
SERMONS FOR THE DAY. Extra fcap. 8vo. 2*s.* 6*d.*

"*We have seldom read a wiser little book. The Sermons are short,
terse, and full of true spiritual wisdom, expressed with a lucidity and a
moderation that must give them weight even with those who agree least
with their author....... Of the volume as a whole it is hardly possible to
speak with too cordial an appreciation.*"—Spectator.

THE CHRISTIAN CALLING. Sermons. Extra fcap.
8vo. 6*s.*

**Donaldson.**—THE APOSTOLICAL FATHERS: a Critical
Account of their Genuine Writings and of their Doctrines. By
JAMES DONALDSON, LL.D. Crown 8vo. 7*s.* 6*d.*

**DONALDSON (J., LL.D.)**—*continued.*

*This book was published in* 1864 *as the first volume of a 'Critical History of Christian Literature and Doctrine from the death of the Apostles to the Nicene Council.' The intention was to carry down the history continuously to the time of Eusebius, and this intention has not been abandoned. But as the writers can be sometimes grouped more easily according to subject or locality than according to time, it is deemed advisable to publish the history of each group separately. The Introduction to the present volume serves as an introduction to the whole period.*

**Drake.**—THE TEACHING OF THE CHURCH DURING THE FIRST THREE CENTURIES ON THE DOCTRINES OF THE CHRISTIAN PRIESTHOOD AND SACRIFICE. By the Rev. C. B. DRAKE, M.A., Warden of the Church of England Hall, Manchester. Crown 8vo. 4*s.* 6*d.*

**Eadie.**—Works by JOHN EADIE, D.D., LL.D., Professor of Biblical Literature and Exegesis, United Presbyterian Church :

THE ENGLISH BIBLE. An External and Critical History of the various English Translations of Scripture, with Remarks on the Need of Revising the English New Testament. Two vols. 8vo. 28*s.*

"*Accurate, scholarly, full of completest sympathy with the translators and their work, and marvellously interesting.*"—Literary Churchman.

"*The work is a very valuable one. It is the result of vast labour, sound scholarship, and large erudition.*"—British Quarterly Review.

ST. PAUL'S EPISTLES TO THE THESSALONIANS. A Commentary on the Greek Text. Edited by the Rev. W. YOUNG, M.A., with a Preface by the Rev. Professor CAIRNS, D.D. 8vo. 12*s.*

**Ecce Homo.** A SURVEY OF THE LIFE AND WORK OF JESUS CHRIST. Fourteenth Edition. Crown 8vo. 6*s.*

"*A very original and remarkable book, full of striking thought and delicate perception; a book which has realised with wonderful vigour and freshness the historical magnitude of Christ's work, and which here and there gives us readings of the finest kind of the probable motive of His individual words and actions.*"—Spectator. "*The best and most established believer will find it adding some fresh buttresses to his faith.*"—Literary Churchman. "*If we have not misunderstood him, we have before us a writer who has a right to claim deference from those who think deepest and know most.*"—Guardian.

**Faber.**—SERMONS AT A NEW SCHOOL. By the Rev. ARTHUR FABER, M.A., Head Master of Malvern College. Cr. 8vo. 6s.

"*These are high-toned, earnest Sermons, orthodox and scholarlike, and laden with encouragement and warning, wisely adapted to the needs of school-life.*"—Literary Churchman.

**Farrar.**—Works by the Rev. F. W. FARRAR, D.D., F.R.S., Canon of Westminster, late Head Master of Marlborough College:

THE FALL OF MAN, AND OTHER SERMONS. Third Edition. Crown 8vo. 6s.

*The* Nonconformist *says of these Sermons,* "*Mr. Farrar's Sermons are almost perfect specimens of one type of Sermons, which we may concisely call beautiful. The style of expression is beautiful—there is beauty in the thoughts, the illustrations, the allusions—they are expressive of genuinely beautiful perceptions and feelings.*" *The* British Quarterly *says,* "*Ability, eloquence, scholarship, and practical usefulness, are in these Sermons combined in a very unusual degree.*"

THE WITNESS OF HISTORY TO CHRIST. Being the Hulsean Lectures for 1870. Fourth Edition. Crown 8vo. 5s.

*The following are the subjects of the Five Lectures:—I. "The Antecedent Credibility of the Miraculous." II. "The Adequacy of the Gospel Records." III. "The Victories of Christianity." IV. "Christianity and the Individual." V. "Christianity and the Race." The subjects of the four Appendices are:—A. "The Diversity of Christian Evidences." B. "Confucius." C. "Buddha." D. "Comte."*

SEEKERS AFTER GOD. The Lives of Seneca, Epictetus, and Marcus Aurelius. New Edition. Crown 8vo. 6s.

"*A very interesting and valuable book.*"—Saturday Review.

THE SILENCE AND VOICES OF GOD : University and other Sermons. Third Edition. Crown 8vo. 6s.

"*We can most cordially recommend Dr. Farrar's singularly beautiful volume of Sermons...... For beauty of diction, felicity of style, aptness of illustration and earnest loving exhortation, the volume is without its parallel.*"—John Bull. "*They are marked by great ability, by an honesty which does not hesitate to acknowledge difficulties and by an earnestness which commands respect.*"—Pall Mall Gazette.

"IN THE DAYS OF THY YOUTH." Sermons on Practical Subjects, preached at Marlborough College from 1871—76. Third Edition. Crown 8vo. 9s.

**FARRAR (Rev. F. W.)**—*continued.*

"*All Dr. Farrar's peculiar charm of style is apparent here, all that care and subtleness of analysis, and an even-added distinctness and clearness of moral teaching, which is what every kind of sermon wants, and especially a sermon to boys.*"—Literary Churchman.

ETERNAL HOPE. Five Sermons preached in Westminster Abbey, in 1876. With Preface, Notes, etc. Contents : What Heaven is.—Is Life Worth Living?—'Hell,' What it is not.—Are there few that be saved?—Earthly and Future Consequences of Sin. Sixteenth Thousand. Crown 8vo. 6s.

SAINTLY WORKERS. Lenten Lectures delivered in St. Andrew's, Holborn, March and April, 1878. Crown 8vo. 6s.

**Fellowship :** LETTERS ADDRESSED TO MY SISTER MOURNERS. Fcap. 8vo. cloth gilt. 3s. 6d.

**Ferrar.**—A COLLECTION OF FOUR IMPORTANT MSS. OF THE GOSPELS, viz., 13, 69, 124, 346, with a view to prove their common origin, and to restore the Text of their Archetype. By the late W. H. FERRAR, M.A., Professor of Latin in the University of Dublin. Edited by T. K. ABBOTT, M.A., Professor of Biblical Greek, Dublin. 4to., half morocco. 10s. 6d.

**Forbes.**—Works by GRANVILLE H. FORBES, Rector of Broughton :

THE VOICE OF GOD IN THE PSALMS. Cr. 8vo. 6s. 6d.

VILLAGE SERMONS. By a Northamptonshire Rector. Crown 8vo. 6s.

"*Such a volume as the present . . . is as great an accession to the cause of a deep theology as the most refined exposition of its fundamental principles . . . We heartily accept his actual teaching as a true picture of what revelation teaches us, and thank him for it as one of the most profound that was ever made perfectly simple and popular . . . . It is part of the beauty of these sermons that while they apply the old truth to the new modes of feeling they seem to preserve the whiteness of its simplicity . . . . There will be plenty of critics to accuse this volume of inadequacy of doctrine because it says no more than Scripture about vicarious suffering and external retribution. For ourselves we welcome it most cordially as expressing adequately what we believe to be the true burden of the Gospel in a manner which may take hold either of the least or the most cultivated intellect.*"—Spectator.

**Hardwick.**—Works by the Ven. ARCHDEACON HARDWICK :
CHRIST AND OTHER MASTERS.   A Historical Inquiry
into some of the Chief Parallelisms and Contrasts between Christ-
ianity and the Religious Systems of the Ancient World.   New
Edition, revised, and a Prefatory Memoir by the Rev. FRANCIS
PROCTER, M.A.   New Edition.   Cr. 8vo.   10s. 6d.

*The plan of the work is boldly and almost nobly conceived. . . . We com-
mend it to the perusal of all those who take interest in the study of ancient
mythology, without losing their reverence for the supreme authority of the
oracles of the living God."*—Christian Observer.

A HISTORY OF THE CHRISTIAN CHURCH.   Middle
Age.   From Gregory the Great to the Excommunication of Luther,
Edited by WILLIAM STUBBS, M.A., Regius Professor of Modern
History in the University of Oxford.   With Four Maps constructed
for this work by A. KEITH JOHNSTON.   New Edition.   Crown
8vo.   10s. 6d.

*"As a Manual for the student of ecclesiastical history in the Middle
Ages, we know no English work which can be compared to Mr. Hardwick's
book."*—Guardian.

A HISTORY of the CHRISTIAN CHURCH DURING
THE REFORMATION.   New Edition, revised by Professor
STUBBS.   Crown 8vo.   10s. 6d.

*This volume is intended as a sequel and companion to the "History
of the Christian Church during the Middle Age."*

**Hare.**—Works by the late ARCHDEACON HARE :
THE VICTORY OF FAITH.   By JULIUS CHARLES
HARE, M.A., Archdeacon of Lewes.   Edited by Prof. PLUMPTRE.
With Introductory Notices by the late Prof. MAURICE and Dean
STANLEY.   Third Edition.   Crown 8vo.   6s. 6d.

THE MISSION OF THE COMFORTER.   With Notes.
New Edition, edited by Prof. E. H. PLUMPTRE.   Crn. 8vo.   7s. 6d.

**Harris.**—SERMONS.   By the late GEORGE COLLYER
HARRIS, Prebendary of Exeter, and Vicar of St. Luke's, Torquay.
With Memoir by CHARLOTTE M. YONGE, and Portrait.   Extra
fcap. 8vo.   6s.

**Hervey.**—THE GENEALOGIES OF OUR LORD AND
SAVIOUR JESUS CHRIST, as contained in the Gospels of
St. Matthew and St. Luke, reconciled with each other, and shown
to be in harmony with the true Chronology of the Times.   By Lord
ARTHUR HERVEY, Bishop of Bath and Wells.   8vo.   10s. 6d.

**Hort.**—TWO DISSERTATIONS. I. On ΜΟΝΟΓΕΝΗΣ ΘΕΟΣ in Scripture and Tradition. II. On the "Constantinopolitan" Creed and other Eastern Creeds of the Fourth Century. By F. J. A. HORT, D.D., Fellow and Divinity Lecturer of Emmanuel College, Cambridge. 8vo. 7s. 6d.

**Howson (Dean)**—Works by :

BEFORE THE TABLE. An Inquiry, Historical and Theological, into the True Meaning of the Consecration Rubric in the Communion Service of the Church of England. By the Very Rev. J. S. HOWSON, D.D., Dean of Chester. With an Appendix and Supplement containing Papers by the Right Rev. the Bishop of St. Andrew's and the Rev. R. W. KENNION, M.A. 8vo. 7s. 6d.

THE POSITION OF THE PRIEST DURING CONSECRATION IN THE ENGLISH COMMUNION SERVICE. A Supplement and a Reply. Crown 8vo. 2s. 6d.

**Hymni Ecclesiæ.**—Fcap. 8vo. 7s. 6d.
*This collection was edited by Dr. Newman while he lived at Oxford.*

**Hyacinthe.**—CATHOLIC REFORM. By FATHER HYACINTHE. Letters, Fragments, Discourses. Translated by Madame HYACINTHE-LOYSON. With a Preface by the Very Rev. A. P. STANLEY, D.D., Dean of Westminster. Cr. 8vo. 7s. 6d.
*"A valuable contribution to the religious literature of the day, and is especially opportune at a time when a controversy of no ordinary importance upon the very subject it deals with is engaged in all over Europe."*— Daily Telegraph.

**Imitation of Christ.**—FOUR BOOKS. Translated from the Latin, with Preface by the Rev. W. BENHAM, B.D., Vicar of Margate. Printed with Borders in the Ancient Style after Holbein, Dürer, and other Old Masters. Containing Dances of Death, Acts of Mercy, Emblems, and a variety of curious ornamentation. Cr. 8vo. gilt edges. 7s. 6d.

**Jacob.**—BUILDING IN SCIENCE, AND OTHER SERMONS. By J. A. JACOB, M.A., Minister of St. Thomas's, Paddington. Extra fcap. 8vo. 6s.

**Jellett.**—THE EFFICACY OF PRAYER : being the Donnellan Lectures for 1877. By J. H. JELLETT, B.D., Senior Fellow of Trinity College, Dublin, formerly President of the Royal Irish Academy. Second Edition. 8vo. 5s.

**Jennings and Lowe.**—THE PSALMS, with Introductions and Critical Notes. By A. C. JENNINGS, B.A., Jesus College, Cambridge, Tyrwhitt Scholar, Crosse Scholar, Hebrew University Scholar, and Fry Scholar of St. John's College; helped in parts by W. H. LOWE, M.A., Hebrew Lecturer and late Scholar of Christ's College, Cambridge, and Tyrwhitt Scholar. Complete in two vols. crown 8vo. 10s. 6d. each. Vol. 1, Psalms i.—lxxii., with Prolegomena; Vol. 2, Psalms lxxiii.—cl.

**Killen.**—THE ECCLESIASTICAL HISTORY OF IRELAND from the Earliest Period to the Present Time. By W. D. KILLEN, D.D., President of Assembly's College, Belfast, and Professor of Ecclesiastical History. Two vols. 8vo. 25s.

" *Those who have the leisure will do well to read these two volumes. They are full of interest, and are the result of great research.*"—Spectator.

**Kingsley.**—Works by the late Rev. CHARLES KINGSLEY, M.A., Rector of Eversley, and Canon of Westminster :

THE WATER OF LIFE, AND OTHER SERMONS. New Edition. Crown 8vo. 6s.

THE GOSPEL OF THE PENTATEUCH ; AND DAVID. New Edition. Crown. 8vo. 6s.

GOOD NEWS OF GOD. Eighth Edition. Crown 8vo. 6s.

SERMONS FOR THE TIMES. New Edition. Crown 8vo. 6s.

VILLAGE AND TOWN AND COUNTRY SERMONS. New Edition. Crown 8vo. 6s.

SERMONS on NATIONAL SUBJECTS. Second Edition. Fcap. 8vo. 3s. 6d.

THE KING OF THE EARTH, and other Sermons, a Second Series of Sermons on National Subjects. Second Edition. Fcap. 8vo. 3s. 6d.

DISCIPLINE, AND OTHER SERMONS. Second Edition. Fcap. 8vo. 3s. 6d.

WESTMINSTER SERMONS. With Preface. New Edition. Crown 8vo. 6s.

**Kynaston.**—SERMONS PREACHED IN THE COL-
LEGE CHAPEL, CHELTENHAM, during the First Year
of his Office. By the Rev. HERBERT KYNASTON, M.A., Principal of Cheltenham College. Crown 8vo. 6s.

**Lightfoot.**—Works by J. B. LIGHTFOOT, D.D., Bishop of
Durham.

S. PAUL'S EPISTLE TO THE GALATIANS. A Re-
vised Text, with Introduction, Notes, and Dissertations. Fifth
Edition, revised. 8vo. cloth. 12s.

*While the Author's object has been to make this commentary generally
complete, he has paid special attention to everything relating to St. Paul's
personal history and his intercourse with the Apostles and Church of the
Circumcision, as it is this feature in the Epistle to the Galatians which
has given it an overwhelming interest in recent theological controversy.
The* Spectator *says, " There is no commentator at once of sounder judgment and more liberal than Dr. Lightfoot."*

ST. PAUL'S EPISTLE TO THE PHILIPPIANS. A
Revised Text, with Introduction, Notes, and Dissertations. Fourth
Edition, revised. 8vo. 12s.

*"No commentary in the English language can be compared with it in
regard to fulness of information, exact scholarship, and laboured attempts
to settle everything about the epistle on a solid foundation."*—Athenæum.

ST. PAUL'S EPISTLES TO THE COLOSSIANS AND
TO PHILEMON. A Revised Text with Introduction, Notes, etc.
Third Edition, revised. 8vo. 12s.

*" It bears marks of continued and extended reading and research, and
of ampler materials at command. Indeed, it leaves nothing to be desired
by those who seek to study thoroughly the epistles contained in it, and to do
so with all known advantages presented in sufficient detail and in convenient form."*—Guardian.

S. CLEMENT OF ROME. An Appendix containing the
newly discovered portions of the two Epistles to the Corinthians
with Introductions and Notes, and a Translation of the whole.
8vo. 8s. 6d.

ON A FRESH REVISION OF THE ENGLISH NEW
TESTAMENT. Second Edition. Crown 8vo. 6s.

*The Author shews in detail the necessity for a fresh revision of the
authorized version on the following grounds:—*1. *False Readings.* 2.
*Artificial distinctions created.* 3. *Real distinctions obliterated.* 4. *Faults*

*of Grammar.* 5. *Faults of Lexicography.* 6. *Treatment of Proper Names, official titles, etc.* 7. *Archaisms, defects in the English, errors of the press, etc.* "*The book is marked by careful scholarship, familiarity with the subject, sobriety, and circumspection.*"—Athenæum.

**Lorne.**—THE PSALMS LITERALLY RENDERED IN VERSE. By the MARQUIS OF LORNE. With three Illustrations. New Edition. Crown 8vo. 7s. 6d.

**Luckock.**—THE TABLES OF STONE. A Course of Sermons preached in All Saints' Church, Cambridge, by H. M. LUCKOCK, M.A., Canon of Ely. Fcap. 8vo. 3s. 6d.

**Maclaren.**—SERMONS PREACHED at MANCHESTER. By ALEXANDER MACLAREN. Sixth Edition. Fcap. 8vo. 4s. 6d.

*These Sermons represent no special school, but deal with the broad principles of Christian truth, especially in their bearing on practical, every day life. A few of the titles are:—"The Stone of Stumbling," "Love and Forgiveness," "The Living Dead," "Memory in Another World," "Faith in Christ," "Love and Fear," "The Choice of Wisdom," "The Food of the World."*

A SECOND SERIES OF SERMONS. Fourth Edition. Fcap. 8vo. 4s. 6d.

*The* Spectator *characterises them as "vigorous in style, full of thought, rich in illustration, and in an unusual degree interesting."*

A THIRD SERIES OF SERMONS. Third Edition. Fcap. 8vo. 4s. 6d.

"*Sermons more sober and yet more forcible, and with a certain wise and practical spirituality about them it would not be easy to find.*"—Spectator.

WEEK-DAY EVENING ADDRESSES. Delivered in Manchester. Extra Fcap. 8vo. 2s. 6d.

**Maclear.**—Works by the Rev. G. F. MACLEAR, D.D., Head Master of King's College School:

A CLASS-BOOK OF OLD TESTAMENT HISTORY. With Four Maps. New Edition. 18mo. 4s. 6d.

"*The present volume," says the Preface, "forms a Class-Book of Old Testament History from the Earliest Times to those of Ezra and Nehemiah. In its preparation the most recent authorities have been consulted, and wherever it has appeared useful, Notes have been subjoined illustrative of the Text, and, for the sake of more advanced students, references*

**MACLEAR (Dr. G. F.)**—*continued.*

*added to larger works. The Index has been so arranged as to form a concise Dictionary of the Persons and Places mentioned in the course of the Narrative." The Maps, prepared by Stanford, materially add to the value and usefulness of the book. The* British Quarterly Review *calls it "A careful and elaborate, though brief compendium of all that modern research has done for the illustration of the Old Testament. We know of no work which contains so much important information in so small a compass."*

### A CLASS-BOOK OF NEW TESTAMENT HISTORY.
Including the Connexion of the Old and New Testament. New Edition. 18mo. 5s. 6d.

*The present volume forms a sequel to the Author's Class-Book of Old Testament History, and continues the narrative to the close of S. Paul's second imprisonment at Rome. The work is divided into three Books— I. The Connection between the Old and New Testament. II. The Gospel History. III. The Apostolic History. In the Appendix are given Chronological Tables. The* Clerical Journal *says, "It is not often that such an amount of useful and interesting matter on biblical subjects, is found in so convenient and small a compass, as in this well-arranged volume."*

### A CLASS-BOOK OF THE CATECHISM OF THE CHURCH OF ENGLAND. New and Cheaper Edition. 18mo. 1s. 6d.

*The present work is intended as a sequel to the two preceding books. "Like them, it is furnished with notes and references to larger works, and it is hoped that it may be found, especially in the higher forms of our Public Schools, to supply a suitable manual of instruction in the chief doctrines of our Church, and a useful help in the preparation of Candidates for Confirmation." The* Literary Churchman *says, "It is indeed the work of a scholar and divine, and as such, though extremely simple, it is also extremely instructive. There are few clergy who would not find it useful in preparing Candidates for Confirmation; and there are not a few who would find it useful to themselves as well."*

### A FIRST CLASS-BOOK OF THE CATECHISM OF THE CHURCH OF ENGLAND, with Scripture Proofs for Junior Classes and Schools. New Edition. 18mo. 6d.

*This is an epitome of the larger Class-book, meant for junior students and elementary classes. The book has been carefully condensed, so as to contain clearly and fully, the most important part of the contents of the larger book.*

**MACLEAR (Dr. G. F.)**—*continued.*

A SHILLING-BOOK of OLD TESTAMENT HISTORY. New Edition. 18mo. cloth limp. 1s.

*This Manual bears the same relation to the larger Old Testament History, that the book just mentioned does to the larger work on the Catechism. It consists of Ten Books, divided into short chapters, and subdivided into sections, each section treating of a single episode in the history, the title of which is given in bold type.*

A SHILLING-BOOK of NEW TESTAMENT HISTORY. New Edition. 18mo. cloth limp. 1s.

A MANUAL OF INSTRUCTION FOR CONFIRMATION AND FIRST COMMUNION, with Prayers and Devotions. 32mo. cloth extra, red edges. 2s.

*This is an enlarged and improved edition of 'The Order of Confirmation.' To it have been added the Communion Office, with Notes and Explanations, together with a brief form of Self Examination and Devotions selected from the works of Cosin, Ken, Wilson, and others.*

THE ORDER OF CONFIRMATION, with Prayers and Devotions. 32mo. cloth. 6d.

THE FIRST COMMUNION, with Prayers and Devotions for the Newly Confirmed. 32mo. 6d.

THE HOUR OF SORROW ; or, The Order for the Burial of the Dead. With Prayers and Hymns. 32mo. cloth extra. 2s.

APOSTLES OF MEDIÆVAL EUROPE. Cr. 8vo. 4s. 6d.

*In two Introductory Chapters the author notices some of the chief characteristics of the mediæval period itself ; gives a graphic sketch of the devastated state of Europe at the beginning of that period, and an interesting account of the religions of the three great groups of vigorous barbarians— the Celts, the Teutons, and the Sclaves—who had, wave after wave, overflowed its surface. He then proceeds to sketch the lives and work of the chief of the courageous men who devoted themselves to the stupendous task of their conversion and civilization, during a period extending from the 5th to the 13th century ; such as St. Patrick, St. Columba, St. Columbanus, St. Augustine of Canterbury, St. Boniface, St. Olaf, St. Cyril, Raymond Sull, and others. "Mr. Maclear will have done a great work if his admirable little volume shall help to break up the dense ignorance which is still prevailing among people at large."—Literary Churchman.*

**Macmillan.**—Works by the Rev. HUGH MACMILLAN, LL.D. F.R.S.E. (For other Works by the same Author, see CATALOGUE OF TRAVELS and SCIENTIFIC CATALOGUE).

**MACMILLAN** (Rev. H., LL.D.)—*continued.*

THE TRUE VINE; or, the Analogies of our Lord's Allegory. Third Edition. Globe 8vo. 6s.

*The* Nonconformist *says, " It abounds in exquisite bits of description, and in striking facts clearly stated." The* British Quarterly *says, " Readers and preachers who are unscientific will find many of his illustrations as valuable as they are beautiful."*

BIBLE TEACHINGS IN NATURE. Twelfth Edition. Globe 8vo. 6s.

*In this volume the author has endeavoured to shew that the teaching of Nature and the teaching of the Bible are directed to the same great end; that the Bible contains the spiritual truths which are necessary to make us wise unto salvation, and the objects and scenes of Nature are the pictures by which these truths are illustrated. " He has made the world more beautiful to us, and unsealed our ears to voices of praise and messages of love that might otherwise have been unheard."*—British Quarterly Review. *"Dr. Macmillan has produced a book which may be fitly described as one of the happiest efforts for enlisting physical science in the direct service of religion."*—Guardian.

THE SABBATH OF THE FIELDS. A Sequel to " Bible Teachings in Nature." Second Edition. Globe 8vo. 6s.

*" This volume, like all Dr. Macmillan's productions, is very delightful reading, and of a special kind. Imagination, natural science, and religious instruction are blended together in a very charming way."*—British Quarterly Review.

THE MINISTRY OF NATURE. Fourth Edition. Globe 8vo. 6s.

*" Whether the reader agree or not with his conclusions, he will acknowledge he is in the presence of an original and thoughtful writer."*—Pall Mall Gazette. *" There is no class of educated men and women that will not profit by these essays."*—Standard.

OUR LORD'S THREE RAISINGS FROM THE DEAD. Globe 8vo. 6s.

**M'Clellan.**—THE NEW TESTAMENT. A New Translation on the Basis of the Authorised Version, from a Critically revised Greek Text, with Analyses, copious References and Illustrations from original authorities, New Chronological and Analytical Harmony of the Four Gospels, Notes and Dissertations. A contribution to Christian Evidence. By JOHN BROWN M'CLELLAN, M.A., late Fellow of Trinity College, Cambridge. In Two

**M'CLELLAN (J. B.)**—*continued.*

Vols. Vol. I.—The Four Gospels with the Chronological and Analytical Harmony. 8vo. 30*s.*

"*One of the most remarkable productions of recent times,*" *says the* Theological Review, "*in this department of sacred literature;*" *and the* British Quarterly Review *terms it* "*a thesaurus of first-hand investigations.*" "*Of singular excellence, and sure to make its mark on the criticism of the New Testament.*"—John Bull.

**Maurice.**—Works by the late Rev. F. DENISON MAURICE, M.A., Professor of Moral Philosophy in the University of Cambridge :

*The* Spectator *says,*—"*Few of those of our own generation whose names will live in English history or literature have exerted so profound and so permanent an influence as Mr. Maurice.*"

THE PATRIARCHS AND LAWGIVERS OF THE OLD TESTAMENT. Third and Cheaper Edition. Crown 8vo. 5*s.*

*The Nineteen Discourses contained in this volume were preached in the chapel of Lincoln's Inn during the year* 1851. *The texts are taken from the books of Genesis, Exodus, Numbers, Deuteronomy, Joshua, Judges, and Samuel, and involve some of the most interesting biblical topics discussed in recent times.*

THE PROPHETS AND KINGS OF THE OLD TESTAMENT. Third Edition, with new Preface. Crown 8vo. 10*s.* 6*d.*

*Mr. Maurice, in the spirit which animated the compilers of the Church Lessons, has in these Sermons regarded the Prophets more as preachers of righteousness than as mere predictors—an aspect of their lives which, he thinks, has been greatly overlooked in our day, and than which, there is none we have more need to contemplate. He has found that the Old Testament Prophets, taken in their simple natural sense, clear up many of the difficulties which beset us in the daily work of life; make the past intelligible, the present endurable, and the future real and hopeful.*

THE GOSPEL OF THE KINGDOM OF HEAVEN. A Series of Lectures on the Gospel of St. Luke. Crown 8vo. 9*s.*

*Mr. Maurice, in his Preface to these Twenty-eight Lectures, says,—* "*In these Lectures I have endeavoured to ascertain what is told us respecting the life of Jesus by one of those Evangelists who proclaim Him to be the Christ, who says that He did come from a Father, that He did baptize with the Holy Spirit, that He did rise from the dead. I have chosen the*

**MAURICE (Rev. F. D.)**—*continued.*

*one who is most directly connected with the later history of the Church, who was not an Apostle, who professedly wrote for the use of a man already instructed in the faith of the Apostles. I have followed the course of the writer's narrative, not changing it under any pretext. I have adhered to his phraseology, striving to avoid the substitution of any other for his."*

THE GOSPEL OF ST. JOHN. A Series of Discourses. Third and Cheaper Edition. Crown 8vo. 6s.

*The* Literary Churchman *thus speaks of this volume: "Thorough honesty, reverence, and deep thought pervade the work, which is every way solid and philosophical, as well as theological, and abounding with suggestions which the patient student may draw out more at length for himself."*

THE EPISTLES OF ST. JOHN. A Series of Lectures on Christian Ethics. Second and Cheaper Edition. Cr. 8vo. 6s.

*These Lectures on Christian Ethics were delivered to the students of the Working Men's College, Great Ormond Street, London, on a series of Sunday mornings. Mr. Maurice believes that the question in which we are most interested, the question which most affects our studies and our daily lives, is the question, whether there is a foundation for human morality, or whether it is dependent upon the opinions and fashions of different ages and countries. This important question will be found amply and fairly discussed in this volume, which the* National Review *calls "Mr. Maurice's most effective and instructive work. He is peculiarly fitted by the constitution of his mind, to throw light on St. John's writings." Appended is a note on "Positivism and its Teacher."*

EXPOSITORY SERMONS ON THE PRAYER-BOOK. The Prayer-book considered especially in reference to the Romish System. Second Edition. Fcap. 8vo. 5s. 6d.

*After an Introductory Sermon, Mr. Maurice goes over the various parts of the Church Service, expounds in eighteen Sermons, their intention and significance, and shews how appropriate they are as expressions of the deepest longings and wants of all classes of men.*

WHAT IS REVELATION? A Series of Sermons on the Epiphany; to which are added, Letters to a Theological Student on the Bampton Lectures of Mr. Mansel. Crown 8vo. 10s. 6d.

*Both Sermons and Letters were called forth by the doctrine maintained by Mr. Mansel in his Bampton Lectures, that Revelation cannot be a direct Manifestation of the Infinite Nature of God. Mr. Maurice maintains*

**MAURICE** (Rev. F. D.)—*continued.*

*the opposite doctrine, and in his Sermons explains why, in spite of the high authorities on the other side, he must still assert the principle which he discovers in the Services of the Church and throughout the Bible.*

### SEQUEL TO THE INQUIRY, "WHAT IS REVELA-TION?" Letters in Reply to Mr. Mansel's Examination of "Strictures on the Bampton Lectures." Crown 8vo. 6s.

*This, as the title indicates, was called forth by Mr. Mansel's examination of Mr. Maurice's Strictures on his doctrine of the Infinite.*

### THEOLOGICAL ESSAYS. Third Edition. Crown 8vo. 10s. 6d.

*"The book," says Mr. Maurice, "expresses thoughts which have been working in my mind for years; the method of it has not been adopted carelessly; even the composition has undergone frequent revision." There are seventeen Essays in all, and although meant primarily for Unitarians, to quote the words of the* Clerical Journal, *"it leaves untouched scarcely any topic which is in agitation in the religious world; scarcely a moot point between our various sects; scarcely a plot of debateable ground between Christians and Infidels, between Romanists and Protestants, between Socinians and other Christians, between English Churchmen and Dissenters on both sides. Scarce is there a misgiving, a difficulty, an aspiration stirring amongst us now—now, when men seem in earnest as hardly ever before about religion, and ask and demand satisfaction with a fearlessness which seems almost awful when one thinks what is at stake—which is not recognised and grappled with by Mr. Maurice."*

### THE DOCTRINE OF SACRIFICE DEDUCED FROM THE SCRIPTURES. Crown 8vo. 7s. 6d.

### THE RELIGIONS OF THE WORLD, AND THEIR RELATIONS TO CHRISTIANITY. Fifth Edition. Crown 8vo. 5s.

### ON THE LORD'S PRAYER. Fourth Edition. Fcap. 8vo. 2s. 6d.

### ON THE SABBATH DAY; the Character of the Warrior, and on the Interpretation of History. Fcap. 8vo. 2s. 6d.

### THE LORD'S PRAYER, THE CREED, AND THE COMMANDMENTS. A Manual for Parents and Schoolmasters. To which is added the Order of the Scriptures. 18mo. cloth limp. 1s.

### DIALOGUES ON FAMILY WORSHIP. Crown 8vo. 6s.

**MAURICE (Rev. F. D.)**—*continued.*

SOCIAL MORALITY. Twenty-one Lectures delivered in the University of Cambridge. New and Cheaper Edition. Cr. 8vo. 10s. 6d.

"*Whilst reading it we are charmed by the freedom from exclusiveness and prejudice, the large charity, the loftiness of thought, the eagerness to recognise and appreciate whatever there is of real worth extant in the world, which animates it from one end to the other. We gain new thoughts and new ways of viewing things, even more, perhaps, from being brought for a time under the influence of so noble and spiritual a mind.*" —Athenæum.

THE CONSCIENCE: Lectures on Casuistry, delivered in the University of Cambridge. Second and Cheaper Edition. Crown 8vo. 5s.

*The* Saturday Review *says:* "*We rise from the perusal of these lectures with a detestation of all that is selfish and mean, and with a living impression that there is such a thing as goodness after all.*"

LECTURES ON THE ECCLESIASTICAL HISTORY OF THE FIRST AND SECOND CENTURIES. 8vo. 10s. 6d.

LEARNING AND WORKING. Six Lectures delivered in Willis's Rooms, London, in June and July, 1854.—THE RELIGION OF ROME, and its Influence on Modern Civilisation. Four Lectures delivered in the Philosophical Institution of Edinburgh, in December, 1854. Crown 8vo. 5s.

SERMONS PREACHED IN COUNTRY CHURCHES. Crown 8vo. 10s. 6d.

"*Earnest, practical, and extremely simple.*"—Literary Churchman. "*Good specimens of his simple and earnest eloquence. The Gospel incidents are realized with a vividness which we can well believe made the common people hear him gladly. Moreover they are sermons which must have done the hearers good.*"—John Bull.

**Moorhouse.**—Works by JAMES MOORHOUSE, M.A., Bishop of Melbourne :

SOME MODERN DIFFICULTIES RESPECTING the FACTS OF NATURE AND REVELATION. Fcap. 8vo. 2s. 6d.

JACOB. Three Sermons preached before the University of Cambridge in Lent 1870. Extra fcap. 8vo. 3s. 6d.

**O'Brien.**—PRAYER. Five Sermons preached in the Chapel of Trinity College, Dublin. By JAMES THOMAS O'BRIEN, D.D., Bishop of Ossory and Ferns. 8vo. 6s.

*"It is with much pleasure and satisfaction that we render our humble tribute to the value of a publication whose author deserves to be remembered with such deep respect."*—Church Quarterly Review.

**Palgrave.**—HYMNS. By FRANCIS TURNER PALGRAVE. Third Edition, enlarged. 18mo. 1s. 6d.

*This is a collection of twenty original Hymns, which the Literary Churchman speaks of as "so choice, so perfect, and so refined,—so tender in feeling, and so scholarly in expression."*

**Paul of Tarsus.** An Inquiry into the Times and the Gospel of the Apostle of the Gentiles. By a GRADUATE. 8vo. 10s. 6d.

*"Turn where we will throughout the volume, we find the best fruit of patient inquiry, sound scholarship, logical argument, and fairness of conclusion. No thoughtful reader will rise from its perusal without a real and lasting profit to himself, and a sense of permanent addition to the cause of truth."*—Standard.

**Philochristus.**—MEMOIRS OF A DISCIPLE OF THE LORD. Second Edition. 8vo. 12s.

*"The winning beauty of this book and the fascinating power with which the subject of it appeals to all English minds will secure for it many readers."*—Contemporary Review.

**Picton.**—THE MYSTERY OF MATTER; and other Essays. By J. ALLANSON PICTON, Author of "New Theories and the Old Faith." Cheaper Edition. With New Preface. Crown 8vo. 6s.

*Contents—The Mystery of Matter: The Philosophy of Ignorance: The Antithesis of Faith and Sight: The Essential Nature of Religion: Christian Pantheism.*

**Plumptre.**—MOVEMENTS IN RELIGIOUS THOUGHT. Sermons preached before the University of Cambridge, Lent Term, 1879. By E. H. PLUMPTRE, D.D., Professor of Divinity, King's College, London, Prebendary of St. Paul's, etc. Fcap. 8vo. 3s. 6d.

**Prescott.**—THE THREEFOLD CORD. Sermons preached before the University of Cambridge. By J. E. PRESCOTT, B.D. Fcap. 8vo. 3s. 6d.

**Procter.**—A HISTORY OF THE BOOK OF COMMON PRAYER: With a Rationale of its Offices. By FRANCIS PROCTER, M.A. Thirteenth Edition, revised and enlarged. Cr. 8vo. 10s. 6d.

*The Athenæum says:—"The origin of every part of the Prayer-book has been diligently investigated,—and there are few questions or facts connected with it which are not either sufficiently explained, or so referred to that persons interested may work out the truth for themselves."*

**Procter and Maclear.**—AN ELEMENTARY INTRO-DUCTION TO THE BOOK OF COMMON PRAYER. Re-arranged and Supplemented by an Explanation of the Morning and Evening Prayer and the Litany. By F. PROCTER, M.A., and G. F. MACLEAR, D.D. New Edition. Enlarged by the addition of the Communion Service and the Baptismal and Confirmation Offices. 18mo. 2s. 6d.

*The* Literary Churchman *characterizes it as "by far the completest and most satisfactory book of its kind we know. We wish it were in the hands of every schoolboy and every schoolmaster in the kingdom."*

**Psalms of David** CHRONOLOGICALLY ARRANGED. An Amended Version, with Historical Introductions and Explanatory Notes. By FOUR FRIENDS. Second and Cheaper Edition, much enlarged. Crown 8vo. 8s. 6d.

*One of the chief designs of the Editors, in preparing this volume, was to restore the Psalter as far as possible to the order in which the Psalms were written. They give the division of each Psalm into strophes, and of each strophe into the lines which composed it, and amend the errors of translation. The* Spectator *calls it "one of the most instructive and valuable books that have been published for many years."*

**Psalter (Golden Treasury).**—THE STUDENT'S EDITION. Being an Edition of the above with briefer Notes. 18mo. 3s. 6d.

*The aim of this edition is simply to put the reader as far as possible in possession of the plain meaning of the writer. "It is a gem," the* Non-conformist *says.*

**Pulsford.**—SERMONS PREACHED IN TRINITY CHURCH, GLASGOW. By WILLIAM PULSFORD, D.D. Cheaper Edition. Crown 8vo. 4s. 6d.

**Ramsay.**—THE CATECHISER'S MANUAL; or, the Church Catechism Illustrated and Explained, for the Use of Clergymen, Schoolmasters, and Teachers. By ARTHUR RAMSAY, M.A. Second Edition. 18mo. 1s. 6d.

**Rays of Sunlight for Dark Days.** A Book of Selections for the Suffering. With a Preface by C. J. VAUGHAN, D.D. 18mo. Eighth Edition. 3s. 6d. Also in morocco, old style.

*Dr. Vaughan says in the Preface, after speaking of the general run of Books of Comfort for Mourners, "It is because I think that the little volume now offered to the Christian sufferer is one of greater wisdom and*

*of deeper experience, that I have readily consented to the request that I
would introduce it by a few words of Preface." The book consists of a
series of very brief extracts from a great variety of authors, in prose and
poetry, suited to the many moods of a mourning or suffering mind.
"Mostly gems of the first water."*—Clerical Journal.

**Reynolds.**—NOTES OF THE CHRISTIAN LIFE. A
Selection of Sermons by HENRY ROBERT REYNOLDS, B.A.,
President of Cheshunt College, and Fellow of University College,
London.   Crown 8vo.   7s. 6d.

**Roberts.**—DISCUSSIONS ON THE GOSPELS. By the
Rev. ALEXANDER ROBERTS, D.D.   Second Edition, revised and
enlarged.   8vo.   16s.

**Robinson.**—MAN IN THE IMAGE OF GOD; and other
Sermons preached in the Chapel of the Magdalen, Streatham,
1874—76. By H. G. ROBINSON, M.A., Prebendary of York.
Crown 8vo.   7s. 6d.

**Romanes.**—CHRISTIAN PRAYER AND GENERAL
LAWS, being the Burney Prize Essay for 1873.   With an Appendix, examining the views of Messrs. Knight, Robertson, Brooke,
Tyndall, and Galton. By GEORGE J. ROMANES, M.A.   Crown
8vo.   5s.

**Salmon.**—THE REIGN OF LAW, and other Sermons,
preached in the Chapel of Trinity College, Dublin.   By the Rev.
GEORGE SALMON, D.D., Regius Professor of Divinity in the
University of Dublin.   Crown 8vo.   6s.

*"Well considered, learned, and powerful discourses."*—Spectator.

**Sanday.**—THE GOSPELS IN THE SECOND CEN-
TURY.   An Examination of the Critical part of a Work entitled
"Supernatural Religion." By WILLIAM SANDAY, M.A., late
Fellow of Trinity College, Oxford.   Crown 8vo.   8s. 6d.

*"A very important book for the critical side of the question as to the
authenticity of the New Testament, and it is hardly possible to conceive a
writer of greater fairness, candour, and scrupulousness."*—Spectator.

**Selborne.**—THE BOOK OF PRAISE : From the Best
English Hymn Writers.   Selected and arranged by Lord SELBORNE.
With Vignette by WOOLNER.   18mo.   4s. 6d.

**SELBORNE (Lord)**—*continued.*

*It has been the Editor's desire and aim to adhere strictly, in all cases in which it could be ascertained, to the genuine uncorrupted text of the authors themselves. The names of the authors and date of composition of the hymns, when known, are affixed, while notes are added to the volume, giving further details. The Hymns are arranged according to subjects. "There is not room for two opinions as to the value of the 'Book of Praise.'"* —Guardian. *"Approaches as nearly as one can conceive to perfection."* —Nonconformist.

BOOK OF PRAISE HYMNAL. *See* end of this Catalogue.

**Service.**—SALVATION HERE AND HEREAFTER. Sermons and Essays. By the Rev. JOHN SERVICE, D.D., Minister of Inch. Fourth Edition. Crown 8vo. 6s.

*"We have enjoyed to-day a rare pleasure, having just closed a volume of sermons which rings true metal from title page to finis, and proves that another and very powerful recruit has been added to that small band of ministers of the Gospel who are not only abreast of the religious thought of their time, but have faith enough and courage enough to handle the questions which are the most critical, and stir men's minds most deeply, with frankness and thoroughness."*—Spectator.

**Shipley.**—A THEORY ABOUT SIN, in relation to some Facts of Daily Life. Lent Lectures on the Seven Deadly Sins. By the Rev. ORBY SHIPLEY, M.A. Crown 8vo. 7s. 6d.

*"Two things Mr. Shipley has done, and each of them is of considerable worth. He has grouped these sins afresh on a philosophic principle..... and he has applied the touchstone to the facts of our moral life... so wisely and so searchingly as to constitute his treatise a powerful antidote to self-deception."*—Literary Churchman.

**Smith.**—PROPHECY A PREPARATION FOR CHRIST. Eight Lectures preached before the University of Oxford, being the Bampton Lectures for 1869. By R. PAYNE SMITH, D.D., Dean of Canterbury. Second and Cheaper Edition. Crown 8vo. 6s.

*The author's object in these Lectures is to shew that there exists in the Old Testament an element, which no criticism on naturalistic principles can either account for or explain away: that element is Prophecy. The author endeavours to prove that its force does not consist merely in its predictions. "These Lectures overflow with solid learning."*—Record.

**Smith.**—CHRISTIAN FAITH. Sermons preached before the University of Cambridge. By W. SAUMAREZ SMITH, M.A., Principal of St. Aidan's College, Birkenhead. Fcap. 8vo. 3s. 6d.

**Stanley.**—Works by the Very Rev. A. P. STANLEY, D.D., Dean of Westminster :

THE ATHANASIAN CREED, with a Preface on the General Recommendations of the RITUAL COMMISSION. Cr. 8vo. 2s.

*"Dr. Stanley puts with admirable force the objections which may be made to the Creed; equally admirable, we think, in his statement of its advantages."*—Spectator.

THE NATIONAL THANKSGIVING. Sermons preached in Westminster Abbey. Second Edition. Crown 8vo. 2s. 6d.

ADDRESSES AND SERMONS AT ST. ANDREW'S in 1872, 1875 and 1876. Crown 8vo. 5s.

**Stewart and Tait.**—THE UNSEEN UNIVERSE ; or, Physical Speculations on a Future State. By Professors BALFOUR STEWART and P. G. TAIT. Sixth Edition, Revised and Enlarged. Crown 8vo. 6s.

*"A most remarkable and most interesting volume, which, probably more than any that has appeared in modern times, will affect religious thought on many momentous questions—insensibly it may be, but very largely and very beneficially."*—Church Quarterly. *" This book is one which well deserves the attention of thoughtful and religious readers...... It is a perfectly safe enquiry, on scientific grounds, into the possibilities of a future existence."*—Guardian.

**Swainson.**—Works by C. A. SWAINSON, D.D., Canon of Chichester :

THE CREEDS OF THE CHURCH in their Relations to Holy Scripture and the Conscience of the Christian 8vo. cloth. 9s.

THE AUTHORITY OF THE NEW TESTAMENT, and other LECTURES, delivered before the University of Cambridge. 8vo. cloth. 12s.

**Taylor.**—THE RESTORATION OF BELIEF. New and Revised Edition. By ISAAC TAYLOR, Esq. Crown 8vo. 8s. 6d.

**Temple.**—SERMONS PREACHED IN THE CHAPEL of RUGBY SCHOOL. By F. TEMPLE, D.D., Bishop of Exeter. New and Cheaper Edition. Extra fcap. 8vo. 4s. 6d.

*This volume contains Thirty-five Sermons on topics more or less intimately connected with every-day life. The following are a few of the subjects discoursed upon:—"Love and Duty;" "Coming to Christ;"*

**TEMPLE (Dr.)**—*continued.*

*"Great Men;" "Faith;" "Doubts;" "Scruples;" "Original Sin;"
"Friendship;" "Helping Others;" "The Discipline of Temptation;"
"Strength a Duty;" "Worldliness;" "Ill Temper;" "The Burial of
the Past."*

A SECOND SERIES OF SERMONS PREACHED IN
THE CHAPEL OF RUGBY SCHOOL. Second Edition.
Extra fcap. 8vo. 6s.

*This Second Series of Forty-two brief, pointed, practical Sermons, on
topics intimately connected with the every-day life of young and old, will be
acceptable to all who are acquainted with the First Series. The following
are a few of the subjects treated of:—"Disobedience," "Almsgiving,"
"The Unknown Guidance of God," "Apathy one of our Trials," "High
Aims in Leaders," "Doing our Best," "The Use of Knowledge," "Use
of Observances," "Martha and Mary," "John the Baptist," "Severity
before Mercy," "Even Mistakes Punished," "Morality and Religion,"
"Children," "Action the Test of Spiritual Life," "Self-Respect," "Too
Late," "The Tercentenary."*

A THIRD SERIES OF SERMONS PREACHED IN
RUGBY SCHOOL CHAPEL IN 1867—1869. Extra fcap.
8vo. 6s.

*This Third Series of Bishop Temple's Rugby Sermons, contains thirty-six
brief discourses, including the "Good-bye" sermon preached on his leaving
Rugby to enter on the office he now holds.*

**Thring.**—Works by Rev. EDWARD THRING, M.A. :
SERMONS DELIVERED AT UPPINGHAM SCHOOL.
Crown 8vo. 5s.

THOUGHTS ON LIFE-SCIENCE. New Edition, enlarged and revised. Crown 8vo. 7s. 6d.

**Trench.**—Works by R. CHENEVIX TRENCH, D.D., Arch-
bishop of Dublin :
NOTES ON THE PARABLES OF OUR LORD.
Thirteenth Edition. 8vo. 12s.

*This work has taken its place as a standard exposition and interpreta-
tion of Christ's Parables. The book is prefaced by an Introductory Essay
in four chapters:—I. On the definition of the Parable. II. On Teaching by Parables. III. On the Interpretation of the Parables. IV. On
other Parables besides those in the Scriptures. The author then proceeds
to take up the Parables one by one, and by the aid of philology, history,
antiquities, and the researches of travellers, shews forth the significance,*

**TRENCH** (Archbishop)—*continued.*

*beauty, and applicability of each, concluding with what he deems its true moral interpretation. In the numerous Notes are many valuable references, illustrative quotations, critical and philological annotations, etc., and appended to the volume is a classified list of fifty-six works on the Parables.*

## NOTES ON THE MIRACLES OF OUR LORD.
### Eleventh Edition, revised. 8vo. 12s.

*In the 'Preliminary Essay' to this work, all the momentous and interesting questions that have been raised in connection with Miracles, are discussed with considerable fulness. The Essay consists of six chapters:—I. On the Names of Miracles, i.e. the Greek words by which they are designated in the New Testament. II. The Miracles and Nature—What is the difference between a Miracle and any event in the ordinary course of Nature? III. The Authority of Miracles—Is the Miracle to command absolute obedience? IV. The Evangelical, compared with the other cycles of Miracles. V. The Assaults on the Miracles—1. The Jewish. 2. The Heathen (Celsus etc.). 3. The Pantheistic (Spinosa etc.). 4. The Sceptical (Hume). 5. The Miracles only relatively miraculous (Schleiermacher). 6. The Rationalistic (Paulus). 7. The Historico-Critical (Woolston, Strauss). VI. The Apologetic Worth of the Miracles. The author then treats the separate Miracles as he does the Parables.*

## SYNONYMS OF THE NEW TESTAMENT. Eighth
### Edition, enlarged. 8vo. cloth. 12s.

*This Edition has been carefully revised, and a considerable number of new Synonyms added. Appended is an Index to the Synonyms, and an Index to many other words alluded to or explained throughout the work. "He is," the* Athenæum *says, " a guide in this department of knowledge to whom his readers may intrust themselves with confidence. His sober judgment and sound sense are barriers against the misleading influence of arbitrary hypotheses."*

## ON THE AUTHORIZED VERSION OF THE NEW
### TESTAMENT. Second Edition. 8vo. 7s.

*After some Introductory Remarks, in which the propriety of a revision is briefly discussed, the whole question of the merits of the present version is gone into in detail, in eleven chapters. Appended is a chronological list of works bearing on the subject, an Index of the principal Texts considered, an Index of Greek Words, and an Index of other Words referred to throughout the book.*

## STUDIES IN THE GOSPELS. Fourth Edition, revised.
### 8vo. 10s. 6d.

*This book is published under the conviction that the assertion often made is untrue,—viz. that the Gospels are in the main plain and easy,*

**TRENCH (Archbishop)**—*continued.*

*and that all the chief difficulties of the New Testament are to be found in the Epistles. These "Studies," sixteen in number, are the fruit of a much larger scheme, and each Study deals with some important episode mentioned in the Gospels, in a critical, philosophical, and practical manner. Many references and quotations are added to the Notes. Among the subjects treated are:—The Temptation; Christ and the Samaritan Woman; The Three Aspirants; The Transfiguration; Zacchæus; The True Vine; The Penitent Malefactor; Christ and the Two Disciples on the way to Emmaus.*

COMMENTARY ON THE EPISTLES to the SEVEN CHURCHES IN ASIA. Third Edition, revised. 8vo. 8s. 6d.

*The present work consists of an Introduction, being a commentary on Rev. i. 4—20, a detailed examination of each of the Seven Epistles, in all its bearings, and an Excursus on the Historico-Prophetical Interpretation of the Epistles.*

THE SERMON ON THE MOUNT. An Exposition drawn from the writings of St. Augustine, with an Essay on his merits as an Interpreter of Holy Scripture. Third Edition, enlarged. 8vo. 10s. 6d.

*The first half of the present work consists of a dissertation in eight chapters on "Augustine as an Interpreter of Scripture," the titles of the several chapters being as follow:—I. Augustine's General Views of Scripture and its Interpretation. II. The External Helps for the Interpretation of Scripture possessed by Augustine. III. Augustine's Principles and Canons of Interpretation. IV. Augustine's Allegorical Interpretation of Scripture. V. Illustrations of Augustine's Skill as an Interpreter of Scripture. VI. Augustine on John the Baptist and on St. Stephen. VII. Augustine on the Epistle to the Romans. VIII. Miscellaneous Examples of Augustine's Interpretation of Scripture. The latter half of the work consists of Augustine's Exposition of the Sermon on the Mount, not however a mere series of quotations from Augustine, but a connected account of his sentiments on the various passages of that Sermon, interspersed with criticisms by Archbishop Trench.*

SHIPWRECKS OF FAITH. Three Sermons preached before the University of Cambridge in May, 1867. Fcap. 8vo. 2s. 6d.

*These Sermons are especially addressed to young men. The subjects are "Balaam," "Saul," and "Judas Iscariot," These lives are set forth as beacon-lights, "to warn us off from perilous reefs and quicksands, which have been the destruction of many, and which might only too easily be ours." The* John Bull *says, "they are, like all he writes, affectionate and earnest discourses."*

**TRENCH (Archbishop)**—*continued.*

SERMONS Preached for the most part in Ireland. 8vo.
10s. 6d.

*This volume consists of Thirty-two Sermons, the greater part of which
were preached in Ireland; the subjects are as follow:—Jacob, a Prince
with God and with Men—Agrippa—The Woman that was a Sinner—
Secret Faults—The Seven Worse Spirits—Freedom in the Truth—Joseph
and his Brethren—Bearing one another's Burdens—Christ's Challenge to
the World—The Love of Money—The Salt of the Earth—The Armour of
God—Light in the Lord—The Jailer of Philippi—The Thorn in the Flesh
—Isaiah's Vision—Selfishness—Abraham interceding for Sodom—Vain
Thoughts—Pontius Pilate—The Brazen Serpent—The Death and Burial
of Moses—A Word from the Cross—The Church's Worship in the
Beauty of Holiness—Every Good Gift from Above—On the Hearing of
Prayer—The Kingdom which cometh not with Observation—Pressing
towards the Mark—Saul—The Good Shepherd—The Valley of Dry Bones
—All Saints.*

LECTURES ON MEDIEVAL CHURCH HISTORY.
Being the Substance of Lectures delivered in Queen's College,
London. Second Edition, revised. 8vo. 12s.

*Contents:—The Middle Ages Beginning—The Conversion of Eng-
land—Islam—The Conversion of Germany—The Iconoclasts—The
Crusades—The Papacy at its Height—The Sects of the Middle Ages—
The Mendicant Orders—The Waldenses—The Revival of Learning—
Christian Art in the Middle Ages, &c., &c.*

**Tulloch.**—THE CHRIST OF THE GOSPELS AND
THE CHRIST OF MODERN CRITICISM. Lectures on
M. RENAN'S "Vie de Jésus." By JOHN TULLOCH, D.D.,
Principal of the College of St. Mary, in the University of St.
Andrew's. Extra fcap. 8vo. 4s. 6d.

**Vaughan.**—Works by the very Rev. CHARLES JOHN VAUGHAN,
D.D., Dean of Llandaff and Master of the Temple:

CHRIST SATISFYING THE INSTINCTS OF HU-
MANITY. Eight Lectures delivered in the Temple Church.
Second Edition. Extra fcap. 8vo. 3s. 6d.

*"We are convinced that there are congregations, in number unmistakably
increasing, to whom such Essays as these, full of thought and learning,
are infinitely more beneficial, for they are more acceptable, than the recognised type of sermons."*—John Bull.

THE BOOK AND THE LIFE, and other Sermons,
preached before the University of Cambridge. Third Edition.
Fcap. 8vo. 4s. 6d.

**VAUGHAN** (Dr. C. J.)—*continued.*

TWELVE DISCOURSES on SUBJECTS CONNECTED WITH THE LITURGY and WORSHIP of the CHURCH OF ENGLAND. Fcap. 8vo. 6s.

LESSONS OF LIFE AND GODLINESS. A Selection of Sermons preached in the Parish Church of Doncaster. Fourth and Cheaper Edition. Fcap. 8vo. 3s. 6d.

*This volume consists of Nineteen Sermons, mostly on subjects connected with the every-day walk and conversation of Christians. The* Spectator *styles them "earnest and human. They are adapted to every class and order in the social system, and will be read with wakeful interest by all who seek to amend whatever may be amiss in their natural disposition or in their acquired habits."*

WORDS FROM THE GOSPELS. A Second Selection of Sermons preached in the Parish Church of Doncaster. Third Edition. Fcap. 8vo. 4s. 6d.

*The* Nonconformist *characterises these Sermons as " of practical earnestness, of a thoughtfulness that penetrates the common conditions and experiences of life, and brings the truths and examples of Scripture to bear on them with singular force, and of a style that owes its real elegance to the simplicity and directness which have fine culture for their roots."*

LIFE'S WORK AND GOD'S DISCIPLINE. Three Sermons. Third Edition. Fcap. 8vo. 2s. 6d.

THE WHOLESOME WORDS OF JESUS CHRIST. Four Sermons preached before the University of Cambridge in November 1866. Second Edition. Fcap. 8vo. 3s. 6d.

*Dr. Vaughan uses the word "Wholesome" here in its literal and original sense, the sense in which St. Paul uses it, as meaning healthy, sound, conducing to right living; and in these Sermons he points out and illustrates several of the "wholesome" characteristics of the Gospel, —the Words of Christ. The* John Bull *says this volume is " replete with all the author's well-known vigour of thought and richness of expression."*

FOES OF FAITH. Sermons preached before the University of Cambridge in November 1868. Second Edition. Fcap. 8vo. 3s. 6d.

*The "Foes of Faith" preached against in these Four Sermons are:— I. "Unreality." II. "Indolence." III. "Irreverence." IV. "Inconsistency."*

LECTURES ON THE EPISTLE to the PHILIPPIANS. Third and Cheaper Edition. Extra fcap. 8vo. 5s.

*Each Lecture is prefaced by a literal translation from the Greek of the paragraph which forms its subject, contains first a minute explanation*

**VAUGHAN (Dr. C. J.)**—*continued.*

*of the passage on which it is based, and then a practical application of the verse or clause selected as its text.*

### LECTURES ON THE REVELATION OF ST. JOHN.
Fourth Edition.  Two Vols.  Extra fcap. 8vo.  9s.

*In this Edition of these Lectures, the literal translations of the passages expounded will be found interwoven in the body of the Lectures themselves. "Dr. Vaughan's Sermons," the* Spectator *says, "are the most practical discourses on the Apocalypse with which we are acquainted." Prefixed is a Synopsis of the Book of Revelation, and appended is an Index of passages illustrating the language of the Book.*

### EPIPHANY, LENT, AND EASTER.  A Selection of
Expository Sermons.  Third Edition.  Crown 8vo.  10s. 6d.

### THE EPISTLES OF ST. PAUL.  For English Readers.
PART I., containing the FIRST EPISTLE TO THE THESSALONIANS.
Second Edition.  8vo.  1s. 6d.

*It is the object of this work to enable English readers, unacquainted with Greek, to enter with intelligence into the meaning, connection, and phraseology of the writings of the great Apostle.*

### ST. PAUL'S EPISTLE TO THE ROMANS.  The Greek
Text, with English Notes.  Fourth Edition.  Crown 8vo.  7s. 6d.

*The* Guardian *says of the work,—"For educated young men his commentary seems to fill a gap hitherto unfilled. . . . As a whole, Dr. Vaughan appears to us to have given to the world a valuable book of original and careful and earnest thought bestowed on the accomplishment of a work which will be of much service and which is much needed."*

### THE CHURCH OF THE FIRST DAYS.
Series I.   The Church of Jerusalem.   Third Edition.
"  II.   The Church of the Gentiles.  Third Edition.
"  III.   The Church of the World.   Third Edition.
Fcap. 8vo.  4s. 6d. each.

*The* British Quarterly *says, "These Sermons are worthy of all praise, and are models of pulpit teaching."*

### COUNSELS for YOUNG STUDENTS.  Three Sermons
preached before the University of Cambridge at the Opening of the Academical Year 1870-71.  Fcap. 8vo.  2s. 6d.

*The titles of the Three Sermons contained in this volume are:—I. "The Great Decision."   II. "The House and the Builder."   III. "The Prayer and the Counter-Prayer."   They all bear pointedly, earnestly, and sympathisingly upon the conduct and pursuits of young students and young men generally.*

**VAUGHAN** (Dr. C. J.)—*continued.*

NOTES FOR LECTURES ON CONFIRMATION, with suitable Prayers. Tenth Edition. Fcap. 8vo. 1*s.* 6*d.*

THE TWO GREAT TEMPTATIONS. The Temptation of Man, and the Temptation of Christ. Lectures delivered in the Temple Church, Lent 1872. Second Edition. Extra fcap. 8vo. 3*s.* 6*d.*

WORDS FROM THE CROSS: Lent Lectures, 1875; and Thoughts for these Times: University Sermons, 1874. Extra fcap. 8vo. 4*s.* 6*d.*

ADDRESSES TO YOUNG CLERGYMEN, delivered at Salisbury in September and October, 1875. Extra fcap. 8vo. 4*s.* 6*d.*

HEROES OF FAITH : Lectures on Hebrews xi. Extra fcap. 8vo. 6*s.*

THE YOUNG LIFE EQUIPPING ITSELF FOR GOD'S SERVICE : Sermons before the University of Cambridge. Sixth Edition. Extra fcap. 8vo. 3*s.* 6*d.*

THE SOLIDITY OF TRUE RELIGION ; and other Sermons. Second Edition. Extra fcap. 8vo. 3*s.* 6*d.*

SERMONS IN HARROW SCHOOL CHAPEL (1847). 8vo. 10*s.* 6*d.*

NINE SERMONS IN HARROW SCHOOL CHAPEL (1849). Fcap. 8vo. 5*s.*

"MY SON, GIVE ME THINE HEART," SERMONS Preached before the Universities of Oxford and Cambridge, 1876 —78. Fcap. 8vo. 5*s.*

**Vaughan (E. T.)**—SOME REASONS OF OUR CHRISTIAN HOPE. Hulsean Lectures for 1875. By E. T. VAUGHAN, M.A., Rector of Harpenden. Crown 8vo. 6*s.* 6*d.*

"*His words are those of a well-tried scholar and a sound theologian, and they will be read widely and valued deeply by an audience far beyond the range of that which listened to their masterly pleading at Cambridge.*" —Standard.

**Vaughan (D. J.)**—Works by CANON VAUGHAN, of Leicester :

SERMONS PREACHED IN ST. JOHN'S CHURCH, LEICESTER, during the Years 1855 and 1856. Cr. 8vo. 5*s.* 6*d.*

**VAUGHAN (D. J.)**—*continued.*

CHRISTIAN EVIDENCES AND THE BIBLE. New Edition, revised and enlarged. Fcap. 8vo. cloth. 5*s.* 6*d.*

THE PRESENT TRIAL OF FAITH. Sermons preached in St. Martin's Church, Leicester. Crown 8vo. 9*s.*

**Venn.**—ON SOME OF THE CHARACTERISTICS OF BELIEF, Scientific and Religious. Being the Hulsean Lectures for 1869. By the Rev. J. VENN, M.A. 8vo. 6*s.* 6*d.*

*These discourses are intended to illustrate, explain, and work out into some of their consequences, certain characteristics by which the attainment of religious belief is prominently distinguished from the attainment of belief upon most other subjects.*

**Warington.**—THE WEEK OF CREATION; or, The Cosmogony of Genesis considered in its Relation to Modern Science. By GEORGE WARINGTON, Author of "The Historic Character of the Pentateuch vindicated." Crown 8vo. 4*s.* 6*d.*

*"A very able vindication of the Mosaic Cosmogony by a writer who unites the advantages of a critical knowledge of the Hebrew text and of distinguished scientific attainments."*—Spectator.

**Westcott.**—Works by BROOKE FOSS WESTCOTT, D.D., Regius Professor of Divinity in the University of Cambridge; Canon of Peterborough:

*The* London Quarterly, *speaking of Mr. Westcott, says, "To a learning and accuracy which command respect and confidence, he unites what are not always to be found in union with these qualities, the no less valuable faculties of lucid arrangement and graceful and facile expression."*

AN INTRODUCTION TO THE STUDY OF THE GOSPELS. Fifth Edition. Crown 8vo. 10*s.* 6*d.*

*The author's chief object in this work has been to shew that there is a true mean between the idea of a formal harmonization of the Gospels and the abandonment of their absolute truth. After an Introduction on the General Effects of the course of Modern Philosophy on the popular views of Christianity, he proceeds to determine in what way the principles therein indicated may be applied to the study of the Gospels.*

A GENERAL SURVEY OF THE HISTORY OF THE CANON OF THE NEW TESTAMENT during the First Four Centuries. Fourth Edition, revised, with a Preface on "Supernatural Religion." Crown 8vo. 10*s.* 6*d.*

*The object of this treatise is to deal with the New Testament as a whole, and that on purely historical grounds. The separate books of which it is*

**WESTCOTT** (Dr.)—*continued.*

*composed are considered not individually, but as claiming to be parts of the apostolic heritage of Christians. The Author has thus endeavoured to connect the history of the New Testament Canon with the growth and consolidation of the Catholic Church, and to point out the relation existing between the amount of evidence for the authenticity of its component parts and the whole mass of Christian literature. "The treatise," says the British Quarterly, "is a scholarly performance, learned, dispassionate, discriminating, worthy of his subject and of the present state of Christian literature in relation to it."*

### THE BIBLE IN THE CHURCH. A Popular Account of the Collection and Reception of the Holy Scriptures in the Christian Churches. Sixth Edition. 18mo. 4s. 6d.

### A GENERAL VIEW OF THE HISTORY OF THE ENGLISH BIBLE. Second Edition. Crown 8vo. 10s. 6d.

*The* Pall Mall Gazette *calls the work "A brief, scholarly, and, to a great extent, an original contribution to theological literature."*

### THE CHRISTIAN LIFE, MANIFOLD AND ONE. Six Sermons preached in Peterborough Cathedral. Crown 8vo. 2s. 6d.

*The Six Sermons contained in this volume are the first preached by the author as a Canon of Peterborough Cathedral. The subjects are:—I. "Life consecrated by the Ascension." II. "Many Gifts, One Spirit." III. "The Gospel of the Resurrection." IV. "Sufficiency of God." V. "Action the Test of Faith." VI. "Progress from the Confession of God."*

### THE GOSPEL OF THE RESURRECTION. Thoughts on its Relation to Reason and History. Third Edition, enlarged. Crown 8vo. 6s.

*The present Essay is an endeavour to consider some of the elementary truths of Christianity, as a miraculous Revelation, from the side of History and Reason. The author endeavours to shew that a devout belief in the Life of Christ is quite compatible with a broad view of the course of human progress and a frank trust in the laws of our own minds. In the third edition the author has carefully reconsidered the whole argument, and by the help of several kind critics has been enabled to correct some faults and to remove some ambiguities, which had been overlooked before.*

### ON THE RELIGIOUS OFFICE OF THE UNIVERSITIES. Crown 8vo. 4s. 6d.

*"There is certainly no man of our time—no man at least who has obtained the command of the public ear—whose utterances can compare with those of Professor Westcott for largeness of views and comprehensiveness of*

*grasp......There is wisdom, and truth, and thought enough, and a harmony and mutual connection running through them all, which makes the collection of more real value than many an ambitious treatise."*—Literary Churchman.

**Wilkins.**—THE LIGHT OF THE WORLD. An Essay, by A. S. WILKINS, M.A., Professor of Latin in Owens College, Manchester. Second Edition. Crown 8vo. 3s. 6d.

*"It would be difficult to praise too highly the spirit, the burden, the conclusions, or the scholarly finish of this beautiful Essay."*—British Quarterly Review.

**Wilson.**—THE BIBLE STUDENT'S GUIDE TO THE MORE CORRECT UNDERSTANDING of the ENGLISH TRANSLATION OF THE OLD TESTAMENT, by Reference to the Original Hebrew. By WILLIAM WILSON, D.D., Canon of Winchester. Second Edition, carefully revised. 4to. 25s.

*"The author believes that the present work is the nearest approach to a complete Concordance of every word in the original that has yet been made: and as a Concordance, it may be found of great use to the Bible student, while at the same time it serves the important object of furnishing the means of comparing synonymous words, and of eliciting their precise and distinctive meaning. The knowledge of the Hebrew language is not absolutely necessary to the profitable use of the work. The plan of the work is simple: every word occurring in the English Version is arranged alphabetically, and under it is given the Hebrew word or words, with a full explanation of their meaning, of which it is meant to be a translation, and a complete list of the passages where it occurs. Following the general work is a complete Hebrew and English Index, which is, in effect, a Hebrew-English Dictionary.*

**Worship (The) of God and Fellowship among Men.** Sermons on Public Worship. By Professor MAURICE, and others. Fcap. 8vo. 3s. 6d.

**Yonge (Charlotte M.)**—Works by CHARLOTTE M. YONGE, Author of "The Heir of Redclyffe:"

SCRIPTURE READINGS FOR SCHOOLS AND FAMILIES. 5 vols. Globe 8vo. 1s. 6d. With Comments, 3s. 6d. each.

FIRST SERIES. Genesis to Deuteronomy.

SECOND SERIES. From Joshua to Solomon.

THIRD SERIES. The Kings and Prophets.

FOURTH SERIES. The Gospel Times.

FIFTH SERIES. Apostolic Times.

**YONGE (Charlotte M.)**—*continued.*

*Actual need has led the author to endeavour to prepare a reading book convenient for study with children, containing the very words of the Bible, with only a few expedient omissions, and arranged in Lessons of such length as by experience she has found to suit with children's ordinary power of accurate attentive interest. The verse form has been retained because of its convenience for children reading in class, and as more resembling their Bibles; but the poetical portions have been given in their lines. Professor Huxley at a meeting of the London School-board, particularly mentioned the Selection made by Miss Yonge, as an example of how selections might be made for School reading. " Her Comments are models of their kind."*—Literary Churchman.

## THE PUPILS OF ST. JOHN THE DIVINE. New Edition. Crown 8vo. 6s.

*"Young and old will be equally refreshed and taught by these pages, in which nothing is dull, and nothing is far-fetched."*—Churchman.

## PIONEERS AND FOUNDERS; or, Recent Workers in the Mission Field. With Frontispiece and Vignette Portrait of Bishop HEBER. Crown 8vo. 6s.

*The missionaries whose biographies are here given, are—John Eliot, the Apostle of the Red Indians; David Brainerd, the Enthusiast; Christian F. Schwartz, the Councillor of Tanjore; Henry Martyn, the Scholar-Missionary; William Carey and Joshua Marshman, the Serampore Missionaries; the Judson Family; the Bishops of Calcutta—Thomas Middleton, Reginald Heber, Daniel Wilson; Samuel Marsden, the Australian Chaplain and Friend of the Maori; John Williams, the Martyr of Erromango; Allen Gardener, the Sailor Martyr; Charles Frederick Mackenzie, the Martyr of Zambesi.*

# THE "BOOK OF PRAISE" HYMNAL,

COMPILED AND ARRANGED BY

## LORD SELBORNE.

*In the following four forms :—*

**A.** Beautifully printed in Royal 32mo., limp cloth, price 6d.

**B.**       ,,      ,,    Small 18mo., larger type, cloth limp, 1s.

**C.** Same edition on fine paper, cloth, 1s. 6d.

**Also an edition with Music, selected, harmonized, and composed by JOHN HULLAH, in square 18mo., cloth, 3s. 6d.**

*The large acceptance which has been given to "The Book of Praise" by all classes of Christian people encourages the Publishers in entertaining the hope that this Hymnal, which is mainly selected from it, may be extensively used in Congregations, and in some degree at least meet the desires of those who seek uniformity in common worship as a means towards that unity which pious souls yearn after, and which our Lord prayed for in behalf of his Church. "The office of a hymn is not to teach controversial Theology, but to give the voice of song to practical religion. No doubt, to do this, it must embody sound doctrine; but it ought to do so, not after the manner of the schools, but with the breadth, freedom, and simplicity of the Fountain-head." On this principle has Sir R. Palmer proceeded in the preparation of this book.*

The arrangement adopted is the following :—

PART I. *consists of Hymns arranged according to the subjects of the Creed—"God the Creator," "Christ Incarnate," "Christ Crucified," "Christ Risen," "Christ Ascended," "Christ's Kingdom and Judgment," etc.*

PART II. *comprises Hymns arranged according to the subjects of the Lord's Prayer.*

PART III. *Hymns for natural and sacred seasons.*

*There are 320 Hymns in all.*

CAMBRIDGE :—PRINTED BY J. PALMER.